Kubernetes Mastery:
From Zero to Certified Administrator

Raul Butuc

Contents

Contents

7

Chapter 1

Introduction

1.1 Course Overview

1.1.1 Objectives and Goals

Kubernetes has emerged as the de facto standard for container orchestration, revolutionizing the way we deploy, manage, and scale containerized applications. This book, **Kubernetes Mastery: From Zero to Certified Administrator**, is designed to take you on a comprehensive journey from the basics of Kubernetes to advanced administration and operations. Whether you're a beginner just getting started with Kubernetes or an experienced professional looking to deepen your knowledge, this book provides the insights and hands-on experience needed to master Kubernetes administration.

Note Throughout this book, we will be using Ubuntu for our local machine operating system.

Objectives The primary objectives of this book are:

- To provide a solid foundation in Kubernetes concepts, architecture, and operations.

- To equip readers with the necessary skills to deploy, manage, and troubleshoot Kubernetes clusters.

- To explore advanced topics in Kubernetes, including networking, security, and storage solutions.

- To prepare readers for the Certified Kubernetes Administrator (CKA) exam with practical examples and exercises.

- To offer real-world case studies and best practices from industry experts.

Goals By the end of this book, you will:

- Understand the core components and architecture of Kubernetes.

- Be able to set up and configure a Kubernetes environment using various tools and cloud providers.

- Gain proficiency in managing Kubernetes resources such as pods, services, deployments, and more.

- Develop skills in monitoring, logging, and securing Kubernetes clusters.

- Learn how to scale applications and manage cluster operations efficiently.

- Be prepared to handle real-world challenges and scenarios in Kubernetes administration.

- Have access to a variety of practical exercises and demos to reinforce learning.

This book is structured to build your knowledge progressively, starting with the basics and moving towards more complex and advanced topics. Each chapter includes detailed explanations, hands-on exercises, and practical examples to help you apply what you learn. Additionally, you'll find quizzes and exercises at the end of each chapter to test your understanding and ensure you're ready to move on to the next topic.

Embark on this journey with confidence, knowing that you have a comprehensive guide to help you become a proficient Kubernetes administrator. Whether you're aiming to pass the CKA exam, manage Kubernetes in a production environment, or simply enhance your skills, this book is your ultimate resource. Let's get started on the path to becoming a Kubernetes hero.

1.1.2 Course Structure

This book is divided into several chapters, each designed to build on the knowledge and skills acquired in the previous chapters. The structure is as follows:

Chapter 1: Introduction This chapter provides an overview of the course, including its objectives, goals, and the overall structure. It also introduces Kubernetes, its history, and its benefits.

Chapter 2: Setting up the Environment This chapter covers the prerequisites for learning Kubernetes, including system requirements, cloud provider options, and the installation of necessary tools. It also guides you through setting up your first Kubernetes cluster using tools like Minikube and KIND.

Chapter 3: Kubernetes Architecture Here, you will learn about the core components and architecture of Kubernetes, including nodes, control plane components, and node components. This chapter also covers the API server, etcd, kubelet, kube proxy, controller managers, scheduler, and container runtimes.

Chapter 4: Core Kubernetes Resources This chapter delves into the fundamental resources of Kubernetes, such as namespaces, pods, services, volumes, configmaps, secrets, deployments, statefulsets, daemonsets, replicasets, jobs, and cronjobs. Each resource is explained in detail with examples.

Chapter 5: Controllers and Operators You will explore the lifecycle of controllers, implementing custom controllers, and the reconciliation loop. This chapter also introduces Kubernetes operators, the operator pattern, and building operators with the Operator SDK.

Chapter 6: Networking in Kubernetes This chapter explains Kubernetes networking concepts, including pod-to-pod communication, service networking, DNS, container network interfaces (CNIs), and service mesh. It also covers network policies and their implementation.

Chapter 7: Advanced Storage Solutions This chapter covers advanced storage topics, including the Container Storage Interface (CSI), integrating external storage solutions, dynamic volume provisioning, and storage patterns. It also discusses best practices for storage in stateful applications.

Chapter 8: Cluster Operations You will learn about autoscaling strategies, cluster federation, and multi-cluster management. This chapter also covers disaster recovery, redundancy, and best practices for managing Kubernetes clusters.

Chapter 9: Security Best Practices This chapter focuses on securing Kubernetes environments, including pod security admissions, network segmentation, node and control plane hardening, image security, audit logging, and encryption.

Chapter 10: Advanced Development Practices You will explore advanced development topics such as GitOps, CI/CD in Kubernetes, DevSecOps, canary deployments, blue-green deployments, and A/B testing.

Chapter 11: Performance and Optimization This chapter covers tuning Kubernetes for high performance, optimizing costs in cloud environments, load testing, and simulating failures.

Chapter 12: Disaster Recovery and Business Continuity You will learn about backup strategies, planning and practicing disaster recovery scenarios, and business continuity planning in Kubernetes environments.

Chapter 13: Ecosystem and Integration This chapter explores Helm for package management, operators, and integrating Kubernetes with the cloud-native landscape and other CNCF projects.

Chapter 14: Real-World Case Studies   This chapter provides adoption stories from large enterprises, lessons from production failures, and innovative uses of Kubernetes in different industries.

Chapter 15: Conclusion   The final chapter offers tips for the Certified Kubernetes Administrator (CKA) exam, further reading and learning resources, and acknowledgements.

Each chapter includes detailed explanations, practical examples, and hands-on exercises to reinforce learning. Quizzes and exercises at the end of each chapter help you test your understanding and ensure you're ready to progress to the next topic. This structured approach ensures a comprehensive learning experience, guiding you from a novice to an expert Kubernetes administrator.

1.1.3   Expected Outcomes

By the end of this book, you will have achieved the following outcomes:

Comprehensive Understanding of Kubernetes   You will gain a thorough understanding of Kubernetes concepts, architecture, and components. This includes knowledge of control plane components, node components, and the Kubernetes API.

Proficiency in Kubernetes Deployment and Management   You will be able to set up and configure Kubernetes environments using various tools and cloud providers. This includes deploying, managing, and scaling applications within a Kubernetes cluster.

Skill in Managing Kubernetes Resources   You will become proficient in managing core Kubernetes resources such as pods, services, deployments, volumes, configmaps, secrets, and more. You will also learn advanced resource management techniques using controllers and operators.

Expertise in Kubernetes Networking   You will develop a solid understanding of Kubernetes networking, including pod-to-pod communication, service networking, DNS, and container network interfaces.

You will also learn about implementing and managing network policies and service meshes.

Advanced Storage Solutions You will gain expertise in Kubernetes storage solutions, including the Container Storage Interface (CSI), dynamic volume provisioning, and various storage patterns. You will understand how to integrate and manage external storage solutions effectively.

Efficient Cluster Operations You will learn to implement autoscaling strategies, manage multi-cluster environments, and ensure disaster recovery and redundancy. This includes practical knowledge of monitoring, logging, and optimizing cluster performance.

Security Best Practices You will understand and apply security best practices in Kubernetes, including pod security admissions, network segmentation, node and control plane hardening, image security, and encryption. You will also learn how to implement audit logging and access monitoring.

Advanced Development and Deployment Practices You will acquire skills in advanced development practices such as GitOps, CI/CD pipelines, DevSecOps, and various deployment strategies like canary deployments, blue-green deployments, and A/B testing.

Performance Tuning and Optimization You will be able to optimize Kubernetes for high performance and cost-efficiency. This includes knowledge of load testing, performance tuning, and simulating failures to ensure resilience.

Disaster Recovery and Business Continuity You will be equipped with strategies for disaster recovery and business continuity in Kubernetes environments. This includes planning and practicing disaster recovery scenarios and implementing robust backup solutions.

Integration with the Cloud Native Ecosystem You will learn to integrate Kubernetes with the broader cloud-native landscape, including tools like Helm, and understand the role of CNCF projects and other integrations.

Preparation for the Certified Kubernetes Administrator (CKA) Exam The book will prepare you for the CKA exam with practical examples, exercises, and exam tips, increasing your chances of achieving certification.

Overall, you will emerge as a proficient Kubernetes administrator, capable of managing Kubernetes in both development and production environments, handling real-world challenges, and implementing best practices to ensure efficient and secure operations. This comprehensive knowledge will enable you to contribute effectively to your organization and advance your career in Kubernetes administration.

1.2 Why Kubernetes?

1.2.1 History and Origins

Kubernetes, often abbreviated as K8s, has a fascinating history that traces back to the early days of container technology and the evolution of cloud computing. Understanding the origins of Kubernetes provides valuable context for its design principles and widespread adoption.

The Rise of Containers The concept of containers dates back to the early 2000s with technologies like FreeBSD Jails and Solaris Zones, which allowed applications to run in isolated environments on a shared operating system. However, it wasn't until the launch of Docker in 2013 that containers gained significant traction. Docker provided a user-friendly platform for packaging applications and their dependencies into lightweight, portable containers that could run consistently across different environments.

Google's Internal Tools While Docker was making waves in the broader tech community, Google had already been using container technology internally for many years. Google developed several internal tools for managing containers at scale, including Borg, a cluster management system, and Omega, its successor. These systems were designed to efficiently manage vast numbers of containers across Google's data centers, ensuring high availability, resource efficiency, and scalability.

The Birth of Kubernetes In 2014, inspired by the success of Borg and Omega, Google decided to open-source a new project based on its internal container management experience. This project was Kubernetes. Kubernetes was designed to be a robust, extensible platform for orchestrating containers, providing a powerful set of features for automating deployment, scaling, and operations of application containers across clusters of hosts.

Community and Ecosystem Growth Kubernetes was donated to the newly formed Cloud Native Computing Foundation (CNCF) in 2015, which helped foster a vibrant, collaborative community around the project. The CNCF's stewardship ensured that Kubernetes evolved through contributions from a wide range of companies and developers, rapidly becoming the leading container orchestration platform. The ecosystem around Kubernetes also flourished, with numerous tools and projects emerging to extend its capabilities.

Milestones and Adoption Since its inception, Kubernetes has seen numerous milestones and widespread adoption across industries. Key milestones include:

- **2015:** Kubernetes 1.0 is released, and Google donates Kubernetes to the CNCF.

- **2016:** Major cloud providers, including Google, AWS, and Microsoft, begin offering managed Kubernetes services.

- **2018:** Kubernetes becomes the first CNCF project to graduate, indicating its maturity and widespread adoption.

- **2020:** Kubernetes surpasses 100,000 commits and 2,000 contributors, reflecting its vibrant and growing community.

Impact on the Industry Kubernetes has had a profound impact on the software industry, driving the adoption of cloud-native architectures and microservices. It has enabled organizations to deploy and manage applications with greater agility, scalability, and resilience. The standardization provided by Kubernetes has also facilitated a more consistent development and operational experience across different environments, from on-premises data centers to public clouds.

Understanding the history and origins of Kubernetes highlights its evolution from an internal Google project to a cornerstone of modern cloud-native infrastructure. This context sets the stage for exploring the technical details and practical applications of Kubernetes in the subsequent chapters.

1.2.2 Evolution of Infrastructure Management

The evolution of infrastructure management has been marked by significant milestones that have transformed how we deploy, manage, and scale applications. Understanding this evolution helps contextualize the emergence and significance of Kubernetes in modern software development and operations.

Physical Servers and Manual Management In the early days of IT infrastructure, applications were deployed on physical servers. Each server ran a single application, and resources were often underutilized. Managing infrastructure was a manual and labor-intensive process, involving tasks such as racking servers, configuring hardware, and installing software. This approach was inefficient, costly, and lacked scalability.

Virtualization The introduction of virtualization technology in the early 2000s revolutionized infrastructure management. Virtualization allowed multiple virtual machines (VMs) to run on a single physical server, improving resource utilization and isolation between applications. Hypervisors like VMware, Hyper-V, and Xen became popular, enabling more efficient use of hardware and simplifying disaster recovery through VM snapshots and migrations.

Cloud Computing The advent of cloud computing brought another paradigm shift. Cloud providers like Amazon Web Services (AWS), Microsoft Azure, and Google Cloud Platform (GCP) offered on-demand access to a vast pool of resources, enabling organizations to scale infrastructure up or down based on demand. This pay-as-you-go model reduced the need for large upfront investments in hardware. Infrastructure as a Service (IaaS) and Platform as a Service (PaaS) models further abstracted the underlying hardware, allowing developers to focus on building applications without worrying about infrastructure management.

Configuration Management and Automation As infrastructure became more complex, the need for automation and consistency grew. Configuration management tools like Puppet, Chef, and Ansible emerged to automate the provisioning and management of infrastructure. These tools enabled the definition of infrastructure as code (IaC), allowing for version control, repeatability, and automated deployments. This era also saw the rise of continuous integration and continuous deployment (CI/CD) practices, further streamlining the software development lifecycle.

Containers and Microservices Containers, popularized by Docker, provided a lightweight and portable way to package applications and their dependencies. Containers offered faster start-up times compared to VMs and consumed fewer resources. This led to the adoption of microservices architectures, where applications are composed of small, loosely coupled services that can be developed, deployed, and scaled independently. Containers facilitated the consistent deployment of microservices across different environments.

Container Orchestration With the increasing adoption of containers, the need for robust orchestration solutions became evident. Managing the lifecycle of containers, ensuring high availability, scaling, and handling networking and storage required sophisticated tools. Several orchestration platforms were developed, including Docker Swarm, Apache Mesos, and Kubernetes. Kubernetes quickly emerged as the leader due to its comprehensive feature set, strong community support, and extensibility.

Kubernetes: The De Facto Standard Kubernetes addressed many challenges associated with container orchestration by providing a declarative approach to managing infrastructure. It automated the deployment, scaling, and operations of application containers across clusters of hosts. Kubernetes introduced concepts such as pods, services, deployments, and namespaces, which abstracted the complexities of infrastructure management and provided a powerful framework for building cloud-native applications.

The Future of Infrastructure Management The evolution of infrastructure management continues as organizations adopt hybrid and multi-cloud strategies, serverless computing, and edge computing. Kubernetes plays a central role in these advancements by providing a consistent platform for running applications across diverse environments. The ongoing development of the Kubernetes ecosystem and related CNCF projects ensures that infrastructure management will become even more automated, scalable, and efficient.

Understanding the evolution of infrastructure management highlights the transformative impact of Kubernetes and sets the stage for mastering its capabilities in modern application deployment and operations.

1.2.3 Kubernetes Architecture Overview

Understanding the architecture of Kubernetes is essential to mastering its administration and effectively managing clusters. Kubernetes is a powerful, extensible platform designed to automate the deployment, scaling, and operation of application containers. Its architecture is built on several key components that work together to provide a robust and scalable system. This section provides a comprehensive overview of the main components and how they interact.

Master Node (Control Plane) The master node, also known as the control plane, is responsible for managing the Kubernetes cluster. It consists of several components that handle the orchestration of workloads, maintain the desired state, and ensure the health and scalability of the cluster.

API Server The API Server acts as the central management entity of the Kubernetes control plane. It exposes the Kubernetes API, which is used by all other components to communicate and manage the cluster's state. The API Server validates and processes RESTful API requests, updates the cluster state in etcd, and serves as the gateway for administrative actions.

etcd   etcd is a distributed key-value store used to persist the state of the Kubernetes cluster. It stores configuration data, metadata, and the desired state of all resources. etcd ensures strong consistency and reliability, which is crucial for maintaining the cluster's integrity.

Controller Manager   The Controller Manager runs various controller processes that regulate the state of the cluster. Controllers continuously monitor the state of the cluster, compare it to the desired state, and make necessary adjustments. Key controllers include:

- **Node Controller:** Manages node status and performs health checks.

- **Replication Controller:** Ensures that the specified number of pod replicas are running.

- **Endpoints Controller:** Manages the endpoints objects and keeps them in sync with services and pods.

- **Service Account and Token Controllers:** Create default accounts and manage API access tokens.

Scheduler   The Scheduler is responsible for assigning pods to nodes based on resource requirements and constraints. It continuously monitors the cluster for unassigned pods and matches them to suitable nodes, ensuring optimal resource utilization and workload distribution.

Cloud Controller Manager   The Cloud Controller Manager integrates Kubernetes with cloud provider APIs, allowing the cluster to interact with underlying cloud services. It manages cloud-specific resources such as load balancers, storage volumes, and networking configurations.

Worker Nodes   Worker nodes are the machines where containers are deployed and run. Each worker node contains the necessary components to manage and execute containerized applications.

Kubelet   The Kubelet is the primary agent running on each worker node. It registers the node with the cluster, ensures that containers are running as expected, and reports node status to the API Server. The Kubelet also monitors the health of pods and manages their lifecycle.

Kube Proxy The Kube Proxy maintains network rules on each worker node, enabling communication between pods and services. It ensures that network traffic is correctly routed to and from containerized applications, supporting various service types such as ClusterIP, NodePort, and LoadBalancer.

Container Runtime The Container Runtime is responsible for running containers on the worker node. Kubernetes supports multiple container runtimes, including Docker, containerd, and CRI-O. The Container Runtime Interface (CRI) standardizes the interaction between the Kubelet and container runtimes.

Pods Pods are the smallest deployable units in Kubernetes and represent a single instance of a running process. A pod can contain one or more containers that share the same network namespace and storage volumes. Pods are ephemeral, meaning they can be created and destroyed dynamically based on the cluster's needs.

Services Services provide a stable network endpoint for accessing a group of pods. They abstract away the underlying pods and offer load balancing, ensuring that traffic is distributed evenly across the available pod instances. Kubernetes supports different service types, including ClusterIP, NodePort, LoadBalancer, and ExternalName.

Volumes Volumes in Kubernetes provide persistent storage for pods. Unlike container storage, volumes have a lifecycle independent of individual containers, ensuring data persistence across container restarts. Kubernetes supports various volume types, including emptyDir, hostPath, and Persistent Volumes (PVs) backed by cloud storage solutions.

Namespaces Namespaces allow for the logical partitioning of cluster resources. They provide a mechanism to create isolated environments within a single cluster, facilitating multi-tenancy and resource management. Namespaces help in organizing and managing resources efficiently, enabling different teams or projects to work within the same cluster without interference.

Deployments Deployments are used to manage the lifecycle of applications in Kubernetes. They define the desired state for application deployment and provide mechanisms for rolling updates, rollbacks, and scaling. Deployments ensure that the specified number of pod replicas are running and handle updating the application seamlessly.

ConfigMaps and Secrets ConfigMaps and Secrets are used to manage configuration data for applications. ConfigMaps store non-sensitive configuration information, while Secrets store sensitive data such as passwords and API keys. Both provide a way to decouple configuration from application code, making it easier to manage and update configurations without modifying container images.

Kubernetes Extensions Kubernetes is highly extensible, allowing custom resources and controllers to be added to the system. Custom Resource Definitions (CRDs) enable the creation of new resource types, while Admission Controllers and Webhooks provide mechanisms for enforcing custom policies and modifying resource requests.

Conclusion The Kubernetes architecture is designed to provide a robust, scalable, and flexible platform for managing containerized applications. Understanding the interplay between the various components of the control plane and worker nodes is crucial for effective Kubernetes administration. This architectural overview lays the foundation for exploring more detailed aspects of Kubernetes in the subsequent chapters.

1.2.4   Benefits of Kubernetes

Kubernetes offers numerous benefits that have contributed to its widespread adoption and popularity in the world of container orchestration. Understanding these benefits can help you appreciate why Kubernetes has become the de facto standard for managing containerized applications.

Automated Deployment and Scaling Kubernetes automates the deployment and scaling of applications, allowing you to manage containerized workloads efficiently. By defining the desired state in Kubernetes manifests, you can let Kubernetes handle the complexities of maintaining that state. This includes automatically scaling applications up or down based on resource usage and demand, ensuring optimal performance and resource utilization.

Self-Healing Capabilities Kubernetes provides robust self-healing capabilities to ensure the reliability and availability of applications. If a container or pod fails, Kubernetes automatically restarts, replaces, or reschedules it to maintain the desired state. This minimizes downtime and reduces the need for manual intervention, enhancing the overall resilience of your applications.

Service Discovery and Load Balancing Kubernetes simplifies service discovery and load balancing through its built-in service abstraction. Services in Kubernetes provide a stable network endpoint for accessing a group of pods, and Kubernetes automatically handles load balancing traffic across these pods. This ensures that applications remain accessible and can handle varying levels of traffic without manual configuration.

Declarative Configuration Management Kubernetes uses declarative configuration management, allowing you to define the desired state of your applications and infrastructure using manifests written in YAML or JSON. This approach provides a clear, version-controlled, and auditable way to manage configurations, making it easier to replicate environments, apply changes, and roll back if necessary.

Efficient Resource Utilization Kubernetes optimizes the use of underlying infrastructure resources through features like resource requests and limits, node affinity, and taints and tolerations. By scheduling workloads based on available resources and constraints, Kubernetes ensures efficient utilization of CPU, memory, and storage, reducing waste and lowering operational costs.

Extensibility and Modularity Kubernetes is designed to be highly extensible and modular. It supports custom resource definitions (CRDs), which allow you to create and manage your own resource types. Additionally, Kubernetes provides extension points such as admission controllers and custom controllers, enabling you to enforce policies, extend functionality, and integrate with external systems seamlessly.

Portability Across Environments Kubernetes provides a consistent platform for running applications across different environments, including on-premises data centers, public clouds, and hybrid environments. This portability ensures that applications can be deployed and managed in a consistent manner, regardless of the underlying infrastructure, facilitating a true multi-cloud strategy.

Enhanced Security Kubernetes includes various security features to protect applications and infrastructure. These features include role-based access control (RBAC), network policies, pod security admissions, and secrets management. By leveraging these capabilities, you can enforce security best practices, isolate workloads, and protect sensitive data within your Kubernetes clusters.

Ecosystem and Community Support The Kubernetes ecosystem is vast and continually growing, with numerous tools, plugins, and extensions available to enhance its capabilities. The strong and active community around Kubernetes contributes to its rapid development, frequent updates, and a wealth of resources, such as documentation, tutorials, and forums, to support users at all levels.

Streamlined Development and Operations Kubernetes bridges the gap between development and operations (DevOps) by providing a unified platform for managing the entire lifecycle of applications. Developers can define application requirements and configurations using manifests, while operations teams can manage infrastructure and ensure compliance. This alignment streamlines workflows, reduces friction, and accelerates the deployment of new features.

Cost Savings By improving resource utilization and automating many aspects of application management, Kubernetes can lead to significant cost savings. Organizations can optimize their infrastructure investments, reduce manual management overhead, and leverage the scalability of Kubernetes to match resources with demand dynamically.

Innovation and Agility Kubernetes enables organizations to innovate faster and respond more quickly to changing market demands. Its flexibility and automation capabilities allow teams to experiment, iterate, and deploy new features with confidence. This agility is crucial in today's fast-paced digital landscape, where the ability to adapt and innovate can be a key competitive advantage.

In summary, Kubernetes offers a comprehensive set of features that enhance the deployment, management, and scaling of containerized applications. Its benefits extend across various aspects of IT operations, from improving reliability and resource utilization to enhancing security and enabling innovation. These advantages make Kubernetes an essential tool for modern application development and infrastructure management.

Chapter 2

Setting up the Environment

2.1   Prerequisites

2.1.1   System Requirements

Before diving into Kubernetes, it's crucial to ensure that your system meets the necessary requirements. Setting up a proper environment is the first step towards a smooth learning experience and successful Kubernetes management. Here, we will cover the essential hardware, software, and network requirements to get you started.

Hardware Requirements   While Kubernetes can run on a variety of systems, having adequate hardware resources is essential for a seamless experience. Here are the recommended hardware specifications:

- **CPU:** A minimum of 2 CPUs is recommended. However, for running multiple nodes and more complex setups, 4 or more CPUs will provide better performance.

- **Memory:** At least 4GB of RAM is required. For more advanced setups, especially those involving multiple nodes, 8GB or more is ideal to ensure smooth operation.

- **Storage:** A minimum of 20GB of free disk space is necessary. Ensure you have additional space for container images and logs.

Software Requirements Kubernetes relies on several software components and tools. Ensuring that you have the correct versions installed is crucial for compatibility and performance.

- **Operating System:** Kubernetes supports a range of operating systems, including Linux (preferred), macOS, and Windows. The most commonly used distributions are Ubuntu, CentOS, and Debian.

- **Container Runtime:** Kubernetes supports various container runtimes. Docker is widely used, but containerd and CRI-O are also popular choices. Ensure you have the latest stable version installed.

- **Kubeadm, Kubelet, and Kubectl:** These are essential tools for setting up and managing Kubernetes clusters. You can install them using package managers like apt for Debian-based systems or yum for Red Hat-based systems.

```
sudo apt-get update
sudo apt-get install -y kubelet kubeadm kubectl
sudo apt-mark hold kubelet kubeadm kubectl
```

- **Virtualization Software:** If you plan to use Minikube or KIND for local development, you will need virtualization software such as VirtualBox, VMware, or Hyper-V (Windows).

Network Requirements Networking is a critical aspect of Kubernetes. Ensure your environment meets the following network prerequisites:

- **Network Connectivity:** Nodes in a Kubernetes cluster must be able to communicate with each other. Ensure there are no firewalls or network policies blocking traffic between nodes.

- **Ports:** Kubernetes uses several ports for communication between components. Make sure the following ports are open:

  - **6443:** Kubernetes API server
  - **2379-2380:** etcd server client API
  - **10250:** Kubelet API
  - **10251:** kube-scheduler

- **10252:** kube-controller-manager
- **10255:** Read-only Kubelet API (optional)
- **10256:** kube-proxy

- **DNS Configuration:** Kubernetes relies on DNS for service discovery. Ensure that DNS resolution is configured correctly on all nodes.

Cloud Providers If you plan to use a cloud provider for your Kubernetes cluster, make sure you meet their specific requirements. Most major cloud providers, including AWS, Azure, and Google Cloud, offer managed Kubernetes services with their own set of prerequisites and setup procedures.

- **AWS:** Ensure you have an AWS account with the necessary IAM permissions. Install and configure the AWS CLI.

- **Azure:** Ensure you have an Azure account with the necessary permissions. Install and configure the Azure CLI.

- **Google Cloud:** Ensure you have a Google Cloud account with the necessary permissions. Install and configure the Google Cloud SDK.

Optional Tools Several optional tools can enhance your Kubernetes experience. While not strictly required, they can be highly beneficial:

- **Helm:** A package manager for Kubernetes, useful for managing complex applications.

- **Minikube:** A tool for running a local Kubernetes cluster, ideal for learning and development.

- **KIND (Kubernetes IN Docker):** A tool for running Kubernetes clusters in Docker containers, useful for testing and CI/CD pipelines.

- **K9s:** A terminal UI to interact with your Kubernetes clusters.

Summary Ensuring that your system meets these hardware, software, and network requirements will provide a solid foundation for your Kubernetes journey. Proper preparation helps avoid common pitfalls and ensures a smoother experience as you set up and manage your Kubernetes environment. With the right setup, you'll be well-equipped to dive into the hands-on aspects of Kubernetes administration.

2.1.2 Cloud Providers and Their Kubernetes Offerings

Cloud providers offer managed Kubernetes services that simplify the deployment, management, and scaling of Kubernetes clusters. These services handle much of the underlying infrastructure, allowing you to focus on your applications. Here, we will explore the Kubernetes offerings from the major cloud providers: Amazon Web Services (AWS), Microsoft Azure, and Google Cloud Platform (GCP).

Amazon Web Services (AWS) Amazon Elastic Kubernetes Service (EKS) is AWS's managed Kubernetes service. EKS provides a highly available and secure environment for running Kubernetes clusters.

Key Features of EKS:

- **Fully Managed Control Plane:** AWS manages the Kubernetes control plane, ensuring high availability and scalability.

- **Integration with AWS Services:** EKS integrates seamlessly with other AWS services such as IAM for authentication, CloudWatch for logging and monitoring, and ELB for load balancing.

- **Security and Compliance:** EKS supports advanced security features like VPC isolation, security groups, and IAM roles. It also complies with various regulatory standards.

- **Auto-scaling:** EKS supports cluster auto-scaling and horizontal pod auto-scaling to automatically adjust resource allocation based on demand.

Getting Started with EKS: To get started with EKS, you need an AWS account and the AWS CLI installed and configured. The following steps provide a high-level overview of setting up an EKS cluster:

1. Create an EKS cluster using the AWS Management Console or the AWS CLI.

2. Configure kubectl to connect to the EKS cluster.

3. Launch worker nodes and join them to the cluster.

4. Deploy applications to the cluster using kubectl.

Microsoft Azure Azure Kubernetes Service (AKS) is Microsoft's managed Kubernetes service. AKS simplifies cluster management by offloading many operational tasks to Azure.

Key Features of AKS:

- **Fully Managed Kubernetes:** Azure handles the control plane and infrastructure management, allowing you to focus on your applications.

- **Integration with Azure Services:** AKS integrates with Azure services such as Azure Active Directory (AAD) for identity management, Azure Monitor for monitoring, and Azure DevOps for CI/CD pipelines.

- **Security and Compliance:** AKS offers features like RBAC, Azure Policy for governance, and integration with Azure Security Center.

- **Scale and Performance:** AKS supports cluster auto-scaling, node auto-upgrade, and multiple node pools for optimal performance.

Getting Started with AKS: To get started with AKS, you need an Azure account and the Azure CLI installed and configured. The following steps outline the process of setting up an AKS cluster:

1. Create an AKS cluster using the Azure portal or the Azure CLI.

2. Configure kubectl to connect to the AKS cluster.

3. Set up node pools and configure scaling options.

4. Deploy applications to the cluster using kubectl.

Google Cloud Platform (GCP)   Google Kubernetes Engine (GKE) is Google's managed Kubernetes service. GKE offers a robust and scalable environment for running Kubernetes clusters.

Key Features of GKE:

- **Managed Kubernetes Control Plane:** GKE provides a fully managed control plane with automatic updates and scaling.

- **Integration with GCP Services:** GKE integrates with GCP services such as Stackdriver for logging and monitoring, IAM for access control, and Cloud Build for CI/CD.

- **Security and Compliance:** GKE supports advanced security features like Workload Identity, Binary Authorization, and VPC-native clusters.

- **Scalability and Performance:** GKE supports auto-scaling, preemptible VMs for cost savings, and regional clusters for high availability.

Getting Started with GKE: To get started with GKE, you need a Google Cloud account and the Google Cloud SDK installed and configured. The following steps provide a high-level overview of setting up a GKE cluster:

1. Create a GKE cluster using the Google Cloud Console or the gcloud CLI.

2. Configure kubectl to connect to the GKE cluster.

3. Set up node pools and configure scaling options.

4. Deploy applications to the cluster using kubectl.

Other Cloud Providers and Solutions   In addition to the major cloud providers, there are other platforms and solutions offering managed Kubernetes services:

- **IBM Cloud Kubernetes Service:** IBM's managed Kubernetes offering with integration to IBM Cloud services.

- **Oracle Cloud Infrastructure (OCI) Container Engine for Kubernetes:** Oracle's managed Kubernetes service designed for enterprise workloads.

- **DigitalOcean Kubernetes:** A simple and cost-effective managed Kubernetes service for small to medium-sized applications.

- **VMware Tanzu Kubernetes Grid:** VMware's enterprise-grade Kubernetes solution for both on-premises and cloud environments.

Choosing the Right Provider   Selecting the right cloud provider for your Kubernetes environment depends on various factors, including your existing infrastructure, application requirements, and budget. Consider the following when making your decision:

- **Integration Needs:** Choose a provider that offers seamless integration with your existing services and tools.

- **Performance and Scalability:** Ensure the provider can meet your performance and scalability requirements.

- **Cost:** Compare pricing models and choose a provider that fits your budget.

- **Support and Documentation:** Evaluate the quality of support and documentation provided by the cloud provider.

In summary, managed Kubernetes services from cloud providers like AWS, Azure, and GCP offer a convenient and powerful way to deploy and manage Kubernetes clusters. By leveraging these services, you can focus on building and running your applications while the provider handles the underlying infrastructure and management tasks.

2.1.3   Installing Necessary Tools (kubectl, minikube, kind, etc.)

To effectively work with Kubernetes, you need several essential tools that facilitate cluster management, deployment, and troubleshooting. This section covers the installation and basic usage of key tools such as kubectl, Minikube, KIND, and k9s.

Installing kubectl   *kubectl* is the command-line tool for interacting with Kubernetes clusters. It allows you to deploy applications, inspect and manage cluster resources, and view logs.

Installation Steps:

1. Download the latest release of kubectl:

```
curl -LO "https://dl.k8s.io/release/$(curl -L -s https://
dl.k8s.io/release/stable.txt)/bin/linux/amd64/kubectl"
```

2. Make the binary executable:

```
chmod +x ./kubectl
```

3. Move the binary to a directory in your PATH:

```
sudo mv ./kubectl /usr/local/bin/kubectl
```

4. Test the installation:

```
kubectl version --client
```

Installing Minikube   Minikube is a tool that runs a single-node Kubernetes cluster on your local machine, ideal for development and testing.

Installation Steps:

1. Download the latest release of Minikube:

   ```
   curl -LO https://storage.googleapis.com/minikube/releases
   /latest/minikube-linux-amd64
   ```

2. Install Minikube:

   ```
   sudo install minikube-linux-amd64 /usr/local/bin/minikube
   ```

3. Start Minikube:

   ```
   minikube start
   ```

4. Verify the installation:

   ```
   minikube status
   ```

Installing KIND (Kubernetes IN Docker)   KIND is a tool for running local Kubernetes clusters using Docker containers. It is particularly useful for testing and CI/CD pipelines.

Installation Steps:

1. Install KIND using Go (requires Go to be installed):

   ```
   GO111MODULE="on" go get sigs.k8s.io/kind@v0.11.1
   ```

2. Move the binary to a directory in your PATH:

   ```
   sudo mv $(go env GOPATH)/bin/kind /usr/local/bin/kind
   ```

3. Create a Kubernetes cluster:

   ```
   kind create cluster
   ```

4. Verify the installation:

   ```
   kubectl cluster-info --context kind-kind
   ```

Installing k9s k9s is a terminal-based UI for interacting with your Kubernetes clusters. It provides an intuitive interface for navigating through Kubernetes resources and performing various operations.

Installation Steps:

1. Download the latest release of k9s:

   ```
   curl -Lo k9s.tgz https://github.com/derailed/k9s/releases/
   download/v0.24.10/k9s_Linux_x86_64.tar.gz
   ```

2. Extract the binary:

   ```
   tar -xzf k9s.tgz
   ```

3. Move the binary to a directory in your PATH:

   ```
   sudo mv k9s /usr/local/bin/k9s
   ```

4. Verify the installation:

   ```
   k9s version
   ```

Using kubectl *kubectl* is the primary tool for managing Kubernetes clusters. Here are some common commands:

- Get cluster information:

  ```
  kubectl cluster-info
  ```

- List nodes:

  ```
  kubectl get nodes
  ```

- Deploy an application:

  ```
  kubectl apply -f application.yaml
  ```

- View pod logs:

  ```
  kubectl logs pod-name
  ```

Using Minikube   Minikube is excellent for local development and testing. Here are some basic operations:

- Start Minikube:

```
minikube start
```

- Access the Minikube dashboard:

```
minikube dashboard
```

- Stop Minikube:

```
minikube stop
```

Using KIND   KIND is useful for running Kubernetes clusters in Docker. Here are some basic commands:

- Create a cluster:

```
kind create cluster
```

- Delete a cluster:

```
kind delete cluster
```

Using k9s   k9s provides a powerful, user-friendly interface for managing Kubernetes resources:

- Launch k9s:

```
k9s
```

- Navigate resources: Use arrow keys to navigate and enter to select.

- View logs: Press 'l' to view logs of a selected pod.

- Execute commands: Use ':' to enter commands in k9s.

- Filter/search: Use '/' to filter/search in k9s.

Summary   Installing and familiarizing yourself with these tools is crucial for efficient Kubernetes administration. Each tool serves a specific purpose, from deploying applications and managing clusters to providing an intuitive interface for troubleshooting and monitoring. With these tools in hand, you'll be well-equipped to handle the various tasks involved in Kubernetes management.

2.2   First Cluster

2.2.1   Minikube and KIND: Local Cluster Setup

Setting up a local Kubernetes cluster is an excellent way to get hands-on experience with Kubernetes without needing a cloud provider. In this section, we'll walk you through setting up your first Kubernetes cluster using Minikube and KIND on an Ubuntu 20.04 system.

Minikube Setup   Minikube is a tool that runs a single-node Kubernetes cluster on your local machine. It is ideal for development, testing, and learning purposes.

Prerequisites: Ensure that your system meets the following requirements:

- A computer with at least 2 CPUs, 2GB of free memory, and 20GB of free disk space.

- Virtualization support enabled in the BIOS.

- Docker installed (Minikube can also work with other hypervisors like VirtualBox, but Docker is recommended).

Installation Steps:

1. Install Docker:

   ```
   sudo apt-get update

   sudo apt-get install -y apt-transport-https
       ca-certificates curl software-properties-common
   ```

```
curl -fsSL https://download.docker.com/linux/ubuntu/gpg |
    sudo apt-key add -

sudo add-apt-repository "deb [arch=amd64] https://
download.docker.com/linux/ubuntu focal stable"

sudo apt-get update

sudo apt-get install -y docker-ce

sudo usermod -aG docker $USER

newgrp docker
```

2. Install Minikube:

```
curl -LO https://storage.googleapis.com/minikube/releases
/latest/minikube-linux-amd64

sudo install minikube-linux-amd64 /usr/local/bin/minikube
```

3. Start Minikube:

```
minikube start --driver=docker
```

4. Verify the installation:

```
kubectl get nodes
```

Basic Minikube Commands:

- Open the Kubernetes dashboard:

```
minikube dashboard
```

- Stop Minikube:

```
minikube stop
```

- Delete Minikube cluster:

```
minikube delete
```

KIND Setup KIND (Kubernetes IN Docker) is a tool for running local Kubernetes clusters using Docker containers. It is particularly useful for testing Kubernetes clusters and CI/CD pipelines.

Prerequisites: Ensure that your system has Docker installed (refer to the Minikube prerequisites for Docker installation steps).

Installation Steps:

1. Install KIND:

   ```
   curl -Lo ./kind https://kind.sigs.k8s.io/dl/v0.11.1/
   kind-linux-amd64

   chmod +x ./kind

   sudo mv ./kind /usr/local/bin/kind
   ```

2. Create a Kubernetes cluster with KIND:

   ```
   kind create cluster
   ```

3. Verify the installation:

   ```
   kubectl get nodes
   ```

Basic KIND Commands:

- List existing KIND clusters:

  ```
  kind get clusters
  ```

- Delete a KIND cluster:

  ```
  kind delete cluster
  ```

- Create a cluster with a specific configuration:

  ```
  kind create cluster --config config.yaml
  ```

Troubleshooting Common Issues:

- **Minikube fails to start:** Ensure Docker is running and you have virtualization support enabled in your BIOS.

- **KIND cluster creation issues:** Check Docker logs for any errors and ensure Docker has sufficient resources allocated.

- **Network issues:** Verify that no firewalls or network policies are blocking communication between nodes.

Conclusion: Setting up a local Kubernetes cluster using Minikube and KIND provides a great way to start learning Kubernetes in a hands-on manner. These tools offer a convenient and straightforward way to deploy and manage a Kubernetes cluster on your local machine, enabling you to experiment and develop your skills without requiring a cloud environment. Once you're comfortable with local setups, you can transition to managing Kubernetes in production environments with greater confidence.

2.2.2 Deploying Your First Cluster

Now that you have the necessary tools installed, it's time to deploy your first Kubernetes cluster. In this section, we will guide you through the process of deploying a cluster using Minikube and KIND. These tools provide an excellent starting point for learning Kubernetes and experimenting with its features.

Deploying a Cluster with Minikube Minikube is designed to run a single-node Kubernetes cluster on your local machine, making it perfect for development and testing.

Starting Minikube: To start Minikube, simply run the following command:

```
minikube start --driver=docker
```

Minikube will download the necessary images and configure your local Kubernetes cluster. This process may take a few minutes depending on your internet speed and system performance.

Verifying the Cluster: After Minikube starts, you can verify that your cluster is up and running with:

```
kubectl get nodes
```

This command should display a list of nodes in your cluster, typically showing a single node with a status of 'Ready'.

Deploying an Application: Let's deploy a simple application to verify that everything is working correctly. Create a YAML file named 'hello-minikube.yaml' with the following content:

```yaml
apiVersion: apps/v1
kind: Deployment
metadata:
  name: hello-minikube
spec:
  replicas: 1
  selector:
    matchLabels:
      app: hello-minikube
  template:
    metadata:
      labels:
        app: hello-minikube
    spec:
      containers:
      - name: hello-minikube
        image: k8s.gcr.io/echoserver:1.4
        ports:
        - containerPort: 8080
```

Deploy the application using kubectl:

```
kubectl apply -f hello-minikube.yaml
```

Check the status of the deployment:

```
kubectl get deployments
```

Exposing the Application: To access the application, expose it using a Service:

```
kubectl expose deployment hello-minikube --type=NodePort
--port=8080
```

Get the URL of the exposed service:

```
minikube service hello-minikube --url
```

Open the provided URL in your web browser to see the application running.

Deploying a Cluster with KIND KIND (Kubernetes IN Docker) runs Kubernetes clusters in Docker containers, which is great for testing and CI/CD pipelines.

Creating a KIND Cluster: Create a Kubernetes cluster with KIND using the following command:

```
kind create cluster
```

KIND will set up a Kubernetes cluster within Docker containers. This process is typically faster than Minikube.

Verifying the Cluster: Verify that the KIND cluster is running:

```
kubectl get nodes
```

This should show a single node similar to the Minikube setup.

Deploying an Application: Use the same 'hello-minikube.yaml' file to deploy an application in KIND:

```
kubectl apply -f hello-minikube.yaml
```

Check the deployment status:

```
kubectl get deployments
```

Exposing the Application: Expose the application using a Service:

```
kubectl expose deployment hello-minikube --type=NodePort
--port=8080
```

Get the list of services to find the port number:

```
kubectl get services
```

Open the application in your browser by accessing 'localhost' and the NodePort listed:

```
http://localhost:<node-port-value>
```

eg:

```
http://localhost:30126
```

Conclusion: Deploying your first Kubernetes cluster with Minikube and KIND is a significant milestone. These tools provide a simple and effective way to start working with Kubernetes locally. By following the steps outlined above, you have successfully set up a cluster, deployed an application, and exposed it to access from your local machine. This foundational experience will prepare you for more advanced Kubernetes concepts and operations.

2.2.3   Cluster Validation and Troubleshooting

Once your Kubernetes cluster is up and running, it's crucial to validate its functionality and troubleshoot any issues that may arise. This section provides guidelines and common practices for validating your cluster and resolving potential problems.

Cluster Validation   Validating your Kubernetes cluster ensures that all components are functioning correctly and that the cluster is ready to handle workloads.

Check Node Status: Verify that all nodes in your cluster are in a 'Ready' state:

```
kubectl get nodes
```

Each node should be listed with the status 'Ready'. If any node is not ready, further investigation is required.

Check Pod Status: Ensure that all pods are running as expected:

```
kubectl get pods --all-namespaces
```

Look for pods in 'Running' or 'Completed' status. Pods in 'Pending' or 'Failed' status may indicate issues with scheduling or resource allocation.

Check System Component Status: Verify the health of key Kubernetes components:

```
kubectl get componentstatuses
```

This command checks the status of components such as the scheduler, controller manager, and etcd. All components should be 'Healthy'.

Check API Server Status: Ensure the Kubernetes API server is accessible:

```
kubectl cluster-info
```

This command provides information about the cluster, including the API server endpoint. Ensure that the API server is running and accessible.

Troubleshooting Common Issues   Despite best efforts, issues may arise in your Kubernetes cluster. Here are some common problems and their troubleshooting steps:

Node Not Ready: If a node is not in the 'Ready' state, check the node's status and logs:

```
kubectl describe node <node-name>
```

```
kubectl logs <node-name>
```

Look for issues related to resource allocation, network connectivity, or node components like kubelet and kube-proxy.

Pod Stuck in Pending: If a pod is stuck in the 'Pending' state, it may be due to insufficient resources or scheduling constraints:

```
kubectl describe pod <pod-name>
```

Check for messages indicating why the pod cannot be scheduled, such as resource limits or node affinity rules.

Pod CrashLoopBackOff: If a pod is repeatedly crashing, investigate the pod's logs and events:

```
kubectl logs <pod-name>
```

```
kubectl describe pod <pod-name>
```

Look for error messages or misconfigurations in the container image, environment variables, or command arguments.

API Server Issues: If the Kubernetes API server is unreachable, check the API server logs and system resource usage on the master node:

```
kubectl logs -n kube-system kube-apiserver-<node-name>
```

Ensure there are no resource constraints or network issues affecting the API server.

Networking Issues: If there are network connectivity issues between pods or nodes, verify the configuration of network policies and the network plugin (CNI) used by the cluster:

```
kubectl get networkpolicy --all-namespaces
```

```
kubectl describe pod <pod-name>
```

Ensure that network policies are correctly defined and that the CNI plugin is functioning properly.

Using Diagnostic Tools   Several tools can help diagnose and troubleshoot Kubernetes clusters effectively:

k9s: k9s provides a terminal-based UI for interacting with your Kubernetes clusters, making it easier to navigate and manage resources.

```
k9s
```

Use k9s to view resource status, logs, and perform administrative tasks interactively.

kube-ops-view: kube-ops-view is a visual tool for monitoring the status of your Kubernetes cluster.

```
kubectl apply -f https://raw.githubusercontent.com/hjacobs/
kube-ops-view/master/deploy/kubernetes/kube-ops-view.yaml
```

Access the kube-ops-view dashboard to get an overview of node and pod health.

Conclusion: Validating and troubleshooting your Kubernetes cluster are essential steps to ensure its smooth operation. By following the guidelines and utilizing the diagnostic tools mentioned above, you can quickly identify and resolve issues, maintaining a healthy and efficient Kubernetes environment. As you become more familiar with these practices, you'll develop a deeper understanding of Kubernetes and become proficient in managing complex clusters.

2.2.4   Kubernetes Dashboard Introduction

The Kubernetes Dashboard is a web-based UI that allows you to manage and monitor your Kubernetes clusters. It provides a user-friendly interface for deploying applications, monitoring cluster resources, and managing cluster configurations. In this section, we'll introduce the Kubernetes Dashboard, explain how to deploy it, and highlight its key features.

Installing the Kubernetes Dashboard The Kubernetes Dashboard can be easily installed using a single command. To deploy the dashboard, follow these steps:

   1. Deploy the Kubernetes Dashboard:

```
kubectl apply -f https://raw.githubusercontent.com/
kubernetes/dashboard/v2.2.0/aio/deploy/recommended.yaml
```

This command downloads and applies the recommended YAML configuration for the dashboard.

2. Verify the installation:

```
kubectl get pods -n kubernetes-dashboard
```

Ensure that the dashboard pod is running and has a status of 'Running'.

Accessing the Kubernetes Dashboard To access the Kubernetes Dashboard, you need to create a proxy to the API server. Use the following command:

```
kubectl proxy
```

Once the proxy is running, open the following URL in your web browser:

```
http://localhost:8001/api/v1/namespaces/kubernetes-dashboard/
services/https:kubernetes-dashboard:/proxy/
```

This URL directs you to the Kubernetes Dashboard login page.

Creating a Service Account for Dashboard Access To log in to the Kubernetes Dashboard, you'll need a token. Create a Service Account and assign it the necessary permissions:

1. Create a Service Account:

```
kubectl create serviceaccount dashboard-admin-sa
```

2. Bind the Service Account to the cluster-admin role:

```
kubectl create clusterrolebinding dashboard-admin-sa \
  --clusterrole=cluster-admin \
  --serviceaccount=default:dashboard-admin-sa
```

3. Retrieve the token for the Service Account:

```
kubectl get secret $(kubectl get serviceaccount
dashboard-admin-sa -o jsonpath="{.secrets[0].name}")
-o go-template="{{.data.token | base64decode}}"
```

Copy the token from the output and use it to log in to the Kubernetes Dashboard.

Key Features of the Kubernetes Dashboard The Kubernetes Dashboard provides a wide range of features to help you manage and monitor your clusters:

Cluster Overview: The dashboard provides an overview of the entire cluster, including the number of nodes, namespaces, and workloads running.

Workload Management: You can view and manage various workloads such as deployments, pods, replica sets, and jobs. The dashboard allows you to scale deployments, update images, and delete resources.

Resource Usage: The dashboard displays resource usage metrics, including CPU and memory usage for nodes and pods. This helps in monitoring the performance and health of the cluster.

Namespace Management: You can view and manage different namespaces within your cluster, making it easier to organize and isolate resources for different projects or teams.

Service Management: The dashboard allows you to manage services, view endpoints, and monitor service performance. You can also create and manage ingresses for routing external traffic to your services.

Config and Storage Management: You can manage configuration resources like config maps and secrets, as well as storage resources like persistent volume claims (PVCs) and storage classes.

Logs and Events: The dashboard provides access to logs and events for pods and other resources. This is useful for troubleshooting issues and monitoring the behavior of applications.

Using the Dashboard for Common Tasks Here are some common tasks you can perform using the Kubernetes Dashboard:

Deploying an Application: To deploy an application, click on the 'Deployments' section, and use the 'Create' button to upload a YAML file or fill in the deployment form.

Scaling a Deployment: Navigate to the 'Deployments' section, select the deployment you want to scale, and use the 'Scale' option to adjust the number of replicas.

Viewing Logs: Go to the 'Pods' section, select a pod, and click on the 'Logs' tab to view the pod's logs.

Checking Resource Usage: Use the 'Nodes' and 'Pods' sections to view CPU and memory usage, helping you identify resource bottlenecks or underutilized resources.

Conclusion The Kubernetes Dashboard is a powerful tool that simplifies the management and monitoring of your Kubernetes clusters. Its user-friendly interface makes it easy to deploy applications, monitor resource usage, and troubleshoot issues. By familiarizing yourself with the dashboard, you can efficiently manage your Kubernetes environment and ensure the smooth operation of your applications.

Chapter 3

Kubernetes Architecture

3.1 Nodes and Clusters

3.1.1 Master vs Worker Nodes

Kubernetes clusters consist of two main types of nodes: Master Nodes (Control Plane) and Worker Nodes. Understanding the roles and components of each type is crucial for effectively managing and operating a Kubernetes environment.

Master Nodes (Control Plane) Master nodes are responsible for managing the Kubernetes cluster. They run the control plane components, which handle the orchestration of containers, maintaining the desired state of applications, and managing the overall cluster operations.

Key Components of Master Nodes:

- **API Server (kube-apiserver):** The API Server is the central management entity of the Kubernetes control plane. It exposes the Kubernetes API, which is used by all other components to communicate and manage the cluster's state. The API Server validates and processes RESTful API requests, updates the cluster state in etcd, and serves as the gateway for administrative actions.

- **etcd:** etcd is a distributed key-value store used to persist the state of the Kubernetes cluster. It stores configuration data, metadata, and the desired state of all resources. etcd ensures strong consistency and reliability, which is crucial for maintaining the cluster's integrity.

- **Controller Manager (kube-controller-manager):** The Controller Manager runs various controller processes that regulate the state of the cluster. Controllers continuously monitor the state of the cluster, compare it to the desired state, and make necessary adjustments. Key controllers include:

  - **Node Controller:** Manages node status and performs health checks.
  - **Replication Controller:** Ensures that the specified number of pod replicas are running.
  - **Endpoints Controller:** Manages the endpoints objects and keeps them in sync with services and pods.
  - **Service Account and Token Controllers:** Create default accounts and manage API access tokens.

- **Scheduler (kube-scheduler):** The Scheduler is responsible for assigning pods to nodes based on resource requirements and constraints. It continuously monitors the cluster for unassigned pods and matches them to suitable nodes, ensuring optimal resource utilization and workload distribution.

- **Cloud Controller Manager:** The Cloud Controller Manager integrates Kubernetes with cloud provider APIs, allowing the cluster to interact with underlying cloud services. It manages cloud-specific resources such as load balancers, storage volumes, and networking configurations.

Worker Nodes Worker nodes are the machines where application containers are deployed and run. Each worker node contains the necessary components to manage and execute containerized applications.

Key Components of Worker Nodes:

- **Kubelet:** The Kubelet is the primary agent running on each worker node. It registers the node with the cluster, ensures that containers are running as expected, and reports node status to the API Server. The Kubelet also monitors the health of pods and manages their lifecycle.

- **Kube Proxy:** The Kube Proxy maintains network rules on each worker node, enabling communication between pods and services. It ensures that network traffic is correctly routed to and from containerized applications, supporting various service types such as ClusterIP, NodePort, and LoadBalancer.

- **Container Runtime:** The Container Runtime is responsible for running containers on the worker node. Kubernetes supports multiple container runtimes, including Docker, containerd, and CRI-O. The Container Runtime Interface (CRI) standardizes the interaction between the Kubelet and container runtimes.

Interaction Between Master and Worker Nodes The interaction between master and worker nodes is crucial for the smooth operation of a Kubernetes cluster. The control plane components on the master nodes manage the cluster's state and communicate with the Kubelet on each worker node to ensure that the desired state is maintained.

Key Interactions:

- **Scheduling:** The Scheduler assigns pods to worker nodes based on resource requirements, constraints, and policies defined in the deployment specifications.

- **Health Monitoring:** The Controller Manager continuously monitors the health of nodes and pods. If a node becomes unresponsive, the Node Controller marks it as 'NotReady' and may reschedule the pods to other nodes.

- **Configuration Updates:** Changes to the cluster configuration, such as deploying new applications or scaling existing ones, are managed by the API Server and propagated to the relevant nodes.

- **Logging and Monitoring:** Logs and metrics from the worker nodes are collected and analyzed to monitor the performance and health of the cluster.

Conclusion Understanding the roles and components of master and worker nodes is fundamental to effectively managing a Kubernetes cluster. Master nodes handle the control plane operations, ensuring the desired state of the cluster is maintained, while worker nodes execute the workloads. By comprehending the interaction between these nodes, you can better troubleshoot issues, optimize performance, and ensure the reliability of your Kubernetes environment.

3.1.2   Control Plane Components

The control plane is the brain of the Kubernetes cluster. It manages the overall state of the cluster, makes decisions about scheduling, and responds to events. The control plane components run on the master nodes and are responsible for maintaining the desired state of the cluster as defined by the user. Let's explore each control plane component in detail.

API Server (kube-apiserver) The API Server is the central management component of the Kubernetes control plane. It provides the main entry point for all administrative tasks and is the only component that directly interacts with the etcd key-value store.

Key Functions of the API Server:

- **API Gateway:** It serves as the gateway for all Kubernetes API requests (kubectl, client libraries, etc.) and performs all the CRUD (Create, Read, Update, Delete) operations on the cluster's resources.

- **Authentication and Authorization:** The API Server authenticates user requests and verifies that the user has the necessary permissions to perform the requested actions.

- **Validation and Admission Control:** It validates API requests and applies admission controllers to enforce policies and ensure the integrity of the cluster.

- **Cluster State Management:** The API Server updates etcd with the current state of the cluster and retrieves the desired state to ensure consistency.

etcd etcd is a distributed, reliable key-value store that stores all cluster data. It is a critical component for the consistency and availability of the Kubernetes control plane.

Key Functions of etcd:

- **Cluster State Storage:** etcd stores the entire state of the Kubernetes cluster, including configuration data, secrets, and service discovery information.

- **High Availability:** etcd supports clustering and data replication to ensure high availability and fault tolerance.

- **Strong Consistency:** It provides strong consistency guarantees, ensuring that all nodes see the same data at any given time.

- **Leader Election:** etcd handles leader election processes for distributed systems, which is critical for maintaining the state of the cluster.

Controller Manager (kube-controller-manager) The Controller Manager runs various controller processes that regulate the state of the cluster. Controllers are responsible for ensuring that the cluster's desired state matches the actual state.

Key Controllers in the Controller Manager:

- **Node Controller:** Manages node status and lifecycle, performs health checks, and responds to node failures.

- **Replication Controller:** Ensures that a specified number of pod replicas are running at all times.

- **Endpoints Controller:** Populates the Endpoints object (i.e., joins Services and Pods).

- **Service Account and Token Controllers:** Manages service accounts and their associated tokens for API access.

- **Job Controller:** Manages the lifecycle of job resources to ensure tasks are completed successfully.

Scheduler (kube-scheduler) The Scheduler is responsible for placing pods on suitable nodes based on resource requirements and constraints. It ensures efficient resource utilization and load balancing across the cluster.

Key Functions of the Scheduler:

- **Pod Placement:** The Scheduler assigns pods to nodes based on resource availability, node affinity, taints, tolerations, and other constraints.

- **Resource Optimization:** It ensures optimal use of cluster resources, preventing overloading of nodes while maintaining efficient utilization.

- **Policy Enforcement:** The Scheduler respects policies defined in the pod specifications, such as anti-affinity rules and resource limits.

Cloud Controller Manager The Cloud Controller Manager integrates Kubernetes with cloud provider APIs, allowing the cluster to interact with underlying cloud services. This component abstracts cloud-specific functionality, making Kubernetes more portable and versatile across different environments.

Key Functions of the Cloud Controller Manager:

- **Node Lifecycle Management:** Integrates with cloud provider APIs to manage the lifecycle of nodes, including creation, deletion, and health checks.

- **Service Load Balancing:** Manages cloud load balancers to expose Kubernetes services to external traffic.

- **Persistent Storage:** Integrates with cloud storage services to provide persistent volumes to pods.

- **Networking:** Manages cloud networking resources such as IP addresses and firewall rules.

Conclusion The control plane components are essential for the functioning of a Kubernetes cluster. They work together to maintain the desired state, manage cluster resources, and ensure high availability and reliability. Understanding these components and their interactions is crucial for effective Kubernetes administration and troubleshooting. By mastering the control plane, you can ensure that your Kubernetes clusters are robust, scalable, and responsive to the needs of your applications.

3.1.3 Node Components

Worker nodes are the backbone of a Kubernetes cluster, running the workloads and hosting the containerized applications. Each worker node contains several critical components that manage and execute these workloads. Understanding these node components is essential for effective cluster management and troubleshooting.

Kubelet The Kubelet is the primary node agent that runs on each worker node. It ensures that containers are running in a pod as expected by continuously monitoring the state of the pods and interacting with the Kubernetes control plane.

Key Functions of the Kubelet:

- **Pod Lifecycle Management:** The Kubelet ensures that the containers described in PodSpecs are running and healthy. It starts and stops containers as necessary, based on the pod's desired state.

- **Node Registration:** The Kubelet registers the node with the Kubernetes API server and provides details about the node's resources and status.

- **Health Monitoring:** It performs regular health checks on the pods and reports the status to the control plane.

- **Resource Usage Reporting:** The Kubelet collects and reports resource usage metrics (CPU, memory, etc.) to the control plane, aiding in scheduling and monitoring.

Kube Proxy   The Kube Proxy is responsible for maintaining network rules on each node, enabling seamless communication between pods and services. It handles the routing of traffic destined for services and ensures that network policies are enforced.

Key Functions of the Kube Proxy:

- **Service Discovery and Load Balancing:** The Kube Proxy routes traffic to the appropriate backend pods based on the service's IP address and port. It performs simple load balancing across the available pods.

- **Network Policy Enforcement:** It enforces network policies that control the allowed traffic between different pods and services.

- **Connection Management:** The Kube Proxy manages network connections to ensure high availability and performance, handling tasks like connection tracking and forwarding.

Container Runtime   The Container Runtime is responsible for running the containers on each node. Kubernetes supports multiple container runtimes, including Docker, containerd, and CRI-O. The Container Runtime Interface (CRI) standardizes the interaction between the Kubelet and container runtimes.

Key Functions of the Container Runtime:

- **Container Management:** The runtime is responsible for the lifecycle management of containers, including starting, stopping, and restarting containers as needed.

- **Image Management:** It pulls container images from registries, manages image storage, and ensures that the correct image versions are used for running containers.

- **Resource Isolation:** The runtime uses features of the host operating system, such as cgroups and namespaces, to provide resource isolation for containers, ensuring they run securely and efficiently.

Additional Node Components   Besides the primary components, nodes might also run additional tools and daemons to enhance functionality and monitoring.

cAdvisor: cAdvisor (Container Advisor) is an open-source tool integrated into the Kubelet that provides resource usage and performance metrics for containers. It helps in monitoring container health and resource consumption.

Node Problem Detector: Node Problem Detector (NPD) is a daemon that runs on each node to detect and report various node problems, such as hardware issues, kernel bugs, or other system-level problems that could affect the node's performance and reliability.

Conclusion   The components running on worker nodes are crucial for the operation of a Kubernetes cluster. The Kubelet, Kube Proxy, and Container Runtime work together to manage and execute containerized applications, ensuring that they run smoothly and efficiently. Additional tools like cAdvisor and Node Problem Detector enhance monitoring and reliability. A deep understanding of these components and their roles will enable you to manage and troubleshoot Kubernetes clusters effectively, ensuring that your applications run reliably and perform well.

3.2   API Server

The API Server, known as 'kube-apiserver', is the central management component of the Kubernetes control plane. It acts as the gateway for all interactions within the Kubernetes cluster, handling RESTful requests from users, nodes, and other components, and ensuring that the desired state of the cluster is maintained.

Key Functions of the API Server

1. Handling RESTful API Requests: The API Server exposes the Kubernetes API, which is used for all cluster interactions. It processes CRUD (Create, Read, Update, Delete) operations on Kubernetes resources, ensuring that the desired state specified by users and controllers is applied to the cluster.

2. Authentication and Authorization: The API Server authenticates all incoming requests to ensure they come from legitimate users or components. It supports multiple authentication mechanisms, including client certificates, bearer tokens, and authentication plugins. After authentication, it checks the user's permissions using Role-Based Access Control (RBAC) to authorize the request.

3. Admission Control: Once a request is authenticated and authorized, it goes through a series of admission controllers. These controllers enforce policies on the request, such as resource quotas, security policies, and custom admission hooks. They can modify or deny requests based on predefined rules.

4. Communication with etcd: The API Server is the only component that directly interacts with etcd, the key-value store that maintains the cluster's state. It writes the current state of resources to etcd and retrieves the desired state from etcd to ensure consistency across the cluster.

5. Cluster State Management: The API Server continuously monitors the state of the cluster and ensures that it matches the desired state defined by the user. It coordinates with other control plane components, such as the Scheduler and Controller Manager, to maintain the cluster's health and performance.

API Server Architecture The API Server architecture is designed to handle a high volume of requests efficiently while ensuring security and consistency.

1. Frontend: The frontend handles incoming API requests and performs initial processing, such as authentication, authorization, and admission control. It ensures that only valid and authorized requests proceed further.

2. Backend: The backend processes validated requests and interacts with etcd to read or write data. It also coordinates with other control plane components to ensure that the desired state of the cluster is maintained.

Scalability and High Availability To ensure scalability and high availability, Kubernetes allows running multiple instances of the API Server. These instances can be load-balanced to handle high volumes of traffic and ensure that the API Server remains available even if individual instances fail.

Load Balancing: Load balancers distribute incoming API requests across multiple API Server instances, ensuring even load distribution and high availability. This setup prevents any single instance from becoming a bottleneck or point of failure.

Leader Election: For certain operations that require a single point of control, the API Server uses leader election to designate a leader among multiple instances. The leader coordinates these operations, while other instances remain ready to take over if the leader fails.

Securing the API Server Security is a critical aspect of the API Server, as it handles sensitive operations and data. Several measures are implemented to secure the API Server:

1. TLS Encryption: All communication with the API Server is encrypted using Transport Layer Security (TLS) to protect against eavesdropping and man-in-the-middle attacks.

2. Authentication and Authorization: As mentioned earlier, the API Server supports various authentication mechanisms and uses RBAC for fine-grained access control.

3. Audit Logging: The API Server can be configured to log all API requests, providing an audit trail that helps in monitoring and detecting unauthorized or suspicious activities.

Conclusion The API Server is the cornerstone of the Kubernetes control plane, managing all interactions within the cluster and ensuring the desired state is maintained. Its robust architecture, combined with features like authentication, authorization, admission control, and high availability, makes it a critical component for the secure and efficient operation of Kubernetes clusters. Understanding the API Server's functions and architecture is essential for anyone looking to master Kubernetes administration and ensure the smooth operation of their clusters.

3.3   Etcd: The Cluster Brain

etcd is a distributed, reliable key-value store that serves as the backbone for storing all cluster data in Kubernetes. Often referred to as the "brain" of the Kubernetes cluster, etcd maintains the cluster's configuration, state, and metadata, ensuring consistency and availability. In this section, we'll delve into the role of etcd, its key features, and best practices for managing it.

Role of etcd in Kubernetes etcd is the primary data store for Kubernetes, holding the entire state of the cluster. It stores information about nodes, pods, services, deployments, and other Kubernetes resources.

1. Configuration Data: etcd stores configuration data for all Kubernetes objects. This includes definitions for pods, deployments, services, config maps, secrets, and more. The API Server reads from and writes to etcd to persist the desired state of these objects.

2. State Information: etcd keeps track of the state of all objects in the cluster. This includes the current status of nodes, the number of replicas running for a deployment, and the endpoints associated with a service.

3. Service Discovery: etcd plays a crucial role in service discovery within the cluster. By storing endpoint information, it allows the API Server and other components to discover services and route traffic appropriately.

Key Features of etcd

1. Distributed and Highly Available: etcd is designed to be distributed and fault-tolerant. It uses the Raft consensus algorithm to replicate data across multiple nodes, ensuring that data remains available even if some nodes fail.

2. Strong Consistency: etcd provides strong consistency guarantees, ensuring that reads always return the most recent write. This is critical for maintaining the accuracy and reliability of the cluster state.

3. Watch Mechanism: etcd supports a watch mechanism that allows clients to subscribe to changes in the data store. This feature is extensively used by Kubernetes to react to changes in the cluster state in real-time.

4. Snapshots and Backups: etcd supports taking snapshots of the data store, which can be used for backups and disaster recovery. Regular snapshots help ensure that data can be restored in case of failures.

Setting Up and Managing etcd Proper setup and management of etcd are crucial for the stability and performance of a Kubernetes cluster.

1. Deployment: etcd can be deployed as a standalone cluster or embedded within the Kubernetes control plane nodes. In production environments, it is recommended to run etcd as a separate cluster to isolate its resources and improve security.

2. High Availability: To ensure high availability, deploy etcd in a cluster configuration with an odd number of members (e.g., 3, 5, or 7). This configuration helps achieve quorum for the Raft consensus algorithm and allows the cluster to tolerate node failures.

3. Data Encryption: Enable encryption for data at rest and in transit. This includes using TLS for communication between etcd nodes and clients, and encrypting the data stored on disk.

4. Regular Backups: Schedule regular backups of etcd data to prevent data loss. Use the etcd snapshot tool to take consistent snapshots and store them in a secure location.

5. Monitoring and Alerts: Monitor etcd health and performance using metrics exposed by the etcd API. Set up alerts for key metrics such as latency, disk usage, and node failures to proactively address issues.

Best Practices for etcd Management

1. Resource Allocation: Allocate dedicated resources (CPU, memory, and disk) for etcd to ensure optimal performance. Avoid running resource-intensive workloads on the same nodes as etcd.

2. Security: Implement strong access controls for etcd. Use firewall rules to restrict access to etcd endpoints and employ authentication and authorization mechanisms to secure access.

3. Performance Tuning: Tune etcd performance parameters based on your cluster size and workload. This includes adjusting disk I/O settings, network configurations, and etcd-specific parameters.

Conclusion etcd is a critical component of the Kubernetes control plane, acting as the central data store for all cluster information. Its strong consistency, high availability, and real-time watch capabilities make it indispensable for maintaining the desired state of the cluster. Proper setup, regular backups, and diligent monitoring are essential for ensuring the reliability and performance of etcd in a Kubernetes environment. By understanding and managing etcd effectively, you can ensure the smooth operation and stability of your Kubernetes clusters.

3.4 Kubelet: The Node Agent

The Kubelet is a critical component of the Kubernetes architecture that runs on each worker node. It acts as the primary agent responsible for managing the lifecycle of pods and ensuring that the containers described in the PodSpecs are running and healthy. A deeper understanding of the Kubelet's functionalities, configuration, and interaction with other components is essential for effective Kubernetes administration.

Role of the Kubelet   The Kubelet ensures that the containers running on a node adhere to the desired state specified by the Kubernetes control plane. It constantly monitors the health and status of the pods and containers, ensuring that the node operates as intended.

Key Functions of the Kubelet:

- **Pod Lifecycle Management:** The Kubelet monitors the lifecycle of pods, ensuring that the containers in each pod are running as specified. It starts, stops, and restarts containers as necessary based on the desired state.

- **Node Registration:** When a node is started, the Kubelet registers it with the Kubernetes API server, providing details about the node's resources and status.

- **Health Checks:** The Kubelet performs regular liveness and readiness probes to check the health of the containers. It restarts containers that fail health checks.

- **Log Collection:** The Kubelet collects logs from running containers and makes them available for debugging and monitoring.

- **Metrics Reporting:** The Kubelet gathers and reports resource usage metrics (CPU, memory, etc.) from the node and its pods to the control plane.

- **Secrets and Configuration Management:** The Kubelet handles the distribution and management of secrets and configuration data, ensuring they are securely mounted into the containers.

- **Volumes Management:** The Kubelet manages the mounting and unmounting of volumes specified in the pod specifications.

Interaction with Container Runtime   The Kubelet interacts with the container runtime to manage the containers on its node. Kubernetes supports multiple container runtimes through the Container Runtime Interface (CRI), including Docker, containerd, and CRI-O.

Container Runtime Interface (CRI):

- **Standardization:** The CRI standardizes the communication between the Kubelet and container runtimes, allowing Kubernetes to support different runtimes seamlessly.

- **Management Tasks:** The Kubelet uses CRI to perform tasks such as starting, stopping, and inspecting containers, pulling images, and managing container logs.

- **Monitoring and Health Checks:** The Kubelet relies on the container runtime to report the status of containers and execute health checks.

Detailed Configuration and Deployment The Kubelet can be customized through various configuration options and command-line flags. Proper configuration is crucial for optimizing performance, security, and resource management.

Key Configuration Options:

- `--config`: Specifies the path to the Kubelet's configuration file, which contains settings for resource limits, security policies, and logging options.

- `--kubeconfig`: Specifies the path to the kubeconfig file used to connect to the API server.

- `--pod-manifest-path`: Specifies the path to a directory containing pod manifest files that the Kubelet should run.

- `--register-node`: Controls whether the Kubelet should register the node with the API server.

- `--node-labels`: Sets labels on the node, which can be used for scheduling purposes.

- `--eviction-hard`: Defines hard eviction thresholds for resource usage (e.g., memory, disk space), beyond which the Kubelet will evict pods to free up resources.

- `--cgroup-driver`: Specifies the cgroup driver used by the container runtime (e.g., cgroupfs, systemd).

- `--image-gc-high-threshold`: Defines the threshold for garbage collection of container images to free up disk space.

Pod Lifecycle Management The Kubelet's role in managing pod lifecycles is central to Kubernetes' operation. It ensures that containers are running, terminated properly, and resources are reclaimed efficiently.

Pod Creation and Deletion:

- **Pod Creation:** When the API server schedules a pod to a node, the Kubelet retrieves the pod specification and uses the container runtime to create and start the containers.

- **Pod Deletion:** When a pod is deleted, the Kubelet stops the containers, cleans up resources, and reports the status back to the API server.

Probes and Health Checks: The Kubelet uses liveness and readiness probes to determine the health and availability of containers. Liveness probes ensure that containers are running correctly, while readiness probes determine if a container is ready to serve traffic.

Resource Management and Quality of Service (QoS): The Kubelet enforces resource limits and requests specified in the pod specs to ensure fair resource allocation among containers. It also manages QoS classes (Guaranteed, Burstable, BestEffort) to prioritize resource usage based on pod specifications.

Security and Access Control Ensuring the security of the Kubelet is vital for protecting the integrity of the node and the entire cluster.

TLS Encryption: The Kubelet uses TLS to encrypt communication with the API server and other components, ensuring that data is protected during transit.

Authentication and Authorization: The Kubelet requires authentication for API requests and uses authorization mechanisms to control access to node resources. It can be configured with client certificates, bearer tokens, and authentication plugins.

Pod Security Admission: The Kubelet utilizes Pod Security Admission (PSA) to control the security settings of pods running on the node. PSA is a built-in admission controller that enforces security profiles on namespaces, dictating the security standards that pods must adhere to. The profiles—Privileged, Baseline, and Restricted—define escalating levels of security constraints, from allowing most behaviors in the Privileged profile to strict controls in the Restricted profile, such as running non-root containers, limiting access to host namespaces, and restricting privileged capabilities.

Monitoring and Troubleshooting Effective monitoring and troubleshooting of the Kubelet are crucial for maintaining node health and performance.

Monitoring Tools:

- **cAdvisor:** The Kubelet integrates with cAdvisor to provide detailed resource usage and performance metrics for containers.

- **Prometheus:** Prometheus can scrape metrics from the Kubelet, providing insights into node and pod performance.

- **Logs:** The Kubelet generates logs that can be viewed using tools like 'kubectl logs' or by accessing the log files directly on the node.

Common Issues and Solutions:

- **Pod Not Starting:** Check the Kubelet logs and events for error messages. Ensure that the container runtime is running and that there are no resource constraints.

- **Node Not Ready:** Verify the node's resource usage and health status. Check for network connectivity issues and ensure that the Kubelet is registered with the API server.

- **Performance Degradation:** Monitor resource usage and adjust resource limits or quotas as necessary. Investigate any throttling or contention issues.

Best Practices for Managing the Kubelet Implementing best practices for managing the Kubelet helps ensure the stability and efficiency of your Kubernetes nodes.

Regular Updates: Keep the Kubelet updated to the latest stable version to benefit from performance improvements, new features, and security patches.

Resource Allocation: Allocate sufficient resources (CPU, memory, disk) to the node to ensure that the Kubelet can perform its functions without contention.

Security Hardening: Regularly audit and harden the security settings of the Kubelet. Implement strong authentication and authorization controls, and restrict access to the Kubelet's API.

Monitoring and Alerts: Set up monitoring and alerts for key Kubelet metrics. Proactively address any anomalies or performance issues to maintain node health.

Conclusion The Kubelet is a vital component of the Kubernetes architecture, responsible for managing the lifecycle of pods on each node. By understanding its functions, configuration options, and interactions with the container runtime, you can effectively manage and troubleshoot nodes in a Kubernetes cluster. Proper monitoring, security practices, and resource management of the Kubelet ensure the reliability and performance of the workloads running on your nodes.

3.5 Kube Proxy: Network Proxy on Nodes

The Kube Proxy is a critical network component in the Kubernetes architecture, responsible for maintaining network rules on each node. It ensures seamless communication between pods and services, managing the traffic routing and load balancing within the cluster. Understanding the Kube Proxy's role and functionality is essential for effectively managing Kubernetes networking.

Role of Kube Proxy　The Kube Proxy runs on each worker node and is responsible for implementing the networking rules that enable communication between different services and pods within the Kubernetes cluster. It manages the network connectivity and forwarding rules, ensuring that network traffic reaches the correct endpoints.

Key Functions of Kube Proxy:

- **Service Discovery:** The Kube Proxy handles service discovery, allowing pods to communicate with services using a consistent internal IP address.

- **Load Balancing:** It provides simple load balancing for services by distributing network traffic across multiple backend pods.

- **Network Rules Management:** The Kube Proxy manages the network rules for forwarding traffic to the appropriate pods based on service endpoints.

- **Session Affinity:** It supports session affinity (also known as sticky sessions), ensuring that traffic from a client is directed to the same pod for the duration of the session.

Operational Modes of Kube Proxy　The Kube Proxy can operate in several modes, each using a different method to manage and forward network traffic. The choice of mode can impact performance and the overall network architecture of the cluster.

User-Space Mode:　In user-space mode, the Kube Proxy runs in user space and listens for traffic destined for service IPs. It then forwards the traffic to the appropriate backend pods. This mode is simple to implement but can introduce additional latency and overhead.

IPTables Mode: In IPTables mode, the Kube Proxy configures iptables rules to handle traffic routing directly within the Linux kernel. This mode is more efficient than user-space mode, as it leverages kernel-level packet processing, reducing latency and overhead.

IPVS Mode: IPVS (IP Virtual Server) mode uses the Linux kernel's IPVS module to implement load balancing. IPVS mode provides higher performance and scalability compared to IPTables mode, offering advanced load balancing algorithms and improved throughput.

Configuration and Deployment Configuring the Kube Proxy involves setting various parameters that control its behavior and operational mode. Proper configuration ensures optimal performance and reliability of network traffic within the cluster.

Key Configuration Options:

- `--proxy-mode`: Specifies the proxy mode (user-space, iptables, or ipvs).

- `--cluster-cidr`: Defines the CIDR range for the cluster IP addresses. This is used to route traffic within the cluster.

- `--masquerade-all`: Ensures that traffic originating from the cluster is masqueraded (NATed) for outbound traffic.

- `--healthz-bind-address`: Specifies the address for the Kube Proxy's health check endpoint.

- `--metrics-bind-address`: Specifies the address for the Kube Proxy's metrics endpoint.

Network Traffic Management The Kube Proxy plays a vital role in managing network traffic within the Kubernetes cluster. It ensures that requests from services are routed to the appropriate pods based on service endpoints.

Service Endpoints: The Kube Proxy watches for changes in service and endpoint objects in the Kubernetes API. It updates the network rules to reflect the current state of service endpoints, ensuring that traffic is directed to the correct pod IPs.

Handling Service IPs: The Kube Proxy assigns a stable virtual IP address to each service, which remains constant even if the underlying pods change. This abstraction simplifies service discovery and load balancing.

Traffic Forwarding: The Kube Proxy forwards traffic based on the service's endpoint information. Depending on the proxy mode, this forwarding can be done in user space, using iptables rules, or through the IPVS module.

Security and Performance Considerations Ensuring the security and performance of the Kube Proxy is critical for the reliable operation of the Kubernetes networking stack.

Security:

- **Network Policies:** Implement network policies to control the flow of traffic between pods and services, enhancing security by restricting access based on defined rules.

- **TLS Encryption:** Use TLS to encrypt traffic between services to protect data in transit and ensure secure communication within the cluster.

- **Access Control:** Limit access to the Kube Proxy's metrics and health check endpoints to authorized users and monitoring tools.

Performance:

- **Choosing the Right Proxy Mode:** Select the appropriate proxy mode based on your cluster's performance requirements and workload characteristics. IPVS mode is generally recommended for high-performance clusters.

- **Resource Allocation:** Ensure that nodes have sufficient CPU and memory resources to handle the Kube Proxy's processing load.

- **Monitoring and Optimization:** Continuously monitor the performance of the Kube Proxy using metrics and logs. Optimize configuration settings based on observed performance data.

Monitoring and Troubleshooting Effective monitoring and troubleshooting of the Kube Proxy are essential for maintaining network reliability and performance.

Monitoring Tools:

- **Prometheus:** Use Prometheus to scrape metrics from the Kube Proxy, providing insights into network traffic, rule processing times, and resource usage.

- **Logs:** Access Kube Proxy logs to diagnose issues and understand the state of network rules and traffic forwarding.

- **Health Checks:** Regularly check the health of the Kube Proxy using its healthz endpoint to ensure it is operating correctly.

Common Issues and Solutions:

- **Service Not Reachable:** Verify that the service endpoints are correctly configured and that the Kube Proxy has updated the network rules.

- **High Latency:** Investigate the proxy mode in use and consider switching to a more efficient mode like IPVS. Check for resource contention on the node.

- **Network Policy Violations:** Ensure that network policies are correctly defined and applied. Verify that they are not inadvertently blocking necessary traffic.

Conclusion The Kube Proxy is a vital component of Kubernetes, managing the network rules that enable seamless communication between services and pods. By understanding its role, operational modes, and configuration options, you can effectively manage Kubernetes networking. Proper security measures, performance optimization, and regular monitoring ensure that the Kube Proxy operates reliably, providing a robust network infrastructure for your Kubernetes clusters.

3.6   Controller Managers

3.6.1   Node Controller Manager

The Node Controller Manager is a crucial component of the Kubernetes control plane. It is responsible for managing the lifecycle of nodes, ensuring that the cluster remains healthy, and handling node-specific events. By understanding the Node Controller Manager's functionality and configuration, you can better manage the nodes in your Kubernetes cluster and ensure their reliability.

Role of the Node Controller Manager   The Node Controller Manager's primary role is to monitor the state of nodes in the cluster and take necessary actions to maintain the desired state. It interacts with the API Server to update the status of nodes, manage node labels and taints, and respond to node failures.

Key Functions of the Node Controller Manager:

- **Node Status Monitoring:** Continuously monitors the health and status of all nodes in the cluster. It checks for node conditions such as Ready, NotReady, and Unknown.

- **Node Registration and Deregistration:** Handles the registration of new nodes and the deregistration of nodes that are no longer part of the cluster.

- **Node Health Checks:** Performs health checks on nodes to detect issues such as network partition, resource exhaustion, and hardware failures.

- **Node Eviction:** Evicts pods from nodes that are marked as NotReady for an extended period, allowing pods to be rescheduled on healthy nodes.

- **Node Taint and Toleration Management:** Manages node taints and tolerations to control pod placement and prevent workloads from running on unsuitable nodes.

Node Status Monitoring and Health Checks   Monitoring node status and performing health checks are fundamental responsibilities of the Node Controller Manager. It ensures that the cluster can detect and respond to node failures promptly.

Node Conditions: Nodes in Kubernetes can have several conditions that indicate their health and status:

- **Ready:** Indicates that the node is healthy and ready to accept pods.

- **NotReady:** Indicates that the node is unhealthy or not ready to accept pods. This could be due to issues like network failures or resource exhaustion.

- **Unknown:** Indicates that the node controller has not heard from the node in a configurable amount of time (default is 40 seconds).

- **Other Conditions:**   Includes conditions like MemoryPressure, DiskPressure, and NetworkUnavailable, which provide more granular information about the node's state.

Health Check Mechanisms: The Node Controller Manager uses several mechanisms to perform health checks on nodes:

- **Heartbeat Signals:** Nodes send periodic heartbeat signals to the API Server. The absence of these signals indicates potential node issues.

- **Resource Monitoring:** Monitors node resources such as CPU, memory, and disk space to detect resource exhaustion or anomalies.

- **Node Lease:** Uses the node lease feature, where each node periodically renews its lease. If the lease is not renewed in time, the node is considered unhealthy.

Node Registration and Deregistration   The Node Controller Manager handles the registration of new nodes joining the cluster and the deregistration of nodes that are being removed or have failed.

Node Registration: When a new node is added to the cluster, the Kubelet on the node registers it with the API Server. The Node Controller Manager then updates the node's status and ensures that it is ready to accept pods.

Node Deregistration: Nodes that are no longer part of the cluster or have been permanently removed are deregistered by the Node Controller Manager. This process involves marking the node as 'NotReady' and evicting any remaining pods.

Node Eviction Policies The Node Controller Manager has policies for evicting pods from unhealthy nodes. These policies ensure that workloads are rescheduled onto healthy nodes, maintaining the availability and reliability of applications.

Pod Eviction Timing: The timing of pod evictions is configurable. By default, if a node remains in the 'NotReady' state for more than five minutes, the Node Controller Manager begins evicting pods from that node.

Graceful Eviction: Pods are evicted gracefully, respecting their termination grace periods. This allows applications to shut down cleanly and prevents data loss.

Forced Eviction: In cases where graceful eviction is not possible (e.g., when a node is completely unresponsive), the Node Controller Manager can perform forced evictions to quickly reschedule pods on healthy nodes.

Node Taint and Toleration Management Taints and tolerations are mechanisms used to control pod placement on nodes. The Node Controller Manager manages these to ensure that pods are scheduled on appropriate nodes.

Taints: Taints are applied to nodes to mark them as unsuitable for certain pods. A node can have multiple taints, each indicating a different reason for unsuitability (e.g., 'node.kubernetes.io/unreachable', 'node.kubernetes.io/disk-pressure').

Tolerations: Tolerations are applied to pods, allowing them to be scheduled on nodes with matching taints. Tolerations specify how long a pod can tolerate a taint before being evicted.

Managing Taints and Tolerations: The Node Controller Manager dynamically manages taints and tolerations based on node conditions and resource usage. This ensures that pods are placed on nodes that can meet their requirements and avoid nodes with known issues.

Configuration and Deployment Configuring the Node Controller Manager involves setting various parameters that control its behavior. Proper configuration ensures that node management is efficient and aligns with the cluster's requirements.

Key Configuration Options:

- `--node-monitor-period`: Specifies the frequency at which the Node Controller Manager checks the health of nodes. Default is 5 seconds.

- `--node-monitor-grace-period`: Defines the duration before a node is considered unhealthy if no health signals are received. Default is 40 seconds.

- `--pod-eviction-timeout`: Sets the grace period for evicting pods from unresponsive nodes. Default is 5 minutes.

- `--cluster-name`: Specifies the name of the cluster, used for distinguishing nodes in multi-cluster environments.

- `--enable-taint-manager`: Enables the taint manager, which automatically applies taints based on node conditions.

Monitoring and Troubleshooting Effective monitoring and troubleshooting of the Node Controller Manager are essential for maintaining the health and performance of the nodes in the cluster.

Monitoring Tools:

- **Prometheus:** Use Prometheus to scrape metrics from the Node Controller Manager, providing insights into node status, pod evictions, and resource usage.

- **Logs:** Access Node Controller Manager logs to diagnose issues and understand the state of node management activities.

- **Node Conditions:** Regularly check the conditions of nodes using 'kubectl' to ensure they are healthy and ready.

Common Issues and Solutions:

- **Node Not Ready:** Verify network connectivity, resource availability, and the health of the Kubelet on the node.

- **Frequent Pod Evictions:** Investigate resource constraints or hardware issues on the affected nodes. Adjust resource requests and limits for the pods if necessary.

- **Node Registration Failures:** Ensure that the Kubelet is properly configured and that there are no authentication or network issues preventing node registration.

Conclusion The Node Controller Manager plays a vital role in maintaining the health and stability of a Kubernetes cluster by managing the lifecycle of nodes. Its functions include monitoring node status, performing health checks, handling node registration and deregistration, managing pod evictions, and applying taints and tolerations. By understanding and effectively managing the Node Controller Manager, you can ensure that your Kubernetes cluster remains robust, resilient, and capable of handling the dynamic nature of containerized applications.

3.6.2   Replication Controller Manager

The Replication Controller Manager is a fundamental component of the Kubernetes control plane, responsible for maintaining the desired number of replicas for each ReplicationController object in the cluster. By ensuring that the specified number of pod replicas are running at all times, it guarantees the availability and scalability of applications. Understanding the Replication Controller Manager's role and functionality is essential for effectively managing application workloads in Kubernetes.

Role of the Replication Controller Manager The primary role of the Replication Controller Manager is to manage the lifecycle of pod replicas. It ensures that the specified number of replicas for a given application is always maintained, adjusting the actual state to match the desired state defined by the user.

Key Functions of the Replication Controller Manager:

- **Replica Management:** Ensures that the desired number of pod replicas are running at all times, scaling up or down as necessary.

- **Pod Monitoring:** Continuously monitors the status of pods and takes corrective actions if any pods are deleted, fail, or become unresponsive.

- **Pod Replacement:** Automatically replaces terminated or failed pods to maintain the desired replica count.

- **Load Balancing:** Distributes pod replicas across available nodes to ensure balanced resource utilization and high availability.

How the Replication Controller Manager Works The Replication Controller Manager operates by continuously comparing the current state of pod replicas with the desired state defined in the ReplicationController specification. It takes actions to reconcile any discrepancies, ensuring that the actual number of running pods matches the specified replica count.

Key Concepts:

- **ReplicationController:** An API object that defines the desired number of replicas for a set of pods, along with a pod template that specifies the configuration of the pods.

- **Selector:** A label selector used to identify the set of pods managed by the ReplicationController. The selector matches the labels of the pods to manage their lifecycle.

- **Pod Template:** A template that describes the configuration of the pods to be created by the ReplicationController, including the container image, resources, and other specifications.

Operational Workflow:

1. **Initialization:** When a new ReplicationController object is created, the Replication Controller Manager initializes the desired number of pod replicas based on the pod template.

2. **Continuous Monitoring:** The Replication Controller Manager continuously monitors the status of the pods managed by the ReplicationController, ensuring they are running and healthy.

3. **Scaling:** If the actual number of running pods deviates from the desired replica count, the Replication Controller Manager scales the pods up or down to match the desired state.

4. **Pod Replacement:** If a pod is deleted or fails, the Replication Controller Manager creates a new pod to replace it, maintaining the desired number of replicas.

Configuration and Deployment Configuring and deploying a ReplicationController involves defining the desired number of replicas and the pod template in a YAML or JSON manifest. Proper configuration ensures that applications are highly available and can scale to meet demand.

Example ReplicationController Configuration:

```
apiVersion: v1
kind: ReplicationController
metadata:
  name: example-rc
spec:
  replicas: 3
  selector:
    app: example-app
  template:
```

```
metadata:
  labels:
    app: example-app
spec:
  containers:
  - name: example-container
    image: nginx:1.17.4
    ports:
    - containerPort: 80
    resources:
      limits:
        memory: "128Mi"
        cpu: "500m"
    readinessProbe:
      httpGet:
        path: /
        port: 80
      initialDelaySeconds: 5
      periodSeconds: 10
    livenessProbe:
      httpGet:
        path: /
        port: 80
      initialDelaySeconds: 15
      periodSeconds: 20
    env:
    - name: EXAMPLE_ENV_VAR
      value: "example-value"
    volumeMounts:
    - name: example-volume
      mountPath: /usr/share/nginx/html
  volumes:
  - name: example-volume
    emptyDir: {}
```

Monitoring and Troubleshooting Effective monitoring and troubleshooting of the Replication Controller Manager are essential for maintaining the availability and performance of application workloads.

Monitoring Tools:

- **Prometheus:** Use Prometheus to scrape metrics from the Replication Controller Manager, providing insights into the status of replicas, scaling events, and resource usage.

- **Logs:** Access logs from the Replication Controller Manager to diagnose issues and understand the state of replica management activities.

- **Events:** Monitor Kubernetes events to track changes in the state of ReplicationController objects and respond to anomalies.

Common Issues and Solutions:

- **Pods Not Scaling:** Verify that the desired replica count is correctly specified in the ReplicationController manifest. Check for resource constraints or node availability issues.

- **Pod Failures:** Investigate the logs of failed pods to determine the cause of failure. Ensure that the pod template specifies valid configurations and resources.

- **Resource Exhaustion:** Monitor resource usage and adjust resource limits and requests in the pod template to prevent resource exhaustion and ensure balanced resource utilization.

Advanced Features and Best Practices Leveraging advanced features and following best practices can enhance the functionality and reliability of the Replication Controller Manager.

Using Rolling Updates: Implement rolling updates to update pod templates without downtime. Use deployment strategies that incrementally replace old replicas with new ones, ensuring continuous availability.

Managing Resource Quotas: Define resource quotas to limit the resource consumption of ReplicationController objects, preventing overcommitment and ensuring fair resource allocation across the cluster.

Label Management: Use meaningful and consistent labels in pod templates and selectors to organize and manage replicas effectively. Labels facilitate filtering, grouping, and selecting resources in the cluster.

Conclusion The Replication Controller Manager is a vital component of Kubernetes, responsible for maintaining the desired number of replicas for application workloads. By ensuring that the specified number of pod replicas are running at all times, it guarantees the availability and scalability of applications. Understanding its functions, configuration options, and best practices enables you to manage application workloads effectively and ensure their reliability in a Kubernetes environment.

3.6.3　Endpoints Controller Manager

The Endpoints Controller Manager is a critical component of the Kubernetes control plane, responsible for managing the Endpoints objects that link Services to the pods providing those services. By maintaining the mapping between Services and their associated pods, the Endpoints Controller Manager ensures seamless communication within the cluster. Understanding its role and functionality is essential for managing network routing and service discovery in Kubernetes.

Role of the Endpoints Controller Manager The primary role of the Endpoints Controller Manager is to create and update Endpoints objects in response to changes in Service and pod states. This process ensures that network traffic is correctly routed to the appropriate pods, enabling efficient service discovery and load balancing.

Key Functions of the Endpoints Controller Manager:

- **Endpoints Management:** Creates and updates Endpoints objects that map Services to the pods providing those services.

- **Pod Monitoring:** Continuously monitors the state of pods to detect changes such as creation, deletion, or updates, and adjusts the Endpoints objects accordingly.

- **Service Updates:** Responds to changes in Service specifications, ensuring that Endpoints objects are correctly synchronized with Service definitions.

- **Load Balancing:** Supports load balancing by updating Endpoints objects to reflect the current set of healthy pods for each Service.

How the Endpoints Controller Manager Works The Endpoints Controller Manager operates by continuously watching for changes in Services and pods. When it detects a change, it updates the corresponding Endpoints objects to ensure accurate routing of network traffic.

Key Concepts:

- **Service:** An abstraction that defines a logical set of pods and a policy by which to access them, typically defined by a selector.

- **Endpoints:** An object that lists the IP addresses and ports of the pods currently providing the Service. This object is dynamically updated by the Endpoints Controller Manager.

- **Selector:** A label selector used by the Service to identify the pods it should route traffic to.

Operational Workflow:

1. **Service Creation:** When a new Service is created, the Endpoints Controller Manager creates an initial Endpoints object with the IP addresses and ports of the pods selected by the Service.

2. **Pod Monitoring:** The Endpoints Controller Manager continuously monitors the state of pods. If a pod matching a Service's selector is created, updated, or deleted, the Endpoints object is updated accordingly.

3. **Service Update:** When a Service is updated, such as a change in its selector, the Endpoints Controller Manager updates the corresponding Endpoints object to reflect the new set of pods.

Configuration and Deployment Configuring and deploying Services and their associated Endpoints objects involves defining selectors and port specifications in the Service manifest. Proper configuration ensures that network traffic is correctly routed to the appropriate pods.

Example Service Configuration:

```
apiVersion: v1
kind: Service
metadata:
  name: example-service
spec:
  selector:
    app: example-app
  ports:
    - protocol: TCP
      port: 80
      targetPort: 8080
```

Endpoints Object: The Endpoints object is automatically created and managed by the Endpoints Controller Manager. It does not require manual configuration, but understanding its structure helps in troubleshooting and monitoring.

```
apiVersion: v1
kind: Endpoints
metadata:
  name: example-service
subsets:
  - addresses:
      - ip: 192.168.1.1
      - ip: 192.168.1.2
    ports:
      - port: 8080
```

Monitoring and Troubleshooting Effective monitoring and troubleshooting of the Endpoints Controller Manager are essential for maintaining accurate service discovery and network routing.

Monitoring Tools:

- **Prometheus:** Use Prometheus to scrape metrics from the Endpoints Controller Manager, providing insights into the status of Endpoints objects and network traffic routing.

- **Logs:** Access logs from the Endpoints Controller Manager to diagnose issues and understand the state of Endpoints management activities.

- **Endpoints Objects:** Regularly inspect Endpoints objects using 'kubectl' to ensure they accurately reflect the current state of the Services and pods.

Common Issues and Solutions:

- **Service Not Reachable:** Verify that the Endpoints object for the Service includes the correct pod IP addresses and ports. Check for issues with the Service's selector and pod labels.

- **Outdated Endpoints:** Ensure that the Endpoints Controller Manager is running and has access to the API Server. Check for network connectivity issues or resource constraints.

- **Pod IP Changes:** If pod IP addresses change frequently, consider using a more stable network configuration or persistent IP addresses for critical services.

Advanced Features and Best Practices   Leveraging advanced features and following best practices can enhance the functionality and reliability of the Endpoints Controller Manager.

Headless Services: Use headless Services to directly expose pods without a cluster IP. This approach provides greater control over service discovery and can be useful for stateful applications.

Service Annotations: Use Service annotations to customize the behavior of the Endpoints Controller Manager and integrate with external load balancers or service discovery systems.

Label Management: Use consistent and meaningful labels for pods and Services to simplify the management and selection of resources.   Labels facilitate filtering, grouping, and organizing resources in the cluster.

Conclusion   The Endpoints Controller Manager is a vital component of Kubernetes, responsible for maintaining the mapping between Services and their associated pods. By ensuring that network traffic is accurately routed to the appropriate pods, it supports efficient service discovery and load balancing.   Understanding its functions, configuration options, and best practices enables you to manage network routing effectively and ensure the reliability of your Kubernetes services.

3.6.4   Service Account and Token Controllers

The Service Account and Token Controllers are essential components of the Kubernetes control plane that manage the creation and maintenance of service accounts and their associated authentication tokens.   These controllers ensure that pods and other Kubernetes components can securely communicate with the API server and other services within the cluster. Understanding their roles and configurations is crucial for managing security and access control in Kubernetes.

Role of the Service Account and Token Controllers   The primary role of the Service Account and Token Controllers is to manage service accounts, which are special types of accounts used by pods to authenticate with the Kubernetes API server and other services.   These controllers ensure that each service account has a corresponding secret containing an authentication token.

Key Functions of the Service Account and Token Controllers:

- **Service Account Creation:** Automatically creates default service accounts in each namespace when the namespace is created.

- **Token Creation:** Generates and manages authentication tokens for service accounts, storing them in secrets.

- **Token Mounting:** Ensures that authentication tokens are mounted into pods as specified by the service account configuration.

- **Token Rotation:** Manages the lifecycle and rotation of tokens to maintain security and compliance with policies.

How the Service Account and Token Controllers Work The Service Account and Token Controllers operate by continuously monitoring the state of service accounts and their associated secrets. They ensure that each service account has a valid token and that tokens are mounted into pods correctly.

Key Concepts:

- **Service Account:** An account that provides an identity for processes running in a pod, allowing them to authenticate with the Kubernetes API server.

- **Secret:** An object that stores sensitive information, such as authentication tokens, used by service accounts.

- **Token:** An authentication credential issued to a service account, enabling secure communication with the API server.

Operational Workflow:

1. **Service Account Initialization:** When a namespace is created, the Service Account Controller automatically creates a default service account in that namespace.

2. **Token Generation:** The Token Controller generates an authentication token for each service account and stores it in a secret associated with the service account.

3. **Token Mounting:** When a pod is created, the Token Controller ensures that the appropriate service account token is mounted into the pod, allowing it to authenticate with the API server.

4. **Token Rotation:** The Token Controller periodically rotates tokens to maintain security, updating the associated secrets and mounted tokens in pods.

Configuration and Deployment Configuring service accounts and their associated tokens involves defining the necessary permissions and specifying how tokens are used by pods. Proper configuration ensures secure and efficient access control within the cluster.

Example Service Account Configuration:

```
apiVersion: v1
kind: ServiceAccount
metadata:
  name: example-service-account
  namespace: default
```

Using Service Accounts in Pods:

```
apiVersion: v1
kind: Pod
metadata:
  name: example-pod
spec:
  serviceAccountName: example-service-account
  containers:
  - name: example-container
    image: nginx:1.17.4
```

Monitoring and Troubleshooting Effective monitoring and troubleshooting of the Service Account and Token Controllers are essential for maintaining secure and efficient access control within the cluster.

Monitoring Tools:

- **Prometheus:** Use Prometheus to scrape metrics from the Service Account and Token Controllers, providing insights into the status and health of service accounts and tokens.

- **Logs:** Access logs from the Service Account and Token Controllers to diagnose issues and understand the state of service account and token management activities.

- **Secrets and Service Accounts:** Regularly inspect secrets and service accounts using 'kubectl' to ensure they are correctly configured and up-to-date.

Common Issues and Solutions:

- **Token Expiration:** Ensure that tokens are being rotated as expected and that the Token Controller is operational. Investigate any errors in token generation or rotation.

- **Missing Tokens:** Verify that service accounts are correctly associated with pods and that the Token Controller has created the necessary secrets.

- **Access Denied:** Check the permissions associated with the service account to ensure it has the required access rights for the API server and other services.

Advanced Features and Best Practices Leveraging advanced features and following best practices can enhance the security and functionality of service accounts and tokens.

Using RBAC with Service Accounts: Implement Role-Based Access Control (RBAC) to define fine-grained permissions for service accounts. Create roles and role bindings to control what actions service accounts can perform within the cluster.

Token Security: Ensure that tokens are stored securely and are only accessible to authorized pods and components. Use encryption for secrets and restrict access to sensitive information.

Audit Logging: Enable audit logging for API requests to monitor and review actions performed using service account tokens. This helps in detecting and investigating suspicious activities.

Conclusion The Service Account and Token Controllers are vital components of Kubernetes, responsible for managing the creation and maintenance of service accounts and their authentication tokens. By ensuring secure and efficient access control, these controllers enable secure communication within the cluster. Understanding their functions, configuration options, and best practices allows you to manage service accounts effectively and maintain the security and integrity of your Kubernetes environment.

3.7 Scheduler: How Work is Assigned

The Scheduler is a critical component of the Kubernetes control plane that assigns work to nodes in a Kubernetes cluster. It is responsible for placing pods on suitable nodes based on resource requirements, constraints, and policies defined by the cluster operator. Understanding how the Scheduler works and how to configure it is essential for optimizing resource utilization and ensuring the efficient operation of your Kubernetes workloads.

Role of the Scheduler The primary role of the Scheduler is to determine the optimal placement of pods within the cluster. It does this by evaluating the current state of the cluster, considering resource availability, and applying scheduling policies to make informed decisions.

Key Functions of the Scheduler:

- **Pod Placement:** Assigns pods to nodes based on their resource requirements, such as CPU, memory, and storage.

- **Resource Optimization:** Ensures efficient utilization of cluster resources by balancing workloads across available nodes.

- **Policy Enforcement:** Applies constraints and policies, such as node affinity/anti-affinity, taints and tolerations, and pod priority.

- **Scalability:** Supports horizontal scaling by placing new pods on appropriate nodes as workloads increase.

How the Scheduler Works The Scheduler follows a multi-step process to place pods on nodes. It begins by filtering nodes that do not meet the pod's requirements and then ranks the remaining nodes to select the most suitable one.

Scheduling Workflow:

1. **Pod Queue:** The Scheduler maintains a queue of unscheduled pods that need to be placed on nodes.

2. **Filtering:** Filters out nodes that do not meet the pod's requirements. This step considers factors such as node capacity, taints, and node selectors.

3. **Scoring:** Scores the remaining nodes based on various criteria to determine their suitability for the pod. Scoring considers factors like resource availability, affinity rules, and existing workloads.

4. **Binding:** Selects the highest-scoring node and binds the pod to it by updating the pod's specification in the API server.

Configuration and Policies The Scheduler can be customized through various configuration options and policies to control pod placement and optimize resource utilization.

Key Configuration Options:

- `--kubeconfig`: Specifies the path to the kubeconfig file used to connect to the API server.

- `--policy-config-file`: Defines the path to the policy configuration file that specifies scheduling policies.

- `--leader-elect`: Enables leader election for high availability, ensuring that only one instance of the Scheduler is active at a time.

Scheduling Policies:

- **Node Affinity/Anti-Affinity:** Controls pod placement based on node labels, allowing you to specify rules for preferred and required node characteristics.

- **Pod Affinity/Anti-Affinity:** Controls pod placement based on the presence of other pods, enabling you to define rules for co-locating or separating pods.

- **Taints and Tolerations:** Allows nodes to repel specific pods using taints, while pods with matching tolerations can tolerate those taints.

- **Pod Priority:** Assigns priority levels to pods, ensuring that higher-priority pods are scheduled before lower-priority ones during resource contention.

Advanced Scheduling Techniques Kubernetes offers advanced scheduling techniques that enhance the flexibility and efficiency of pod placement.

Inter-Pod Affinity and Anti-Affinity: Inter-pod affinity and anti-affinity rules enable you to control the placement of pods relative to other pods. This is useful for improving data locality, reducing latency, and enhancing fault tolerance.

Topology-Aware Scheduling: Topology-aware scheduling considers the physical topology of the cluster, such as zones and regions, to optimize pod placement for high availability and low latency.

Custom Schedulers: Kubernetes supports custom schedulers, allowing you to implement specialized scheduling logic to meet specific requirements. Custom schedulers can coexist with the default scheduler and handle specific pods based on annotations or labels.

Monitoring and Troubleshooting Effective monitoring and troubleshooting of the Scheduler are crucial for maintaining optimal resource utilization and resolving scheduling issues.

Monitoring Tools:

- **Prometheus:** Use Prometheus to scrape metrics from the Scheduler, providing insights into scheduling latency, pod placement decisions, and resource utilization.

- **Logs:** Access Scheduler logs to diagnose issues and understand the decision-making process for pod placement.

- **Events:** Monitor Kubernetes events to track scheduling activities and detect anomalies.

Common Issues and Solutions:

- **Pods Not Scheduled:** Verify that the cluster has sufficient resources and that the nodes meet the pod's requirements. Check for scheduling constraints such as node selectors and taints.

- **Unbalanced Workloads:** Ensure that the Scheduler is configured to balance workloads effectively. Review affinity and anti-affinity rules and adjust them as necessary.

- **High Scheduling Latency:** Monitor Scheduler performance metrics and investigate potential bottlenecks. Consider increasing the Scheduler's resources or optimizing scheduling policies.

Best Practices for Scheduler Configuration Implementing best practices for Scheduler configuration helps ensure efficient and reliable pod placement.

Resource Requests and Limits: Define resource requests and limits for pods to provide the Scheduler with accurate information for making placement decisions. This helps prevent overcommitment and ensures fair resource allocation.

Scheduling Constraints: Use scheduling constraints such as affinity/anti-affinity rules, taints, and tolerations to control pod placement based on specific requirements. This enhances the efficiency and reliability of workload distribution.

High Availability: Enable leader election for the Scheduler to ensure high availability and prevent single points of failure. This setup ensures that scheduling continues seamlessly even if one instance of the Scheduler fails.

Conclusion The Scheduler is a vital component of Kubernetes that determines the optimal placement of pods within the cluster. By understanding its role, workflow, configuration options, and advanced scheduling techniques, you can optimize resource utilization and ensure the efficient operation of your Kubernetes workloads. Proper monitoring, troubleshooting, and adherence to best practices further enhance the Scheduler's effectiveness, contributing to the overall stability and performance of your Kubernetes environment.

3.8   Cloud Controller Manager

The Cloud Controller Manager (CCM) is a vital component of the Kubernetes control plane that integrates Kubernetes with cloud provider APIs. It allows Kubernetes to interact with the underlying infrastructure provided by cloud services, managing resources such as load balancers, storage volumes, and networking configurations. Understanding the role and functionality of the Cloud Controller Manager is essential for effectively managing Kubernetes clusters in cloud environments.

Role of the Cloud Controller Manager The Cloud Controller Manager abstracts cloud-specific functionality from the core Kubernetes components, making Kubernetes more portable across different cloud providers. It interacts with the cloud provider's API to manage infrastructure resources required by Kubernetes.

Key Functions of the Cloud Controller Manager:

- **Node Lifecycle Management:** Manages the lifecycle of nodes in the cloud, including node creation, deletion, and health checks.

- **Load Balancer Management:** Creates and configures cloud load balancers to expose Kubernetes services to external traffic.

- **Persistent Storage Management:** Integrates with cloud storage services to provision and manage persistent volumes for pods.

- **Network Configuration:** Manages cloud networking resources such as IP addresses and firewall rules.

How the Cloud Controller Manager Works The Cloud Controller Manager operates by interacting with the cloud provider's API to manage infrastructure resources. It consists of several controllers, each responsible for a specific set of cloud resources.

Key Components:

- **Node Controller:** Manages the registration and lifecycle of nodes in the cloud, ensuring that nodes are correctly integrated with the Kubernetes cluster.

- **Route Controller:** Manages routing configurations in the cloud to ensure that network traffic is correctly routed between nodes and pods.

- **Service Controller:** Manages the creation and configuration of cloud load balancers for exposing Kubernetes services to external traffic.

- **Persistent Volume Controller:** Integrates with cloud storage services to provision and manage persistent volumes for pods.

Operational Workflow:

1. **Node Management:** When a new node is added to the cluster, the Node Controller interacts with the cloud provider to register the node and ensure it is ready for use.

2. **Service Exposure:** When a Service of type LoadBalancer is created, the Service Controller configures a cloud load balancer to route external traffic to the service.

3. **Storage Provisioning:** When a PersistentVolumeClaim is created, the Persistent Volume Controller provisions a corresponding volume from the cloud storage service and makes it available to the pod.

4. **Network Configuration:** The Route Controller ensures that the necessary network routes and firewall rules are configured to enable communication between nodes and pods.

Configuration and Deployment Configuring the Cloud Controller Manager involves setting various parameters that control its interaction with the cloud provider's API. Proper configuration ensures efficient resource management and integration with cloud services.

Key Configuration Options:

- `--cloud-provider`: Specifies the cloud provider (e.g., aws, gce, azure) that the Cloud Controller Manager interacts with.

- `--cloud-config`: Defines the path to the cloud provider configuration file, which contains authentication and other necessary settings.

- `--leader-elect`: Enables leader election for high availability, ensuring that only one instance of the Cloud Controller Manager is active at a time.

Monitoring and Troubleshooting Effective monitoring and troubleshooting of the Cloud Controller Manager are essential for maintaining the health and performance of cloud-integrated Kubernetes clusters.

Monitoring Tools:

- **Prometheus:** Use Prometheus to scrape metrics from the Cloud Controller Manager, providing insights into resource provisioning, node status, and service availability.

- **Logs:** Access logs from the Cloud Controller Manager to diagnose issues and understand the interactions with the cloud provider's API.

- **Events:** Monitor Kubernetes events to track changes in cloud resources and detect anomalies.

Common Issues and Solutions:

- **Resource Provisioning Failures:** Verify the cloud provider configuration and ensure that the Cloud Controller Manager has the necessary permissions to create and manage resources.

- **Node Registration Issues:** Ensure that nodes are properly registered and that the cloud provider's API is accessible. Check for network connectivity issues and authentication errors.

- **Load Balancer Configuration Errors:** Verify that the Service specifications are correct and that the cloud load balancer is configured properly. Check for resource quotas or limits imposed by the cloud provider.

Advanced Features and Best Practices Leveraging advanced features and following best practices can enhance the functionality and reliability of the Cloud Controller Manager.

Multi-Region Clusters: Use the Cloud Controller Manager to manage clusters that span multiple regions, ensuring high availability and low latency for globally distributed applications.

Custom Cloud Providers: Implement custom cloud providers for specialized infrastructure needs, allowing the Cloud Controller Manager to interact with non-standard or private cloud environments.

Resource Quotas: Define resource quotas to limit the amount of cloud resources that can be consumed by the cluster, preventing overuse and controlling costs.

Conclusion The Cloud Controller Manager is a crucial component of Kubernetes that integrates with cloud provider APIs to manage infrastructure resources. By understanding its role, configuration options, and best practices, you can effectively manage cloud-integrated Kubernetes clusters. Proper monitoring and troubleshooting further enhance the reliability and performance of your clusters, ensuring seamless interaction with the underlying cloud infrastructure.

3.9 Container Runtimes and CRI

3.9.1 Understanding Container Runtimes

Container runtimes are the underlying technology that enables the running of containers. In a Kubernetes environment, the container runtime is responsible for pulling container images, starting and stopping containers, and managing container resources. Understanding the different container runtimes and their roles is essential for effectively managing containerized applications in Kubernetes.

What is a Container Runtime? A container runtime is a software component that runs and manages containers. It provides the necessary environment and tools to run containers, including isolation, resource management, and interaction with the host operating system.

Key Functions of a Container Runtime:

- **Image Management:** Pulls container images from container registries and manages local image storage.

- **Container Lifecycle Management:** Handles the lifecycle of containers, including creation, starting, stopping, and deletion.

- **Resource Isolation:** Provides isolation for containers through namespaces and control groups (cgroups), ensuring that containers run independently of each other.

- **Networking:** Manages network interfaces and configurations for containers, enabling communication between containers and external systems.

- **Logging and Monitoring:** Collects and provides logs and metrics from running containers for monitoring and troubleshooting purposes.

Types of Container Runtimes Several container runtimes are available, each with its own features and capabilities. Kubernetes supports multiple container runtimes through the Container Runtime Interface (CRI), allowing users to choose the runtime that best fits their needs.

Docker: Docker is one of the most popular and widely used container runtimes. It provides a comprehensive platform for building, shipping, and running containers.

- **Pros:**

  - Widely adopted with extensive community support and tooling.
  - Mature ecosystem with robust features for image management and container orchestration.

- **Cons:**

  - Additional abstraction layers, which may introduce complexity and overhead.
  - Limited integration with certain advanced Kubernetes features.

Containerd: Containerd is a high-performance container runtime that is widely used in production environments. It is designed to provide simplicity, robustness, and portability.

- **Pros:**

  - Lightweight and efficient with minimal overhead.
  - Directly integrated with Kubernetes through the CRI.
  - Strong community support and industry adoption.

- **Cons:**

  - Less feature-rich compared to Docker's full platform, focusing primarily on runtime responsibilities.

CRI-O: CRI-O is an open-source container runtime specifically designed for Kubernetes. It provides a lightweight runtime that adheres closely to the CRI standards.

- **Pros:**

  - Lightweight and optimized for Kubernetes.
  - Direct support for Kubernetes features and extensions.

    – Lower resource consumption compared to Docker.

- **Cons:**

  – Smaller ecosystem and community compared to Docker.

  – May require additional configuration for some use cases.

Other Runtimes: Other container runtimes, such as rkt and gVisor, offer unique features and capabilities for specific use cases. For example, gVisor provides enhanced security through additional isolation layers.

Container Runtime Interface (CRI) The Container Runtime Interface (CRI) is a standardized API used by Kubernetes to interact with container runtimes. It abstracts the underlying runtime implementation, allowing Kubernetes to support multiple container runtimes seamlessly.

Key Benefits of CRI:

- **Flexibility:** Allows users to choose from different container runtimes based on their specific needs and preferences.

- **Interoperability:** Ensures that Kubernetes can work with any CRI-compliant container runtime, promoting compatibility and integration.

- **Decoupling:** Decouples the Kubernetes control plane from the container runtime, enabling independent evolution and improvements of both components.

Configuring Container Runtimes in Kubernetes Configuring the container runtime in Kubernetes involves setting up the desired runtime and ensuring it is properly integrated with the kubelet. Proper configuration ensures that the runtime can manage containers efficiently and securely.

Example Configuration for Containerd:

```
# /etc/default/kubelet
KUBELET_EXTRA_ARGS=--container-runtime=remote
--container-runtime-endpoint=/run/containerd/containerd.sock
```

Monitoring and Troubleshooting Container Runtimes Effective monitoring and troubleshooting of container runtimes are crucial for maintaining the health and performance of containerized applications.

Monitoring Tools:

- **Prometheus:** Use Prometheus to scrape metrics from the container runtime, providing insights into resource usage, container status, and performance.

- **Logs:** Access runtime logs to diagnose issues and understand the state of container management activities.

- **cAdvisor:** Leverage cAdvisor integrated with the kubelet to collect resource usage and performance metrics from containers.

Common Issues and Solutions:

- **Container Startup Failures:** Check the runtime logs for error messages and ensure that the container images are available and correctly configured.

- **Resource Exhaustion:** Monitor resource usage and adjust resource limits and requests to prevent resource contention and exhaustion.

- **Compatibility Issues:** Ensure that the runtime is properly integrated with Kubernetes and that all necessary configurations are applied.

Best Practices for Managing Container Runtimes Implementing best practices for managing container runtimes helps ensure the stability and efficiency of containerized applications in Kubernetes.

Resource Allocation: Define resource requests and limits for containers to ensure fair resource allocation and prevent overcommitment.

Security Hardening: Apply security best practices, such as using non-root users, enabling runtime security features, and regularly updating container images.

Regular Updates: Keep the container runtime updated to the latest stable version to benefit from performance improvements, new features, and security patches.

Conclusion Container runtimes are the backbone of containerized applications in Kubernetes, providing the necessary environment to run and manage containers. By understanding the different types of container runtimes, their roles, and how to configure them, you can effectively manage your Kubernetes workloads. Leveraging the Container Runtime Interface (CRI) ensures flexibility and interoperability, enabling you to choose the best runtime for your needs. Proper monitoring, troubleshooting, and adherence to best practices further enhance the reliability and performance of your containerized applications.

3.9.2   Docker: A Pioneer in Containerization

Docker is one of the most influential technologies in the field of containerization, revolutionizing the way applications are developed, shipped, and deployed. As a pioneer in container technology, Docker has become synonymous with containers and remains a popular choice for container runtime in Kubernetes. Understanding Docker's history, architecture, and features is essential for effectively utilizing containerization in Kubernetes.

History and Evolution of Docker Docker was introduced by Solomon Hykes in 2013 as an open-source project under the company DotCloud (later renamed Docker Inc.). It provided a user-friendly platform for developers to create, deploy, and run applications in containers, encapsulating the application code, dependencies, and environment into a single, portable unit.

Key Milestones in Docker's Evolution:

- **2013:** Docker was launched as an open-source project, quickly gaining popularity among developers and enterprises.

- **2014:** Docker 1.0 was released, marking its readiness for production use.

- **2015:** The Open Container Initiative (OCI) was formed, standardizing container formats and runtimes, with Docker contributing to the specifications.

- **2017:** Docker introduced Moby, a project to advance container technology, emphasizing modularity and open development.

Docker Architecture Docker's architecture is designed to provide a comprehensive platform for building, shipping, and running containers. It consists of several key components that work together to manage the container lifecycle.

Key Components of Docker:

- **Docker Engine:** The core component of Docker, responsible for creating and managing containers. It includes the Docker daemon, CLI, and REST API.

- **Docker Daemon:** A background service that manages Docker objects such as images, containers, networks, and volumes. It listens for API requests and interacts with the container runtime.

- **Docker CLI:** A command-line interface that allows users to interact with the Docker daemon to manage containers, images, and other resources.

- **Docker Images:** Immutable, read-only templates that contain the application code, runtime, libraries, and dependencies needed to run an application.

- **Docker Containers:** Lightweight, portable, and self-sufficient units that encapsulate the application and its dependencies. Containers are instances of Docker images.

- **Docker Hub:** A cloud-based registry service that allows users to store, share, and distribute Docker images. It provides a vast repository of pre-built images for various applications.

Features and Benefits of Docker Docker's features have made it a preferred choice for containerization, providing numerous benefits to developers and operations teams.

Key Features of Docker:

- **Portability:** Docker containers encapsulate all necessary components, making applications portable across different environments and platforms.

- **Isolation:** Containers provide process and file system isolation through namespaces and cgroups, ensuring that applications run independently.

- **Efficiency:** Containers share the host operating system's kernel, resulting in low overhead and efficient resource utilization.

- **Scalability:** Docker enables easy scaling of applications by deploying multiple container instances across distributed systems.

- **Version Control:** Docker images are versioned, allowing users to track changes and roll back to previous versions if needed.

- **Continuous Integration/Continuous Deployment (CI/CD):** Docker integrates seamlessly with CI/CD pipelines, automating the build, test, and deployment processes.

Docker in Kubernetes Docker has played a significant role in the development and adoption of Kubernetes. While Kubernetes has evolved to support multiple container runtimes, Docker remains a popular choice due to its maturity and extensive ecosystem.

Using Docker with Kubernetes:

- **Container Runtime:** Docker can be configured as the container runtime for Kubernetes, managing the lifecycle of containers in the cluster.

- **Image Management:** Kubernetes leverages Docker images stored in container registries, including Docker Hub, to deploy applications.

- **Development and Testing:** Docker provides a consistent environment for developing and testing applications locally before deploying them to a Kubernetes cluster.

Monitoring and Troubleshooting Docker Effective monitoring and troubleshooting of Docker are crucial for maintaining the health and performance of containerized applications.

Monitoring Tools:

- **Docker Logs:** Access logs from Docker containers to diagnose issues and understand the state of the application.

- **Prometheus:** Use Prometheus to scrape metrics from Docker containers, providing insights into resource usage and performance.

- **cAdvisor:** Integrate cAdvisor with Docker to collect resource usage and performance metrics from running containers.

Common Issues and Solutions:

- **Container Startup Failures:** Check Docker logs for error messages and ensure that the container images are available and correctly configured.

- **Resource Exhaustion:** Monitor resource usage and adjust resource limits and requests to prevent resource contention and exhaustion.

- **Network Connectivity Issues:** Verify network configurations and ensure that the necessary ports and protocols are correctly configured.

Best Practices for Using Docker in Kubernetes Implementing best practices for using Docker in Kubernetes helps ensure the stability and efficiency of containerized applications.

Image Management: Use multi-stage builds to optimize Docker images, reduce image size, and improve security by minimizing the attack surface.

Resource Allocation: Define resource requests and limits for Docker containers to ensure fair resource allocation and prevent overcommitment.

Security Hardening: Apply security best practices, such as using non-root users, enabling runtime security features, and regularly updating container images.

Conclusion Docker has been a pioneer in containerization, providing a robust and user-friendly platform for building, shipping, and running containers. By understanding Docker's architecture, features, and integration with Kubernetes, you can effectively manage containerized applications. Proper monitoring, troubleshooting, and adherence to best practices further enhance the reliability and performance of your Docker containers in a Kubernetes environment.

3.9.3   Introduction to CRI: Decoupling Kubernetes from Runtimes

The Container Runtime Interface (CRI) is a key component in Kubernetes that decouples the Kubernetes control plane from the container runtime, providing a standardized API for container management. This decoupling allows Kubernetes to support multiple container runtimes seamlessly, enhancing flexibility and interoperability. Understanding the CRI and its impact on Kubernetes architecture is essential for effectively managing containerized environments.

What is the Container Runtime Interface (CRI)? The CRI is an API that defines how the Kubernetes kubelet interacts with container runtimes. By abstracting the container runtime, CRI enables Kubernetes to use different runtimes interchangeably without altering the core Kubernetes codebase.

Key Objectives of the CRI:

- **Standardization:** Provides a standard interface for container runtimes to integrate with Kubernetes, ensuring consistent behavior across different runtimes.

- **Flexibility:** Allows users to choose from a variety of container runtimes based on specific needs and preferences.

- **Interoperability:** Ensures that Kubernetes can work with any CRI-compliant container runtime, promoting compatibility and integration.

- **Decoupling:** Decouples the Kubernetes control plane from the container runtime, enabling independent evolution and improvements of both components.

How CRI Works The CRI defines a set of gRPC (Google Remote Procedure Call) protocols that the kubelet uses to interact with container runtimes. These protocols cover essential container management operations such as image management, container lifecycle management, and resource management.

Key Components of the CRI:

- **CRI API:** The API that defines the interactions between the kubelet and the container runtime. It includes methods for managing images, containers, and sandboxes.

- **Container Runtime:** The implementation of the CRI API by a container runtime, such as containerd, CRI-O, or other CRI-compliant runtimes.

- **Kubelet:** The Kubernetes agent that uses the CRI API to communicate with the container runtime, managing the lifecycle of containers on each node.

Operational Workflow:

1. **Image Management:** The kubelet uses the CRI API to pull container images from registries and manage local image storage.

2. **Container Management:** The kubelet uses the CRI API to create, start, stop, and delete containers as needed based on the desired state specified by the control plane.

3. **Resource Management:** The kubelet uses the CRI API to monitor and manage resources allocated to containers, ensuring efficient utilization and isolation.

Advantages of Using CRI The adoption of CRI in Kubernetes brings several advantages, enhancing the overall flexibility, performance, and security of containerized applications.

Key Advantages:

- **Enhanced Flexibility:** Users can choose from a variety of container runtimes, selecting the one that best meets their performance, security, and feature requirements.

- **Improved Interoperability:** CRI-compliant runtimes can seamlessly integrate with Kubernetes, ensuring consistent behavior and compatibility.

- **Independent Evolution:** The decoupling of Kubernetes and container runtimes allows each component to evolve independently, enabling rapid innovation and improvements.

- **Reduced Complexity:** The standardized CRI API simplifies the integration of new container runtimes, reducing the complexity of managing containerized environments.

Popular CRI-Compliant Runtimes Several popular container runtimes are CRI-compliant, offering different features and capabilities to meet various use cases.

Containerd: Containerd is a high-performance container runtime that is widely used in production environments. It provides simplicity, robustness, and portability, making it a popular choice for Kubernetes.

CRI-O: CRI-O is an open-source container runtime specifically designed for Kubernetes. It offers a lightweight and efficient runtime that adheres closely to CRI standards, providing seamless integration with Kubernetes.

Other Runtimes: Other CRI-compliant runtimes, such as Kata Containers and gVisor, offer unique features like enhanced security and isolation, catering to specific use cases and requirements.

Configuring CRI in Kubernetes Configuring CRI in Kubernetes involves setting up the desired container runtime and ensuring it is properly integrated with the kubelet. Proper configuration ensures efficient and secure container management.

Example Configuration for Containerd:

```
# /etc/default/kubelet
KUBELET_EXTRA_ARGS=--container-runtime=remote --container-runtime-endpoint
```

Monitoring and Troubleshooting CRI Effective monitoring and troubleshooting of CRI are crucial for maintaining the health and performance of containerized applications in Kubernetes.

Monitoring Tools:

- **Prometheus:** Use Prometheus to scrape metrics from the container runtime, providing insights into resource usage, container status, and performance.

- **Logs:** Access runtime logs to diagnose issues and understand the state of container management activities.

- **cAdvisor:** Leverage cAdvisor integrated with the kubelet to collect resource usage and performance metrics from containers.

Common Issues and Solutions:

- **Container Startup Failures:** Check the runtime logs for error messages and ensure that the container images are available and correctly configured.

- **Resource Exhaustion:** Monitor resource usage and adjust resource limits and requests to prevent resource contention and exhaustion.

- **Compatibility Issues:** Ensure that the runtime is properly integrated with Kubernetes and that all necessary configurations are applied.

Conclusion The Container Runtime Interface (CRI) is a pivotal component in Kubernetes that decouples the control plane from the container runtime, enhancing flexibility, interoperability, and innovation. By understanding CRI and its advantages, you can effectively manage containerized environments in Kubernetes, leveraging the benefits of various CRI-compliant runtimes. Proper configuration, monitoring, and troubleshooting further ensure the reliability and performance of your containerized applications.

3.9.4 Containerd: An Industry-Standard Core Container Runtime

Containerd is a high-performance container runtime that has become an industry-standard for managing the complete lifecycle of containers. As a core component of many container platforms, including Docker and Kubernetes, Containerd provides simplicity, robustness, and efficiency. Understanding its architecture, features, and integration with Kubernetes is essential for leveraging its full potential in containerized environments.

History and Evolution of Containerd Containerd was originally part of Docker but was later spun out as an independent project to provide a simple, robust, and portable runtime for managing containers. It is now a graduated project under the Cloud Native Computing Foundation (CNCF), highlighting its maturity and widespread adoption.

Key Milestones in Containerd's Evolution:

- **2015:** Containerd was introduced as part of Docker to handle the container lifecycle.

- **2017:** Containerd became an independent project under the CNCF, emphasizing its role as a core container runtime.

- **2019:** Containerd graduated from the CNCF, indicating its stability, maturity, and broad community support.

Containerd Architecture Containerd's architecture is designed to provide a comprehensive platform for managing container lifecycles, including image transfer and storage, container execution, supervision, and networking.

Key Components of Containerd:

- **Containerd Daemon:** The core daemon that manages the entire container lifecycle, including image management, container execution, and supervision.

- **CRI Plugin:** An implementation of the Container Runtime Interface (CRI) that allows Containerd to integrate seamlessly with Kubernetes.

- **Snapshotter:** Manages the file system snapshots used by containers, supporting various storage backends like OverlayFS, Btrfs, and ZFS.

- **Content Store:** Manages container images and other content, providing efficient image storage and distribution.

- **Task Service:** Manages container processes, including starting, stopping, and monitoring the lifecycle of containers.

Features and Benefits of Containerd Containerd provides several features that make it a preferred choice for managing containerized applications, particularly in production environments.

Key Features of Containerd:

- **Simplicity and Efficiency:** Containerd is designed to be simple and lightweight, focusing on the core functionalities required to manage containers efficiently.

- **High Performance:** Optimized for performance, Containerd provides fast and reliable container management operations with minimal overhead.

- **Extensibility:** Supports various plugins and extensions, allowing users to customize and extend its capabilities based on their needs.

- **Robust Image Management:** Efficiently handles image storage, distribution, and transfer, supporting multiple image formats and registries.

- **Strong Community Support:** Backed by a robust open-source community and supported by major industry players, ensuring ongoing development and improvements.

Containerd in Kubernetes Containerd integrates seamlessly with Kubernetes through the Container Runtime Interface (CRI), providing a reliable and high-performance runtime for managing containerized workloads in Kubernetes clusters.

Using Containerd with Kubernetes:

- **Container Runtime:** Configured as the container runtime for Kubernetes, Containerd manages the lifecycle of containers in the cluster, ensuring efficient and reliable operations.

- **Image Management:** Kubernetes leverages Containerd's robust image management capabilities to pull and manage container images from various registries.

- **Resource Management:** Containerd ensures efficient resource allocation and isolation, enhancing the performance and stability of Kubernetes workloads.

Configuring Containerd in Kubernetes Configuring Containerd as the container runtime in Kubernetes involves setting up the CRI plugin and ensuring proper integration with the kubelet.

Example Configuration for Containerd:

```
# /etc/default/kubelet
KUBELET_EXTRA_ARGS=--container-runtime=remote
--container-runtime-endpoint=/run/containerd/containerd.sock
```

Monitoring and Troubleshooting Containerd Effective monitoring and troubleshooting of Containerd are crucial for maintaining the health and performance of containerized applications in Kubernetes.

Monitoring Tools:

- **Prometheus:** Use Prometheus to scrape metrics from Containerd, providing insights into resource usage, container status, and performance.

- **Logs:** Access Containerd logs to diagnose issues and understand the state of container management activities.

- **cAdvisor:** Leverage cAdvisor integrated with the kubelet to collect resource usage and performance metrics from containers managed by Containerd.

Common Issues and Solutions:

- **Container Startup Failures:** Check Containerd logs for error messages and ensure that the container images are available and correctly configured.

- **Resource Exhaustion:** Monitor resource usage and adjust resource limits and requests to prevent resource contention and exhaustion.

- **Compatibility Issues:** Ensure that Containerd is properly integrated with Kubernetes and that all necessary configurations are applied.

Best Practices for Using Containerd in Kubernetes Implementing best practices for using Containerd in Kubernetes helps ensure the stability and efficiency of containerized applications.

Resource Allocation: Define resource requests and limits for containers to ensure fair resource allocation and prevent overcommitment.

Security Hardening: Apply security best practices, such as using non-root users, enabling runtime security features, and regularly updating container images.

Regular Updates: Keep Containerd updated to the latest stable version to benefit from performance improvements, new features, and security patches.

Conclusion Containerd is a robust and high-performance container runtime that has become an industry standard for managing containerized applications. By understanding its architecture, features, and integration with Kubernetes, you can effectively leverage Containerd to manage your Kubernetes workloads. Proper monitoring, troubleshooting, and adherence to best practices further enhance the reliability and performance of your containerized environments.

3.9.5 Comparison: Docker vs. Containerd

Docker and Containerd are two prominent container runtimes in the Kubernetes ecosystem. While both are integral to container management, they serve slightly different purposes and have distinct characteristics. Understanding the differences and use cases for Docker and Containerd can help you make informed decisions about which runtime to use in your Kubernetes environment.

Overview of Docker Docker is a comprehensive platform for building, shipping, and running containers. It includes everything needed to manage containers, including a container runtime, image building tools, and a rich set of APIs and CLI tools.

Key Features of Docker:

- **Integrated Platform:** Docker provides an all-in-one solution for container management, including image building, distribution, and runtime.

- **User-Friendly CLI:** Docker's command-line interface is user-friendly and widely adopted, making it easy for developers to get started with containerization.

- **Rich Ecosystem:** Docker has a vast ecosystem of tools, plugins, and community support, including Docker Hub for sharing and distributing container images.

- **Advanced Networking:** Docker includes advanced networking features, such as overlay networks, for complex container communication setups.

Overview of Containerd Containerd is a high-performance container runtime that focuses on the core functionalities required to manage containers. It is designed to be simple, robust, and portable, providing the necessary tools to run containers efficiently.

Key Features of Containerd:

- **Lightweight and Efficient:** Containerd is designed to be lightweight with minimal overhead, making it suitable for high-performance environments.

- **CRI Integration:** Containerd has a built-in CRI plugin, allowing seamless integration with Kubernetes for managing containerized workloads.

- **Modular Design:** Containerd's modular architecture allows for easy customization and extension, enabling users to tailor the runtime to their specific needs.

- **Robust Image Management:** Containerd provides efficient image storage, distribution, and management capabilities, supporting multiple image formats.

Comparative Analysis Comparing Docker and Containerd involves evaluating their design philosophies, performance, features, and integration with Kubernetes.

Design Philosophy:

- **Docker:** Aims to provide a comprehensive platform for container management, encompassing everything from development to deployment.

- **Containerd:** Focuses on being a robust and efficient runtime for managing containers, leaving image building and other functionalities to external tools.

Performance:

- **Docker:** May have additional overhead due to its integrated platform, but provides a rich set of features and tools for container management.

- **Containerd:** Optimized for performance with minimal overhead, making it suitable for high-throughput environments and large-scale deployments.

Integration with Kubernetes:

- **Docker:** Integrates with Kubernetes through the Docker runtime, but requires an additional layer (dockershim) for compatibility with the CRI.

- **Containerd:** Directly integrates with Kubernetes via the CRI plugin, offering seamless and efficient container management without the need for dockershim.

Ecosystem and Community Support:

- **Docker:** Benefits from a large community and extensive ecosystem, with numerous plugins, tools, and resources available.

- **Containerd:** Also enjoys strong community support, particularly within the CNCF, and is backed by major industry players, ensuring ongoing development and improvements.

Use Cases and Recommendations Both Docker and Containerd are powerful container runtimes, but they are suited to different use cases and scenarios.

When to Use Docker:

- **Development and Testing:** Docker's integrated platform and user-friendly CLI make it ideal for development environments where ease of use and a comprehensive toolset are important.

- **Small to Medium Deployments:** For smaller deployments where the additional overhead is negligible, Docker provides a robust solution with rich features and ecosystem support.

- **CI/CD Pipelines:** Docker integrates well with continuous integration and deployment pipelines, simplifying the build, test, and deployment processes.

When to Use Containerd:

- **Production Environments:** Containerd's lightweight and efficient design make it suitable for production environments where performance and resource utilization are critical.

- **Large-Scale Deployments:** For large-scale Kubernetes clusters, Containerd's direct CRI integration and minimal overhead ensure efficient container management.

- **High-Performance Workloads:** Environments requiring high throughput and low latency benefit from Containerd's optimized performance and robust management capabilities.

Conclusion Docker and Containerd are both essential tools in the container ecosystem, each with its own strengths and ideal use cases. Docker provides a comprehensive platform with rich features and a user-friendly interface, making it suitable for development and smaller deployments. Containerd offers a high-performance, lightweight runtime that excels in production and large-scale environments. By understanding the differences and advantages of each, you can choose the best container runtime to meet your specific needs and optimize your Kubernetes deployments.

3.9.6   Other Runtimes: rkt, cri-o, etc.

While Docker and Containerd are among the most commonly used container runtimes in Kubernetes, there are several other runtimes that offer unique features and capabilities suited to specific use cases. Understanding these alternative runtimes, such as rkt and CRI-O, can help you select the best runtime for your specific needs.

rkt: A Security-Focused Container Runtime rkt (pronounced "rocket") is a container runtime developed by CoreOS with a focus on security and composability. It was designed to address some of the perceived shortcomings of Docker, particularly in security and operational complexity.

Key Features of rkt:

- **Pod Native:** rkt treats pods as a first-class concept, aligning closely with Kubernetes' pod model.

- **Security:** Offers advanced security features, such as support for TPM-based (Trusted Platform Module) attestation and better isolation through the use of multiple stages for container execution.

- **Composability:** Designed to be composable with other tools, allowing users to replace components as needed.

- **No Daemon:** Unlike Docker, rkt does not rely on a central daemon. Each container runs as an individual process, enhancing security and simplicity.

Use Cases for rkt:

- **Security-Sensitive Environments:** Ideal for environments that require advanced security features and strict isolation.

- **Customizable Workflows:** Suitable for users who need a highly customizable runtime that can be integrated with other tools.

- **Kubernetes Integration:** Although not as widely adopted as Docker or Containerd, rkt can be used with Kubernetes through the rktnetes integration.

CRI-O: A Kubernetes-Optimized Runtime   CRI-O is an open-source container runtime specifically designed to provide a lightweight and efficient runtime for Kubernetes. It implements the Kubernetes Container Runtime Interface (CRI) and is optimized to work seamlessly with Kubernetes.

Key Features of CRI-O:

- **Kubernetes Focused:** Built from the ground up to integrate with Kubernetes, offering streamlined operations and management.

- **Lightweight:** CRI-O is designed to be a minimal runtime, reducing overhead and improving performance.

- **Extensible:** Supports plugins for various components, allowing users to extend and customize functionality.

- **Secure by Default:** Emphasizes security with support for seccomp, SELinux, and other security features.

Use Cases for CRI-O:

- **Kubernetes Deployments:** Ideal for users looking for a runtime that is tightly integrated and optimized for Kubernetes.

- **Resource-Constrained Environments:** Suitable for environments where minimizing overhead and maximizing performance are critical.

- **Security-Focused Deployments:** Provides robust security features for deployments that require strong isolation and security controls.

Other Container Runtimes Several other container runtimes offer unique capabilities that cater to specific needs and use cases.

Kata Containers: Kata Containers combine the speed and manageability of containers with the security advantages of virtual machines (VMs). They provide lightweight VMs that run containers, offering enhanced isolation.

- **Key Features:**

    - Strong isolation using VM technology.
    - Compatibility with OCI (Open Container Initiative) image formats.
    - Integration with Kubernetes and other orchestration tools.

- **Use Cases:**

- Security-sensitive workloads requiring strong isolation.
- Multi-tenant environments where enhanced isolation is crucial.

gVisor: gVisor is a user-space kernel for running containers, developed by Google. It provides a strong isolation boundary between the host and container, enhancing security.

- **Key Features:**

  - User-space kernel providing enhanced isolation.
  - Compatibility with Docker and Kubernetes.
  - Lightweight and efficient compared to full VMs.

- **Use Cases:**

  - Security-focused deployments needing strong isolation without the overhead of traditional VMs.
  - Environments where running untrusted code requires additional security measures.

Configuring Alternative Runtimes in Kubernetes Configuring alternative runtimes in Kubernetes involves setting up the desired runtime and ensuring it is properly integrated with the kubelet through the Container Runtime Interface (CRI).

Example Configuration for CRI-O:

```
# /etc/default/kubelet
KUBELET_EXTRA_ARGS=--container-runtime=remote
--container-runtime-endpoint=/var/run/crio/crio.sock
```

Monitoring and Troubleshooting Alternative Runtimes Effective monitoring and troubleshooting of alternative runtimes are crucial for maintaining the health and performance of containerized applications.

Monitoring Tools:

- **Prometheus:** Use Prometheus to scrape metrics from the container runtime, providing insights into resource usage, container status, and performance.

- **Logs:** Access runtime logs to diagnose issues and understand the state of container management activities.

- **cAdvisor:** Leverage cAdvisor integrated with the kubelet to collect resource usage and performance metrics from containers.

Common Issues and Solutions:

- **Container Startup Failures:** Check runtime logs for error messages and ensure that container images are available and correctly configured.

- **Resource Exhaustion:** Monitor resource usage and adjust resource limits and requests to prevent resource contention and exhaustion.

- **Compatibility Issues:** Ensure that the runtime is properly integrated with Kubernetes and that all necessary configurations are applied.

Conclusion While Docker and Containerd are widely used container runtimes in Kubernetes, alternative runtimes like rkt, CRI-O, Kata Containers, and gVisor offer unique features and advantages for specific use cases. By understanding the capabilities and ideal use cases for each runtime, you can select the best runtime to meet your specific needs, ensuring efficient and secure management of your containerized applications in Kubernetes. Proper configuration, monitoring, and troubleshooting further enhance the reliability and performance of these runtimes.

3.9.7 Runtime Selection: Considerations for Production Clusters

Selecting the appropriate container runtime for production clusters is a critical decision that can significantly impact the performance, security, and manageability of your Kubernetes environment. Several factors need to be considered to ensure that the chosen runtime aligns with the specific requirements of your applications and infrastructure. This section outlines key considerations and best practices for selecting a container runtime for production clusters.

Performance and Efficiency Performance and efficiency are paramount in production environments where resource utilization and throughput are critical.

Key Considerations:

- **Resource Overhead:** Evaluate the runtime's resource consumption, including CPU and memory overhead. Lightweight runtimes like Containerd and CRI-O are typically preferred for their minimal overhead.

- **Startup Time:** Assess the time taken by the runtime to start containers. Faster startup times can improve the responsiveness of your applications.

- **Throughput:** Consider the runtime's ability to handle high volumes of container operations, ensuring it can meet the demands of your workload.

Security Features Security is a critical aspect of production environments. The container runtime must provide robust security features to protect your applications and data.

Key Considerations:

- **Isolation Mechanisms:** Evaluate the runtime's isolation capabilities, such as namespace separation and cgroup management. Advanced runtimes like gVisor and Kata Containers offer enhanced isolation using additional layers of security.

- **Security Policies:** Ensure the runtime supports security policies such as seccomp, AppArmor, and SELinux. These policies help mitigate security vulnerabilities and enforce best practices.

- **Compliance:** Check if the runtime meets regulatory and compliance requirements relevant to your industry, such as PCI-DSS or HIPAA.

Compatibility and Integration The chosen runtime must integrate seamlessly with your existing infrastructure and toolchain.

Key Considerations:

- **Kubernetes Compatibility:** Ensure the runtime is fully compatible with Kubernetes and supports the Container Runtime Interface (CRI). Containerd and CRI-O are well-integrated with Kubernetes.

- **Ecosystem Integration:** Consider how well the runtime integrates with other tools and services in your ecosystem, such as CI/CD pipelines, monitoring tools, and security scanners.

- **Support and Community:** A strong community and support ecosystem can be invaluable for troubleshooting and ongoing maintenance. Runtimes like Docker and Containerd benefit from robust community support.

Operational Considerations Operational aspects such as ease of management, scalability, and availability are crucial for maintaining a reliable production environment.

Key Considerations:

- **Scalability:** Assess the runtime's ability to scale with your workload. It should handle increasing numbers of containers without significant performance degradation.

- **High Availability:** Consider the runtime's support for high availability configurations. It should ensure minimal downtime and resilience in case of failures.

- **Ease of Use:** Evaluate the ease of installation, configuration, and management. User-friendly runtimes can reduce operational complexity and improve efficiency.

Cost and Licensing Cost and licensing can impact the total cost of ownership and should be factored into the decision-making process.

Key Considerations:

- **Open Source vs. Commercial:** Determine whether an open-source runtime or a commercial offering better suits your needs. Open-source runtimes like Containerd and CRI-O can reduce costs, while commercial options may offer additional support and features.

- **Support Costs:** Consider the costs associated with support, including subscription fees and support contracts. Ensure the level of support aligns with your operational requirements.

- **Licensing Restrictions:** Be aware of any licensing restrictions that may affect your use of the runtime, particularly in large-scale or multi-tenant environments.

Case Studies and Real-World Examples Reviewing case studies and real-world examples can provide valuable insights into the practical applications and performance of different runtimes in production environments.

Example Scenarios:

- **High-Performance Computing:** Containerd is often chosen for high-performance computing environments due to its efficiency and minimal overhead.

- **Multi-Tenant Security:** gVisor or Kata Containers may be selected for multi-tenant environments requiring enhanced security and isolation.

- **CI/CD Integration:** Docker's rich ecosystem and integration capabilities make it a preferred choice for environments with complex CI/CD pipelines.

Conclusion Selecting the right container runtime for production clusters involves a careful evaluation of performance, security, compatibility, operational considerations, and cost. By thoroughly assessing these factors and considering real-world use cases, you can choose a runtime that meets your specific needs, ensuring efficient, secure, and reliable management of your Kubernetes workloads. Proper configuration, ongoing monitoring, and adherence to best practices will further enhance the performance and stability of your production environment.

3.10 Extensibility in Kubernetes

3.10.1 API Extensions: Aggregation Layer

Kubernetes is designed to be highly extensible, allowing users to extend its capabilities without modifying the core codebase. One of the primary methods for achieving this extensibility is through the API Aggregation Layer, which enables the addition of custom APIs to the Kubernetes API server. Understanding how the API Aggregation Layer works and how to use it is essential for extending Kubernetes functionality to meet specific requirements.

What is the API Aggregation Layer? The API Aggregation Layer is a mechanism that allows the Kubernetes API server to serve additional APIs that are not part of the core Kubernetes APIs. It enables the aggregation of multiple API services under a single API endpoint, providing a unified interface for managing different resources.

Key Objectives of the API Aggregation Layer:

- **Extensibility:** Allows the addition of new APIs to Kubernetes without altering the core API server.

- **Modularity:** Facilitates the development and deployment of modular API services that can be independently managed and updated.

- **Interoperability:** Ensures that custom APIs can seamlessly integrate with existing Kubernetes resources and workflows.

How the API Aggregation Layer Works The API Aggregation Layer works by proxying requests from the Kubernetes API server to additional API servers that host the custom APIs. These aggregated APIs appear as part of the core Kubernetes API, making them accessible through the standard Kubernetes API endpoint.

Key Components:

- **API Server:** The core Kubernetes API server that handles requests and proxies them to aggregated API servers as needed.

- **Aggregation API Servers:** Additional API servers that host custom APIs, registered with the core API server through APIService objects.

- **APIService Objects:** Kubernetes resources that register aggregated APIs with the core API server, specifying the group, version, and path of the new APIs.

Operational Workflow:

1. **Register APIService:** Create an APIService object to register the custom API with the core API server. This object includes information about the API group, version, and service endpoint.

2. **Proxy Requests:** The core API server proxies incoming requests to the appropriate aggregated API server based on the registered APIService objects.

3. **Serve Responses:** The aggregated API server processes the requests and returns responses through the core API server, making them appear as part of the Kubernetes API.

Configuring API Extensions   Configuring API extensions using the API Aggregation Layer involves creating APIService objects and setting up the aggregated API servers. Proper configuration ensures that custom APIs are correctly integrated and accessible.

Example APIService Configuration:

```
apiVersion: apiregistration.k8s.io/v1
kind: APIService
metadata:
  name: v1alpha1.mygroup.example.com
spec:
  group: mygroup.example.com
  version: v1alpha1
```

```
service:
  name: my-custom-api
  namespace: custom-apis
insecureSkipTLSVerify: true
groupPriorityMinimum: 1000
versionPriority: 10
```

Monitoring and Troubleshooting API Extensions Effective monitoring and troubleshooting of API extensions are crucial for maintaining the functionality and performance of custom APIs.

Monitoring Tools:

- **Prometheus:** Use Prometheus to scrape metrics from the aggregated API servers, providing insights into request rates, error rates, and performance.

- **Logs:** Access logs from both the core API server and the aggregated API servers to diagnose issues and understand request flows.

- **APIService Status:** Regularly check the status of APIService objects using 'kubectl' to ensure they are correctly registered and operational.

Common Issues and Solutions:

- **Failed API Requests:** Ensure that the aggregated API server is running and accessible. Verify the service endpoint specified in the APIService object.

- **Registration Errors:** Check the configuration of APIService objects for errors, such as incorrect group or version information.

- **Performance Degradation:** Monitor the performance of the aggregated API servers and optimize resource allocation as needed. Ensure that the API servers are scaled appropriately to handle the load.

Best Practices for Using API Aggregation Layer Implementing best practices for using the API Aggregation Layer helps ensure the stability and efficiency of custom APIs in Kubernetes.

Security Considerations: Ensure that communication between the core API server and aggregated API servers is secured using TLS. Avoid using 'insecureSkipTLSVerify' in production environments unless absolutely necessary.

Versioning: Follow best practices for API versioning to ensure backward compatibility and smooth upgrades. Use semantic versioning to manage changes to custom APIs.

Resource Management: Allocate sufficient resources to the aggregated API servers to handle expected loads. Monitor resource usage and scale the servers as needed to maintain performance.

Conclusion The API Aggregation Layer is a powerful feature in Kubernetes that enables the addition of custom APIs, enhancing the platform's extensibility and flexibility. By understanding how the API Aggregation Layer works and following best practices for configuration, monitoring, and troubleshooting, you can effectively extend Kubernetes to meet your specific needs. Proper implementation ensures seamless integration of custom APIs, providing a unified and scalable interface for managing diverse resources in your Kubernetes environment.

3.10.2 Custom Resource Definitions (CRDs)

Custom Resource Definitions (CRDs) are a powerful feature in Kubernetes that enable users to extend the Kubernetes API by defining their own custom resources. CRDs allow you to create, manage, and interact with custom objects just like native Kubernetes resources, providing a flexible way to extend Kubernetes functionality to suit specific needs. Understanding how to define, use, and manage CRDs is crucial for leveraging the full potential of Kubernetes extensibility.

What are Custom Resource Definitions (CRDs)? CRDs are API objects that allow you to define new resource types in Kubernetes. Once a CRD is created, you can use Kubernetes tools and APIs to manage instances of the custom resource, similar to built-in resources like Pods, Services, and Deployments.

Key Objectives of CRDs:

- **Extensibility:** Enable users to extend the Kubernetes API with custom resources tailored to their specific applications and workflows.

- **Flexibility:** Allow for the definition of complex resource types that can represent application-specific concepts or abstractions.

- **Integration:** Seamlessly integrate custom resources with Kubernetes tools, APIs, and controllers.

Defining Custom Resource Definitions Defining a CRD involves creating a YAML or JSON manifest that specifies the name, schema, and validation rules for the custom resource. This manifest is then applied to the Kubernetes cluster to register the new resource type.

Example CRD Definition:

```
apiVersion: apiextensions.k8s.io/v1
kind: CustomResourceDefinition
metadata:
  name: examples.mygroup.example.com
spec:
  group: mygroup.example.com
  versions:
    - name: v1
      served: true
      storage: true
      schema:
        openAPIV3Schema:
          type: object
          properties:
            spec:
              type: object
              properties:
                field1:
                  type: string
                field2:
                  type: integer
```

```
scope: Namespaced
names:
  plural: examples
  singular: example
  kind: Example
  shortNames:
    - ex
```

Using Custom Resources   Once a CRD is defined and applied, you can create and manage instances of the custom resource using standard Kubernetes tools like 'kubectl'.

Example Custom Resource Instance:

```
apiVersion: mygroup.example.com/v1
kind: Example
metadata:
  name: example-instance
spec:
  field1: "value1"
  field2: 42
```

Managing Custom Resources:

- **Creating Instances:** Use 'kubectl apply' to create instances of the custom resource from YAML or JSON manifests.

- **Updating Instances:** Modify the resource definition and use 'kubectl apply' or 'kubectl edit' to update the custom resource.

- **Deleting Instances:** Use 'kubectl delete' to remove instances of the custom resource.

- **Querying Instances:** Use 'kubectl get' to list instances and 'kubectl describe' to get detailed information about a specific instance.

Validation and Schema Enforcement   CRDs support schema validation using OpenAPI v3 schemas. This ensures that custom resources adhere to a predefined structure and validation rules, improving consistency and reliability.

Defining Validation Rules:

- **OpenAPI v3 Schema:** Use OpenAPI v3 schemas to define the structure, data types, and validation rules for custom resources.

- **Required Fields:** Specify required fields to enforce the presence of essential attributes.

- **Type Validation:** Define data types for fields to ensure that values meet expected formats (e.g., string, integer, boolean).

Custom Controllers and CRDs Custom controllers can be used to manage the lifecycle and behavior of custom resources defined by CRDs. Controllers watch for changes to custom resources and take actions to reconcile the current state with the desired state.

Building Custom Controllers:

- **Controller Pattern:** Implement controllers using the Kubernetes controller pattern, which involves watching for resource changes and executing reconciliation logic.

- **Controller Frameworks:** Use frameworks like Kubebuilder or the Operator SDK to simplify the development of custom controllers.

- **Reconciliation Logic:** Define the logic for reconciling the desired state of custom resources with their actual state, performing actions such as creating, updating, or deleting dependent resources.

Advanced Features of CRDs CRDs offer advanced features that enhance their functionality and usability, including subresources, versioning, and conversion.

Subresources:

- **Status Subresource:** Enable the status subresource to manage status information separately from the spec, improving separation of concerns and avoiding conflicts.

- **Scale Subresource:** Implement the scale subresource to allow horizontal scaling of custom resources, integrating with Kubernetes autoscaling mechanisms.

Versioning and Conversion:

- **API Versioning:** Define multiple versions of the custom resource to support backward compatibility and smooth upgrades.

- **Conversion Webhooks:** Implement conversion webhooks to handle the conversion of custom resources between different API versions, ensuring data consistency and compatibility.

Monitoring and Troubleshooting CRDs Effective monitoring and troubleshooting of CRDs are essential for maintaining the health and performance of custom resources.

Monitoring Tools:

- **Prometheus:** Use Prometheus to monitor metrics related to custom controllers and resources, providing insights into their status and performance.

- **Logs:** Access logs from custom controllers to diagnose issues and understand the state of custom resource management activities.

- **Events:** Monitor Kubernetes events to track changes and detect anomalies related to custom resources.

Common Issues and Solutions:

- **Validation Errors:** Ensure that custom resources conform to the defined schema and validation rules. Check the OpenAPI schema for accuracy.

- **Controller Failures:** Diagnose controller failures by reviewing logs and debugging the reconciliation logic. Ensure that the controller has the necessary permissions to manage resources.

- **Resource Conflicts:** Avoid conflicts between custom resources and native Kubernetes resources by using unique names and groups for CRDs.

Best Practices for Using CRDs Implementing best practices for defining and managing CRDs helps ensure their stability and usability.

Design Considerations: Carefully design the schema and validation rules for custom resources to ensure they meet application requirements and provide flexibility for future enhancements.

Documentation: Provide comprehensive documentation for custom resources, including usage examples, API specifications, and troubleshooting guides, to assist users in effectively managing them.

Testing: Thoroughly test custom resources and controllers in a staging environment before deploying them to production, ensuring they behave as expected and do not introduce regressions.

Conclusion Custom Resource Definitions (CRDs) are a powerful tool for extending the Kubernetes API to support custom application-specific resources. By understanding how to define, use, and manage CRDs, you can leverage Kubernetes' extensibility to meet your unique needs. Proper implementation, monitoring, and adherence to best practices ensure that custom resources are reliable, scalable, and maintainable, enhancing the overall functionality of your Kubernetes environment.

3.10.3   Admission Controllers and Webhooks

Admission controllers are an integral part of Kubernetes that intercept requests to the Kubernetes API server before any changes are made to the objects in the cluster. They are used to enforce policies and execute custom business logic, ensuring that the cluster remains in a desired state. Webhooks are a powerful mechanism that extends the functionality of admission controllers by allowing external services to handle admission decisions.

What are Admission Controllers? Admission controllers are plugins that govern and enforce how the cluster is used. After a request to the Kubernetes API server is authenticated and authorized, it passes through a series of admission controllers before being persisted to the cluster state.

Key Functions of Admission Controllers:

- **Validation:** Ensure that resource requests meet specific criteria before they are persisted.

- **Mutation:** Modify resource requests to meet required policies before they are accepted.

- **Enforcement:** Implement security policies, resource quotas, and other constraints.

Types of Admission Controllers There are two main types of admission controllers: validating admission controllers and mutating admission controllers.

Validating Admission Controllers: Validate requests before they are persisted. They can reject requests that do not meet certain criteria.

- **Example:** The 'PodSecurity' admission controller ensures that pods comply with security profiles like 'privileged', 'baseline' or 'restricted' based on the configured namespace security standards.

Mutating Admission Controllers: Modify requests before they are persisted. They can add or change fields in the resource specifications.

- **Example:** The 'DefaultStorageClass' admission controller sets a default storage class for persistent volume claims that do not specify one.

Webhooks for Admission Controllers Admission webhooks are HTTP callbacks that allow you to customize admission control. There are two types of admission webhooks: mutating admission webhooks and validating admission webhooks.

Mutating Admission Webhooks: Modify the incoming resource before it is persisted. They can add or modify fields in the resource specification.

Example Mutating Admission Webhook Configuration:

```yaml
apiVersion: admissionregistration.k8s.io/v1
kind: MutatingWebhookConfiguration
metadata:
  name: example-mutating-webhook
webhooks:
  - name: mutating.example.com
    clientConfig:
      service:
        name: example-webhook-service
        namespace: default
        path: "/mutate"
      caBundle: <base64-encoded-CA-cert>
    rules:
      - operations: ["CREATE", "UPDATE"]
        apiGroups: [""]
        apiVersions: ["v1"]
        resources: ["pods"]
```

Validating Admission Webhooks: Validate the incoming resource and can reject the request if it does not meet certain criteria.

Example Validating Admission Webhook Configuration:

```yaml
apiVersion: admissionregistration.k8s.io/v1
kind: ValidatingWebhookConfiguration
metadata:
  name: example-validating-webhook
webhooks:
  - name: validating.example.com
    clientConfig:
      service:
        name: example-webhook-service
        namespace: default
        path: "/validate"
      caBundle: <base64-encoded-CA-cert>
```

```
rules:
  - operations: ["CREATE", "UPDATE"]
    apiGroups: [""]
    apiVersions: ["v1"]
    resources: ["pods"]
```

Configuring Admission Controllers and Webhooks Admission controllers can be enabled or disabled by setting the `--enable-admission-plugins` and `--disable-admission-plugins` flags in the Kubernetes API server configuration.

Enabling Admission Controllers:

```
--enable-admission-plugins=NamespaceLifecycle,LimitRanger,
ServiceAccount,DefaultStorageClass,ResourceQuota
```

Admission webhooks require additional configuration, including the setup of the webhook service and the creation of the webhook configuration objects.

Monitoring and Troubleshooting Admission Controllers and Webhooks Effective monitoring and troubleshooting of admission controllers and webhooks are essential to ensure they function correctly and enforce the desired policies.

Monitoring Tools:

- **Prometheus:** Use Prometheus to scrape metrics from the API server, providing insights into the performance and impact of admission controllers.

- **Logs:** Access API server logs to diagnose issues related to admission controllers and webhooks.

- **Events:** Monitor Kubernetes events to track the actions of admission controllers and detect anomalies.

Common Issues and Solutions:

- **Webhook Failures:** Ensure that the webhook service is running and accessible. Verify the webhook configuration and certificates.

- **Admission Controller Errors:** Review the API server logs to identify and resolve configuration errors or conflicts.

- **Performance Impact:** Monitor the performance of admission controllers and optimize their configuration to minimize latency and overhead.

Best Practices for Admission Controllers and Webhooks
Implementing best practices for admission controllers and webhooks ensures they are effective and reliable.

Security: Secure communication between the API server and webhooks using TLS. Validate certificates and avoid using insecure configurations in production.

Testing: Thoroughly test admission controllers and webhooks in a staging environment before deploying them to production. Ensure they enforce policies correctly without causing disruptions.

Documentation: Provide clear documentation for the policies and logic implemented by admission controllers and webhooks. This helps users understand their purpose and behavior.

Conclusion Admission controllers and webhooks are essential components of Kubernetes that provide fine-grained control over resource creation and modification. By understanding their roles, configuring them correctly, and following best practices, you can ensure that your Kubernetes cluster operates securely and efficiently, enforcing the necessary policies to maintain the desired state.

3.10.4   Dynamic Admission Control

Dynamic Admission Control in Kubernetes involves using admission controllers that can make real-time decisions about requests to the Kubernetes API server. This approach allows for more flexible and responsive policies that can adapt to changing conditions and requirements. Dynamic admission control is a powerful mechanism for enforcing policies and ensuring compliance within your Kubernetes cluster.

What is Dynamic Admission Control?   Dynamic admission control refers to the use of admission webhooks to enforce policies dynamically at runtime. Unlike static admission controllers, which are configured at the time of API server startup, dynamic admission controllers can be added, updated, or removed without restarting the API server. This flexibility makes them ideal for implementing policies that need to be updated frequently or based on external conditions.

Key Features of Dynamic Admission Control:

- **Real-Time Decisions:** Make admission decisions based on the current state of the cluster and external inputs.

- **Flexibility:** Easily add, modify, or remove policies without restarting the API server.

- **Extensibility:** Integrate with external systems and services to enforce complex policies.

Types of Admission Webhooks   There are two main types of admission webhooks used in dynamic admission control: mutating admission webhooks and validating admission webhooks.

Mutating Admission Webhooks: Modify incoming requests before they are persisted. They can add, remove, or alter fields in the request.

Example Mutating Admission Webhook Configuration:

```
apiVersion: admissionregistration.k8s.io/v1
kind: MutatingWebhookConfiguration
metadata:
  name: example-mutating-webhook
webhooks:
  - name: mutating.example.com
    clientConfig:
      service:
        name: example-webhook-service
        namespace: default
        path: "/mutate"
      caBundle: <base64-encoded-CA-cert>
    rules:
      - operations: ["CREATE", "UPDATE"]
        apiGroups: [""]
        apiVersions: ["v1"]
        resources: ["pods"]
```

Validating Admission Webhooks: Validate incoming requests and can reject them if they do not meet certain criteria.

Example Validating Admission Webhook Configuration:

```
apiVersion: admissionregistration.k8s.io/v1
kind: ValidatingWebhookConfiguration
metadata:
  name: example-validating-webhook
webhooks:
  - name: validating.example.com
    clientConfig:
      service:
        name: example-webhook-service
        namespace: default
        path: "/validate"
      caBundle: <base64-encoded-CA-cert>
    rules:
      - operations: ["CREATE", "UPDATE"]
        apiGroups: [""]
```

```
apiVersions: ["v1"]
resources: ["pods"]
```

Configuring Dynamic Admission Control Configuring dynamic admission control involves setting up the webhook services and creating the webhook configuration objects. These configurations determine how and when the webhooks are called.

Setting Up Webhook Services: The webhook services must be reachable by the Kubernetes API server and able to handle incoming admission requests. They should be secured with TLS to ensure secure communication.

Creating Webhook Configurations: Webhook configurations are Kubernetes resources that register the webhook services with the API server. They specify the rules and conditions under which the webhooks are invoked.

Monitoring and Troubleshooting Dynamic Admission Control Effective monitoring and troubleshooting are crucial to ensure that dynamic admission control works as expected and does not impact cluster performance.

Monitoring Tools:

- **Prometheus:** Use Prometheus to monitor the performance and metrics of the webhook services.

- **Logs:** Access logs from the webhook services and the API server to diagnose issues.

- **Events:** Monitor Kubernetes events to track the actions of admission webhooks and detect anomalies.

Common Issues and Solutions:

- **Webhook Service Unreachable:** Ensure that the webhook service is correctly configured and reachable by the API server. Verify the service endpoints and TLS certificates.

- **Invalid Configuration:** Check the webhook configuration objects for errors and ensure they are correctly specified.

- **Performance Impact:** Monitor the performance impact of admission webhooks and optimize their configuration to minimize latency.

Best Practices for Dynamic Admission Control Implementing best practices for dynamic admission control ensures that it is effective and reliable.

Security: Secure communication between the API server and webhook services using TLS. Validate certificates and avoid insecure configurations in production.

Testing: Thoroughly test admission webhooks in a staging environment before deploying them to production. Ensure they enforce policies correctly without causing disruptions.

Documentation: Provide clear documentation for the policies and logic implemented by admission webhooks. This helps users understand their purpose and behavior.

Conclusion Dynamic admission control is a powerful feature in Kubernetes that allows for flexible and responsive policy enforcement. By using admission webhooks, you can implement complex policies that adapt to changing conditions and integrate with external systems. Proper configuration, monitoring, and adherence to best practices ensure that dynamic admission control is effective and reliable, enhancing the security and compliance of your Kubernetes cluster.

Chapter 4

Core Kubernetes Resources

4.1 Understanding Namespaces

Namespaces are a fundamental concept in Kubernetes that provide a way to partition a single Kubernetes cluster into multiple virtual clusters. This is especially useful for managing complex environments with multiple teams, projects, or applications. Understanding namespaces is essential for effective resource management, isolation, and security in Kubernetes.

What are Namespaces? Namespaces are Kubernetes objects that allow you to create isolated environments within a single Kubernetes cluster. Each namespace provides a separate scope for resources like pods, services, and deployments, enabling better organization and management of cluster resources.

Key Features of Namespaces:

- **Resource Isolation:** Provides logical isolation for resources, allowing different teams or projects to operate independently within the same cluster.

- **Access Control:** Facilitates the application of role-based access control (RBAC) policies to different namespaces, enhancing security and management.

- **Resource Quotas:** Enables the setting of resource limits for namespaces to ensure fair resource allocation and prevent resource exhaustion.

- **Environment Segregation:** Supports the separation of different environments (e.g., development, staging, production) within the same cluster.

Creating and Managing Namespaces   Managing namespaces involves creating, listing, describing, and deleting namespaces using Kubernetes tools and APIs.

Creating a Namespace: You can create a namespace using a YAML manifest or the 'kubectl' command-line tool.

Example Namespace Manifest:

```
apiVersion: v1
kind: Namespace
metadata:
  name: development
```

Creating a Namespace with kubectl:

```
kubectl create namespace development
```

Listing and Describing Namespaces: Use 'kubectl' commands to list and describe namespaces in your cluster.
List All Namespaces:

```
kubectl get namespaces
```

Describe a Specific Namespace:

```
kubectl describe namespace development
```

Deleting a Namespace: You can delete a namespace using 'kubectl'. Deleting a namespace also deletes all resources within that namespace.
Delete a Namespace:

```
kubectl delete namespace development
```

Using Namespaces for Resource Management Namespaces are crucial for managing resources in a multi-tenant environment. They provide a way to allocate resources, apply policies, and organize resources efficiently.

Resource Quotas: Resource quotas limit the amount of resources that can be consumed by a namespace, ensuring fair distribution of cluster resources.

Example Resource Quota Manifest:

```
apiVersion: v1
kind: ResourceQuota
metadata:
  name: dev-quota
  namespace: development
spec:
  hard:
    pods: "10"
    requests.cpu: "4"
    requests.memory: "8Gi"
    limits.cpu: "8"
    limits.memory: "16Gi"
```

Limit Ranges: Limit ranges define default resource limits and requests for containers in a namespace, helping to manage resource usage effectively.

Example Limit Range Manifest:

```
apiVersion: v1
kind: LimitRange
metadata:
  name: dev-limits
  namespace: development
spec:
  limits:
  - default:
      cpu: "1"
      memory: "512Mi"
    defaultRequest:
```

```
    cpu: "0.5"
    memory: "256Mi"
  type: Container
```

Applying Access Control with Namespaces Namespaces facilitate the application of RBAC policies, allowing fine-grained access control over resources.

Creating RoleBindings: RoleBindings associate users or groups with roles within a specific namespace, controlling access to resources.

Example RoleBinding Manifest:

```
apiVersion: rbac.authorization.k8s.io/v1
kind: RoleBinding
metadata:
  name: dev-read-access
  namespace: development
subjects:
- kind: User
  name: jane.doe
  apiGroup: rbac.authorization.k8s.io
roleRef:
  kind: Role
  name: read-only
  apiGroup: rbac.authorization.k8s.io
```

Best Practices for Using Namespaces Implementing best practices for using namespaces helps ensure effective resource management and isolation.

Namespace Naming Conventions: Use clear and consistent naming conventions for namespaces to improve organization and management. For example, use names like 'dev', 'staging', and 'prod' for different environments.

Segregate Environments: Create separate namespaces for different environments (development, staging, production) to isolate resources and manage them independently.

Monitor Resource Usage: Regularly monitor resource usage in each namespace to ensure efficient allocation and prevent resource exhaustion.

Conclusion Namespaces are a fundamental feature in Kubernetes that provide logical isolation, resource management, and access control within a single cluster. By understanding how to create, manage, and use namespaces effectively, you can enhance the organization, security, and efficiency of your Kubernetes environment. Implementing best practices and leveraging namespaces for resource quotas, limit ranges, and RBAC policies further optimizes cluster management and ensures a well-structured and secure infrastructure.

4.2 Pods

4.2.1 Pod Lifecycle

Pods are the smallest and simplest Kubernetes objects. They represent a single instance of a running process in your cluster and can contain one or more containers. Understanding the lifecycle of a pod is crucial for effectively managing applications in Kubernetes.

What is a Pod? A pod encapsulates one or more containers that share storage, network, and a specification on how to run the containers. Pods are designed to support multiple cooperating processes (as containers) that form a cohesive unit of service.

Key Features of Pods:

- **Shared Network:** All containers in a pod share the same network namespace, including the IP address and network ports.

- **Shared Storage:** Containers in a pod can share storage volumes, allowing data to be shared easily between them.

- **Lifecycle Management:** Pods provide a lifecycle for the containers, ensuring they are created, monitored, and terminated correctly.

Pod Lifecycle Phases The lifecycle of a pod consists of several phases, from its creation to its termination. Each phase represents the state of the pod at a given time.

Pending: The pod has been accepted by the Kubernetes system, but one or more of the containers have not been created yet. This phase includes time spent waiting for the scheduler to assign the pod to a node and for the container images to be pulled.

Running: The pod has been bound to a node, and all containers have been created. At least one container is still running, or is in the process of starting or restarting.

Succeeded: All containers in the pod have terminated successfully, and will not be restarted.

Failed: All containers in the pod have terminated, and at least one container has terminated in failure. That is, the container either exited with a non-zero status or was terminated by the system.

Unknown: The state of the pod could not be obtained, typically due to an error in communicating with the node where the pod is running.

Pod Lifecycle Management Managing the lifecycle of pods involves creating, updating, and deleting pods as necessary. Kubernetes provides various mechanisms to manage these operations.

Creating Pods: Pods can be created using YAML manifests or the 'kubectl' command-line tool.

Example Pod Manifest:

```yaml
apiVersion: v1
kind: Pod
metadata:
  name: example-pod
  namespace: default
```

```
spec:
  containers:
  - name: example-container
    image: nginx:1.17.4
    ports:
    - containerPort: 80
```

Creating a Pod with kubectl:

```
kubectl apply -f example-pod.yaml
```

Updating Pods: Pods are immutable once created. To update a pod, you need to delete the existing pod and create a new one with the updated specifications. This process is usually managed by higher-level controllers like Deployments and StatefulSets.

Deleting Pods: Pods can be deleted using the 'kubectl' command. Deleting a pod gracefully terminates all its containers and frees up resources.

Deleting a Pod:

```
kubectl delete pod example-pod
```

Pod Lifecycle Hooks Kubernetes provides lifecycle hooks that allow containers to run code triggered by events during their lifecycle, such as when the container is started or terminated.

PostStart Hook: The PostStart hook is executed immediately after a container is created. This can be used to perform initialization tasks.

Example PostStart Hook:

```
apiVersion: v1
kind: Pod
metadata:
  name: example-pod
spec:
  containers:
```

```
  - name: example-container
    image: nginx:1.17.4
    lifecycle:
      postStart:
        exec:
          command: ["/bin/sh", "-c", "echo Hello, Kubernetes!"]
```

PreStop Hook: The PreStop hook is executed immediately before a container is terminated. This can be used to perform cleanup tasks or send notifications.

Example PreStop Hook:

```
apiVersion: v1
kind: Pod
metadata:
  name: example-pod
spec:
  containers:
  - name: example-container
    image: nginx:1.17.4
    lifecycle:
      preStop:
        exec:
          command: ["/bin/sh", "-c", "echo Goodbye,
Kubernetes!"]
```

Pod Probes Probes are used to check the health and status of containers within a pod. Kubernetes supports three types of probes: liveness, readiness, and startup probes.

Liveness Probe: Determines if a container is running. If the liveness probe fails, the container is killed and restarted.

Example Liveness Probe:

```
apiVersion: v1
kind: Pod
```

```
metadata:
  name: example-pod
spec:
  containers:
  - name: example-container
    image: nginx:1.17.4
    livenessProbe:
      httpGet:
        path: /healthz
        port: 80
      initialDelaySeconds: 10
      periodSeconds: 5
```

Readiness Probe: Indicates whether a container is ready to serve traffic. If the readiness probe fails, the endpoints associated with the container are removed from service.

Example Readiness Probe:

```
apiVersion: v1
kind: Pod
metadata:
  name: example-pod
spec:
  containers:
  - name: example-container
    image: nginx:1.17.4
    readinessProbe:
      httpGet:
        path: /ready
        port: 80
      initialDelaySeconds: 5
      periodSeconds: 5
```

Startup Probe: Indicates whether a container application has started. Useful for applications with long initialization times.

Example Startup Probe:

```
apiVersion: v1
kind: Pod
metadata:
  name: example-pod
spec:
  containers:
  - name: example-container
    image: nginx:1.17.4
    startupProbe:
      httpGet:
        path: /startup
        port: 80
      failureThreshold: 30
      periodSeconds: 10
```

Best Practices for Managing Pod Lifecycles Implementing best practices for managing pod lifecycles ensures stability, performance, and efficient resource utilization.

Use Controllers: Manage pods using higher-level controllers like Deployments, StatefulSets, and DaemonSets. These controllers provide automated management, scaling, and updates for pods.

Define Resource Requests and Limits: Specify resource requests and limits for pods to ensure fair resource allocation and prevent resource contention.

Implement Probes: Use liveness, readiness, and startup probes to monitor the health and status of containers, ensuring that applications are running correctly and can serve traffic.

Graceful Shutdown: Implement lifecycle hooks to handle cleanup and graceful shutdown of containers, improving application stability and data integrity.

Conclusion Understanding the lifecycle of pods is fundamental to managing applications in Kubernetes. By leveraging lifecycle phases, hooks, and probes, you can ensure that your applications are robust, scalable, and resilient. Implementing best practices and using higher-level controllers further enhances the manageability and efficiency of your Kubernetes deployments.

4.2.2 Managing Pods

Managing pods effectively is crucial for maintaining the stability and performance of your applications in Kubernetes. This involves a variety of tasks including creating, updating, scaling, and deleting pods. By leveraging Kubernetes tools and controllers, you can automate and simplify pod management, ensuring that your applications run smoothly.

Creating Pods Pods can be created using YAML manifests or the 'kubectl' command-line tool. Creating pods involves defining the desired state of the pod, including the containers it should run, the resources it needs, and any specific configurations.

Example Pod Manifest:

```
apiVersion: v1
kind: Pod
metadata:
  name: example-pod
  namespace: default
spec:
  containers:
  - name: example-container
    image: nginx:1.17.4
    ports:
    - containerPort: 80
```

Creating a Pod with kubectl:

```
kubectl apply -f example-pod.yaml
```

Updating Pods Pods are immutable once created. To update a pod, you typically need to delete the existing pod and create a new one with the updated specifications. This process is managed by higher-level controllers like Deployments, StatefulSets, and DaemonSets, which handle the replacement of pods seamlessly and ensure minimal downtime.

Updating a Pod:

- **Manual Update:**

    - Delete the existing pod:

      ```
      kubectl delete pod example-pod
      ```

    - Create a new pod with updated specifications:

      ```
      kubectl apply -f updated-pod.yaml
      ```

- **Using Controllers:** Higher-level controllers like Deployments manage updates automatically. You only need to update the controller's specification, and it will handle the replacement of pods.

    - Update the Deployment manifest with the new specifications.
    - Apply the updated Deployment manifest:

      ```
      kubectl apply -f updated-deployment.yaml
      ```

    - The Deployment controller manages the rolling update, ensuring minimal disruption.

Scaling Pods Scaling pods involves adjusting the number of pod replicas to meet the demands of your application. This can be done manually or automatically using Kubernetes controllers like Deployments and ReplicaSets.

Scaling a Deployment:

```
kubectl scale deployment example-deployment --replicas=5
```

Horizontal Pod Autoscaler (HPA): HPA automatically scales the number of pod replicas based on observed CPU utilization or other custom metrics.

Example HPA Configuration:

```
apiVersion: autoscaling/v1
kind: HorizontalPodAutoscaler
metadata:
  name: example-hpa
  namespace: default
spec:
  scaleTargetRef:
    apiVersion: apps/v1
    kind: Deployment
    name: example-deployment
  minReplicas: 1
  maxReplicas: 10
  targetCPUUtilizationPercentage: 80
```

Deleting Pods   Deleting pods can be done using the 'kubectl' command. When a pod is deleted, Kubernetes ensures that all resources associated with the pod are cleaned up properly.

Deleting a Pod:

```
kubectl delete pod example-pod
```

Pod Status and Monitoring   Monitoring the status of pods is essential for ensuring that your applications are running as expected. Kubernetes provides several commands and tools for this purpose.

Checking Pod Status:

```
kubectl get pods
```

Describing a Pod:

```
kubectl describe pod example-pod
```

Logging: Access logs from containers within a pod to diagnose issues and monitor application behavior.

Viewing Pod Logs:

```
kubectl logs example-pod -c example-container
```

Handling Pod Failures Kubernetes automatically handles pod failures through mechanisms like restarts and replacements. Higher-level controllers ensure that the desired state of the application is maintained even in the event of failures.

Restart Policies: Pods can have different restart policies such as Always, OnFailure, and Never, which dictate how Kubernetes handles container restarts.

Example Restart Policy:

```
apiVersion: v1
kind: Pod
metadata:
  name: example-pod
spec:
  restartPolicy: Always
  containers:
  - name: example-container
    image: nginx:1.17.4
```

Best Practices for Managing Pods Implementing best practices for managing pods ensures reliability, scalability, and efficient resource usage.

Use Controllers: Manage pods using higher-level controllers like Deployments, StatefulSets, and DaemonSets. These controllers provide automated management, scaling, and updates for pods.

Define Resource Requests and Limits: Specify resource requests and limits for pods to ensure fair resource allocation and prevent resource contention.

Implement Probes: Use liveness, readiness, and startup probes to monitor the health and status of containers, ensuring that applications are running correctly and can serve traffic.

Graceful Shutdown: Implement lifecycle hooks to handle cleanup and graceful shutdown of containers, improving application stability and data integrity.

Conclusion Managing pods is a fundamental aspect of Kubernetes administration. By leveraging Kubernetes tools and controllers, you can automate and simplify pod management, ensuring that your applications run smoothly and efficiently. Implementing best practices and using monitoring tools further enhances the reliability and performance of your Kubernetes deployments.

4.2.3 Inter-pod Affinity and Anti-affinity

Inter-pod affinity and anti-affinity are advanced scheduling features in Kubernetes that allow you to specify rules about how pods should be placed relative to other pods. These features enable more precise control over pod placement, improving performance, fault tolerance, and resource utilization by controlling the co-location of pods on nodes.

What is Inter-pod Affinity and Anti-affinity? Inter-pod affinity allows you to specify that a pod should be co-located (on the same node) with other pods that meet certain criteria. Conversely, inter-pod anti-affinity specifies that a pod should not be co-located with other pods that meet certain criteria. These rules help manage pod distribution across the cluster based on the specific needs of your applications.

Key Features of Inter-pod Affinity and Anti-affinity:

- **Affinity:** Ensures that pods are scheduled on the same node or within the same topology domain as other specified pods.

- **Anti-affinity:** Ensures that pods are not scheduled on the same node or within the same topology domain as other specified pods.

- **Topology Domains:** Supports specifying rules based on topology domains such as nodes, zones, or regions.

- **Flexibility:** Provides soft and hard constraints to balance between strict requirements and optimal scheduling.

Configuring Inter-pod Affinity Inter-pod affinity rules are specified in the pod's manifest under the 'affinity' section. These rules define the conditions under which pods should be co-located.

Example Inter-pod Affinity Configuration:

```
apiVersion: v1
kind: Pod
metadata:
  name: example-pod
spec:
  affinity:
    podAffinity:
      requiredDuringSchedulingIgnoredDuringExecution:
      - labelSelector:
          matchExpressions:
          - key: app
            operator: In
            values:
            - frontend
        topologyKey: "kubernetes.io/hostname"
  containers:
  - name: example-container
    image: nginx:1.17.4
```

Configuring Inter-pod Anti-affinity Inter-pod anti-affinity rules are also specified in the pod's manifest under the 'affinity' section. These rules define the conditions under which pods should not be co-located.

Example Inter-pod Anti-affinity Configuration:

```
apiVersion: v1
```

```
kind: Pod
metadata:
  name: example-pod
spec:
  affinity:
    podAntiAffinity:
      requiredDuringSchedulingIgnoredDuringExecution:
      - labelSelector:
          matchExpressions:
          - key: app
            operator: In
            values:
            - backend
        topologyKey: "kubernetes.io/hostname"
  containers:
  - name: example-container
    image: nginx:1.17.4
```

Soft and Hard Constraints Affinity and anti-affinity rules can be specified as either soft or hard constraints. Soft constraints (preferredDuringSchedulingIgnoredDuringExecution) allow Kubernetes to prioritize these rules, while hard constraints (requiredDuringSchedulingIgnoredDuringExecution) must be strictly followed.

Example Soft Constraint:

```
apiVersion: v1
kind: Pod
metadata:
  name: example-pod
spec:
  affinity:
    podAffinity:
      preferredDuringSchedulingIgnoredDuringExecution:
      - weight: 1
        podAffinityTerm:
          labelSelector:
```

```
        matchExpressions:
        - key: app
          operator: In
          values:
          - frontend
        topologyKey: "kubernetes.io/hostname"
  containers:
  - name: example-container
    image: nginx:1.17.4
```

Use Cases for Inter-pod Affinity and Anti-affinity Implementing
inter-pod affinity and anti-affinity is beneficial for various scenarios,
enhancing performance, reliability, and resource utilization.

Common Use Cases:

- **Workload Co-location:** Ensuring that related workloads, such as
  a web server and a cache server, are scheduled on the same node to
  minimize latency.

- **High Availability:** Distributing replicas of an application across
  different nodes or zones to improve fault tolerance and availability.

- **Resource Contention:** Avoiding resource contention by ensuring
  that resource-intensive pods are not scheduled on the same node.

Monitoring and Troubleshooting Affinity and Anti-affinity
Effective monitoring and troubleshooting ensure that affinity and
anti-affinity rules are correctly applied and that pod placement meets your
requirements.

Monitoring Tools:

- **Kubernetes Events:** Monitor events related to pod scheduling to
  ensure that affinity and anti-affinity rules are being followed.

- **Logs:** Review scheduler logs for information on pod placement
  decisions and any issues encountered.

- **Metrics:** Use tools like Prometheus to monitor metrics related to pod distribution and resource utilization.

Common Issues and Solutions:

- **Pod Scheduling Failures:** Ensure that there are sufficient resources available to meet the specified affinity or anti-affinity rules. Adjust rules if necessary.

- **Unintended Pod Placement:** Verify the accuracy of label selectors and topology keys used in affinity and anti-affinity rules.

- **Performance Impact:** Monitor the performance impact of affinity and anti-affinity rules and optimize configurations to balance between strict placement and resource utilization.

Best Practices for Using Inter-pod Affinity and Anti-affinity
Implementing best practices for inter-pod affinity and anti-affinity helps ensure optimal pod placement and efficient resource utilization.

Clear Labeling: Use clear and consistent labeling for your pods to make it easier to define and manage affinity and anti-affinity rules.

Balance Soft and Hard Constraints: Balance the use of soft and hard constraints to ensure that affinity and anti-affinity rules are flexible enough to allow efficient scheduling while still meeting critical requirements.

Regular Review: Regularly review and update affinity and anti-affinity rules to adapt to changing application requirements and cluster conditions.

Conclusion Inter-pod affinity and anti-affinity are powerful features in Kubernetes that provide fine-grained control over pod placement. By understanding and effectively implementing these features, you can improve the performance, reliability, and resource utilization of your applications. Regular monitoring, troubleshooting, and adherence to best practices further enhance the effectiveness of your pod placement strategies.

4.3   Services

4.3.1   ClusterIP, NodePort, LoadBalancer, and ExternalName

Services in Kubernetes provide a way to expose applications running on a set of pods as a network service. They abstract the underlying pods and provide stable endpoints to access them, even as the pods scale up and down. Kubernetes supports several types of services, each with its own use case: ClusterIP, NodePort, LoadBalancer, and ExternalName.

ClusterIP   The default type of service in Kubernetes is ClusterIP. It exposes the service on a cluster-internal IP, making it accessible only within the cluster. This type of service is ideal for internal communications between microservices.

Key Features of ClusterIP:

- **Internal Access:** Accessible only within the cluster.

- **Stable Endpoint:** Provides a stable internal IP address for accessing the service.

- **DNS Resolution:** Automatically resolves DNS names to the service's ClusterIP.

Example ClusterIP Service Configuration:

```
apiVersion: v1
kind: Service
metadata:
  name: example-clusterip-service
  namespace: default
spec:
  selector:
    app: example-app
  ports:
    - protocol: TCP
```

```
      port: 80
      targetPort: 8080
  type: ClusterIP
```

Use Cases for ClusterIP:

- **Internal Microservices:** Useful for exposing services that should only be accessed by other services within the cluster.

- **Database Connections:** Internal databases that should not be accessible outside the cluster.

- **Backend Services:** Backend services that only need to communicate with frontend applications or other backend services within the cluster.

NodePort NodePort services expose the service on a static port on each node's IP. This allows the service to be accessed externally using ¡NodeIP¿:¡NodePort¿. NodePort is useful for exposing a service to external traffic without requiring an external load balancer.

Key Features of NodePort:

- **External Access:** Makes the service accessible outside the cluster.

- **Static Port:** Uses a static port on each node.

- **Cluster-wide Access:** Can be accessed via any node's IP.

Example NodePort Service Configuration:

```
apiVersion: v1
kind: Service
metadata:
  name: example-nodeport-service
  namespace: default
spec:
  selector:
    app: example-app
  ports:
```

```
  - protocol: TCP
    port: 80
    targetPort: 8080
    nodePort: 30007
type: NodePort
```

Use Cases for NodePort:

- **Testing and Development:** Exposing services for testing and development purposes.

- **Simple External Access:** Providing external access without the complexity of configuring a load balancer.

- **Intranet Services:** Services intended to be accessible from within an internal network.

LoadBalancer   LoadBalancer services expose the service externally using a cloud provider's load balancer. This type of service automatically provisions a load balancer for the service and provides a stable external IP address. LoadBalancer is ideal for services that need to be accessible from the internet.

Key Features of LoadBalancer:

- **External Load Balancer:** Integrates with cloud provider load balancers.

- **Stable External IP:** Provides a stable external IP for the service.

- **Automated Provisioning:** Automatically creates and manages the load balancer.

Example LoadBalancer Service Configuration:

```
apiVersion: v1
kind: Service
metadata:
  name: example-loadbalancer-service
  namespace: default
```

```
spec:
  selector:
    app: example-app
  ports:
    - protocol: TCP
      port: 80
      targetPort: 8080
  type: LoadBalancer
```

Use Cases for LoadBalancer:

- **Public-facing Services:** Exposing applications such as web servers, APIs, or any service that needs to be accessible from the internet.

- **Managed Cloud Services:** Leveraging cloud provider load balancers for automatic scaling and high availability.

- **High Traffic Applications:** Applications requiring robust load balancing to distribute traffic evenly across multiple pods.

ExternalName   ExternalName services map a service to an external DNS name. This type of service does not provide proxying of traffic but instead returns a CNAME record with the external name. ExternalName is useful for integrating Kubernetes services with external services that have a DNS name.

Key Features of ExternalName:

- **DNS Mapping:** Maps the service to an external DNS name.

- **No Proxying:** Does not proxy traffic, only resolves DNS.

- **Simple Integration:** Easily integrates external services into Kubernetes.

Example ExternalName Service Configuration:

```
apiVersion: v1
kind: Service
```

```
metadata:
  name: example-externalname-service
  namespace: default
spec:
  type: ExternalName
  externalName: example.com
```

Use Cases for ExternalName:

- **Legacy Systems Integration:** Integrating with legacy systems or services that are not running within the Kubernetes cluster.

- **Third-party Services:** Accessing third-party services using a consistent DNS name.

- **Service Migration:** Gradually migrating services from external locations to within the cluster by maintaining a consistent DNS name.

Choosing the Right Service Type   Selecting the appropriate service type depends on the specific needs of your application and the desired level of exposure.

Use Cases:

- **ClusterIP:** Use for internal services that do not need to be exposed outside the cluster.

- **NodePort:** Use for simple, external access to services without requiring a load balancer.

- **LoadBalancer:** Use for services that need to be accessible from the internet, leveraging cloud provider load balancers.

- **ExternalName:** Use for integrating with external services that are identified by a DNS name.

Monitoring and Troubleshooting Services   Effective monitoring and troubleshooting of services ensure that they are operating correctly and efficiently.

Monitoring Tools:

- **Kubernetes Dashboard:** Provides an overview of services and their status.

- **Prometheus:** Use Prometheus to monitor metrics related to services, such as request rates and error rates.

- **Logs:** Access service logs to diagnose issues and monitor traffic patterns.

Common Issues and Solutions:

- **Service Unreachable:** Check the service and pod labels to ensure they match. Verify network policies and firewall rules.

- **Load Balancer Provisioning Issues:** Ensure the cloud provider configuration is correct and that there are no quota limits being exceeded.

- **DNS Resolution Failures:** Verify that the DNS configuration is correct and that the external name resolves as expected.

Best Practices for Managing Services Implementing best practices for managing services ensures reliability and performance.

Clear Naming Conventions: Use clear and consistent naming conventions for services to improve manageability and organization.

Resource Requests and Limits: Define resource requests and limits for services to ensure they have sufficient resources to handle traffic.

Regular Monitoring: Regularly monitor service metrics and logs to detect and address issues proactively.

Conclusion Kubernetes services are a powerful abstraction for exposing applications running on pods. By understanding and effectively using different service types—ClusterIP, NodePort, LoadBalancer, and ExternalName—you can ensure that your applications are accessible as needed. Implementing best practices and leveraging monitoring tools further enhances the reliability and performance of your services.

4.4 Volumes and Persistent Storage

4.4.1 Volume Types

In Kubernetes, volumes provide a way for containers to persist data beyond the life cycle of a pod, share data between containers within a pod, and access storage resources outside of the container environment. Kubernetes supports a variety of volume types, each with its own use case and functionality.

EmptyDir An EmptyDir volume is created when a pod is assigned to a node and exists as long as that pod is running on that node. This volume type is useful for scratch space and temporary storage.

Key Features of EmptyDir:

- **Lifecycle:** Exists as long as the pod is running on the node.

- **Ephemeral:** Data is deleted when the pod is terminated.

- **Use Case:** Temporary storage, cache, or scratch space.

Example EmptyDir Configuration:

```
apiVersion: v1
kind: Pod
metadata:
  name: example-pod
spec:
  containers:
  - name: example-container
    image: nginx:1.17.4
```

```
    volumeMounts:
    - mountPath: /cache
      name: cache-volume
  volumes:
  - name: cache-volume
    emptyDir: {}
```

HostPath   A HostPath volume mounts a file or directory from the host node's filesystem into a pod. This can be useful for integrating with legacy applications or accessing specific host files.

Key Features of HostPath:

- **Host Access:** Direct access to the host's filesystem.

- **Flexibility:** Can mount files, directories, or block devices.

- **Use Case:** Integrating with legacy applications, accessing host-specific files.

Example HostPath Configuration:

```
apiVersion: v1
kind: Pod
metadata:
  name: example-pod
spec:
  containers:
  - name: example-container
    image: nginx:1.17.4
    volumeMounts:
    - mountPath: /data
      name: host-volume
  volumes:
  - name: host-volume
    hostPath:
      path: /path/on/host
      type: Directory
```

PersistentVolume and PersistentVolumeClaim PersistentVolumes (PV) and PersistentVolumeClaims (PVC) provide a way to manage durable storage resources in a Kubernetes cluster. PVs are cluster-wide resources, while PVCs are requests for storage by users.

Key Features of PersistentVolumes and PersistentVolumeClaims:

- **Durable Storage:** Provides persistent storage that outlives pods.

- **Dynamic Provisioning:** Supports dynamic provisioning of storage resources.

- **Use Case:** Databases, shared storage, and any application requiring durable storage.

Example PersistentVolume Configuration:

```
apiVersion: v1
kind: PersistentVolume
metadata:
  name: example-pv
spec:
  capacity:
    storage: 10Gi
  accessModes:
    - ReadWriteOnce
  persistentVolumeReclaimPolicy: Retain
  hostPath:
    path: /mnt/data
```

Example PersistentVolumeClaim Configuration:

```
apiVersion: v1
kind: PersistentVolumeClaim
metadata:
  name: example-pvc
spec:
  accessModes:
    - ReadWriteOnce
```

```
resources:
  requests:
    storage: 10Gi
```

ConfigMap and Secret ConfigMap and Secret volumes are used to inject configuration data and sensitive information into pods. ConfigMaps are used for non-sensitive data, while Secrets are used for sensitive data such as passwords and tokens.

Key Features of ConfigMap and Secret:

- **Configuration Management:** Inject configuration data into pods.

- **Security:** Secrets provide a secure way to manage sensitive information.

- **Use Case:** Application configuration, environment variables, sensitive data injection.

Example ConfigMap Configuration:

```
apiVersion: v1
kind: ConfigMap
metadata:
  name: example-config
data:
  config.json: |
    {
      "key": "value"
    }
```

Example Secret Configuration:

```
apiVersion: v1
kind: Secret
metadata:
  name: example-secret
type: Opaque
data:
```

```
username: dXNlcm5hbWU=
password: cGFzc3dvcmQ=
```

NFS (Network File System) An NFS volume allows a pod to access shared storage provided by an NFS server. This is useful for sharing data between multiple pods and applications.

Key Features of NFS:

- **Shared Storage:** Allows multiple pods to access the same storage.

- **Network-based:** Accessible over the network from multiple nodes.

- **Use Case:** Shared data repositories, shared configuration files.

Example NFS Configuration:

```
apiVersion: v1
kind: Pod
metadata:
  name: example-pod
spec:
  containers:
  - name: example-container
    image: nginx:1.17.4
    volumeMounts:
    - mountPath: /mnt/data
      name: nfs-volume
  volumes:
  - name: nfs-volume
    nfs:
      server: nfs-server.example.com
      path: /path/to/share
```

AWS EBS (Elastic Block Store) An AWS EBS volume is a block storage device provided by Amazon Web Services that can be attached to a single pod. It is useful for applications running on AWS that require persistent storage.

Key Features of AWS EBS:

- **Persistent Storage:** Provides durable block storage.

- **AWS Integration:** Seamlessly integrates with AWS infrastructure.

- **Use Case:** Databases, file storage, any application requiring persistent block storage.

Example AWS EBS Configuration:

```
apiVersion: v1
kind: Pod
metadata:
  name: example-pod
spec:
  containers:
  - name: example-container
    image: nginx:1.17.4
    volumeMounts:
    - mountPath: /mnt/data
      name: ebs-volume
  volumes:
  - name: ebs-volume
    awsElasticBlockStore:
      volumeID: <volume-id>
      fsType: ext4
```

Azure Disk   An Azure Disk volume is a block storage device provided by Microsoft Azure that can be attached to a single pod. It is suitable for applications running on Azure that require persistent storage.

Key Features of Azure Disk:

- **Persistent Storage:** Provides durable block storage.

- **Azure Integration:** Seamlessly integrates with Azure infrastructure.

- **Use Case:** Databases, file storage, any application requiring persistent block storage.

Example Azure Disk Configuration:

```
apiVersion: v1
kind: Pod
metadata:
  name: example-pod
spec:
  containers:
  - name: example-container
    image: nginx:1.17.4
    volumeMounts:
    - mountPath: /mnt/data
      name: azure-disk-volume
  volumes:
  - name: azure-disk-volume
    azureDisk:
      diskName: <disk-name>
      diskURI: <disk-uri>
      fsType: ext4
```

GCE Persistent Disk A GCE Persistent Disk is a block storage device provided by Google Cloud Platform that can be attached to a single pod. It is ideal for applications running on GCP that require persistent storage.

Key Features of GCE Persistent Disk:

- **Persistent Storage:** Provides durable block storage.

- **GCP Integration:** Seamlessly integrates with Google Cloud Platform.

- **Use Case:** Databases, file storage, any application requiring persistent block storage.

Example GCE Persistent Disk Configuration:

```
apiVersion: v1
kind: Pod
metadata:
```

```
name: example-pod
spec:
  containers:
  - name: example-container
    image: nginx:1.17.4
    volumeMounts:
    - mountPath: /mnt/data
      name: gce-pd-volume
  volumes:
  - name: gce-pd-volume
    gcePersistentDisk:
      pdName: <disk-name>
      fsType: ext4
```

Best Practices for Using Volumes Implementing best practices for using volumes ensures data durability, security, and performance.

Use PersistentVolumes and PersistentVolumeClaims: For applications requiring durable storage, use PersistentVolumes (PVs) and PersistentVolumeClaims (PVCs) to manage storage resources effectively.

Secure Sensitive Data: Use Secrets to store and manage sensitive data securely. Avoid storing sensitive information in plain text within pod specifications.

Monitor Storage Usage: Regularly monitor storage usage to ensure that volumes do not run out of space. Use tools like Prometheus and Grafana to set up alerts for storage capacity.

Backup and Recovery: Implement a robust backup and recovery strategy for critical data stored in volumes. Use cloud-native backup solutions or third-party tools to automate backups.

Conclusion Understanding the various volume types in Kubernetes and their use cases is essential for effectively managing storage in your applications. By choosing the right volume type and following best practices, you can ensure data durability, security, and performance in your Kubernetes deployments.

4.4.2   Persistent Volumes and Claims

Persistent Volumes (PVs) and Persistent Volume Claims (PVCs) are integral components of Kubernetes' storage architecture, providing a mechanism for users to request and manage durable storage that persists beyond the lifecycle of individual pods. Understanding how to effectively use PVs and PVCs is crucial for managing stateful applications in Kubernetes.

Persistent Volumes (PVs) A Persistent Volume (PV) is a piece of storage in the cluster that has been provisioned by an administrator or dynamically provisioned using StorageClasses. PVs are a resource in the cluster, similar to a node, and provide an abstraction for physical storage devices such as NFS, iSCSI, or cloud provider-specific storage solutions.

Key Features of Persistent Volumes:

- **Cluster Resource:** PVs are cluster-wide resources managed independently of pods.

- **Storage Abstraction:** Abstracts underlying storage systems, providing a consistent interface.

- **Reclaim Policies:** Define what happens to the PV when its PVC is deleted (Retain, Recycle, Delete).

Example Persistent Volume Configuration:

```
apiVersion: v1
kind: PersistentVolume
metadata:
  name: example-pv
spec:
  capacity:
    storage: 10Gi
  accessModes:
    - ReadWriteOnce
```

```
persistentVolumeReclaimPolicy: Retain
nfs:
  path: /mnt/data
  server: nfs-server.example.com
```

Persistent Volume Claims (PVCs)   A Persistent Volume Claim (PVC) is a request for storage by a user. PVCs are used to request specific size and access modes (e.g., ReadWriteOnce, ReadOnlyMany, ReadWriteMany). The Kubernetes control plane automatically matches PVCs to appropriate PVs based on the requested properties.

Key Features of Persistent Volume Claims:

- **User Requests:** Users create PVCs to request storage without needing to know the underlying storage details.

- **Dynamic Binding:** PVCs are dynamically bound to suitable PVs.

- **Access Modes:** PVCs specify the access modes they require, which must match the PV's capabilities.

Example Persistent Volume Claim Configuration:

```
apiVersion: v1
kind: PersistentVolumeClaim
metadata:
  name: example-pvc
spec:
  accessModes:
    - ReadWriteOnce
  resources:
    requests:
      storage: 10Gi
```

Dynamic Provisioning   Dynamic provisioning allows the automatic creation of PVs based on StorageClasses when a PVC is created. This eliminates the need for administrators to pre-provision storage and simplifies storage management.

Key Features of Dynamic Provisioning:

- **Automation:** Automates the provisioning of storage resources.

- **StorageClasses:** Uses StorageClasses to define different tiers and types of storage.

- **Flexibility:** Supports various backend storage systems, including cloud storage services.

Example StorageClass Configuration:

```
apiVersion: storage.k8s.io/v1
kind: StorageClass
metadata:
  name: example-storageclass
provisioner: kubernetes.io/aws-ebs
parameters:
  type: gp2
  fsType: ext4
```

Example PVC with StorageClass:

```
apiVersion: v1
kind: PersistentVolumeClaim
metadata:
  name: example-pvc
spec:
  storageClassName: example-storageclass
  accessModes:
    - ReadWriteOnce
  resources:
    requests:
      storage: 10Gi
```

Binding and Using PVs and PVCs   Once a PVC is bound to a PV, the PVC can be used as a volume in pod specifications. This allows pods to access the persistent storage specified by the PV.

Example Pod Using a PVC:

```
apiVersion: v1
kind: Pod
metadata:
  name: example-pod
spec:
  containers:
  - name: example-container
    image: nginx:1.17.4
    volumeMounts:
    - mountPath: /mnt/data
      name: storage
  volumes:
  - name: storage
    persistentVolumeClaim:
      claimName: example-pvc
```

Reclaim Policies   Reclaim policies determine what happens to a PV when its PVC is deleted. The policies are:

- **Retain:** Keeps the PV for manual reclamation by the administrator.

- **Recycle:** Deletes the PV's data and makes it available for a new claim.

- **Delete:** Deletes the PV and its data from the underlying storage.

Example PV with Reclaim Policy:

```
apiVersion: v1
kind: PersistentVolume
metadata:
  name: example-pv
spec:
  capacity:
    storage: 10Gi
  accessModes:
    - ReadWriteOnce
  persistentVolumeReclaimPolicy: Retain
```

```
nfs:
  path: /mnt/data
  server: nfs-server.example.com
```

Monitoring and Troubleshooting PVs and PVCs Effective monitoring and troubleshooting are essential to ensure the reliable operation of PVs and PVCs.

Monitoring Tools:

- **Kubernetes Dashboard:** Provides an overview of PV and PVC status.

- **Prometheus:** Monitors storage metrics, such as capacity and usage.

- **Logs:** Access logs for events related to PV and PVC provisioning and binding.

Common Issues and Solutions:

- **PVC Pending:** Ensure there are available PVs that match the PVC's requirements.

- **Binding Failures:** Verify that the StorageClass and provisioning parameters are correct.

- **Storage Exhaustion:** Monitor storage usage and expand capacity as needed.

Best Practices for Using PVs and PVCs Implementing best practices ensures efficient and reliable storage management.

Define Clear Policies: Clearly define reclaim policies based on the application's data retention needs.

Use Dynamic Provisioning: Leverage dynamic provisioning with StorageClasses to automate and simplify storage management.

Monitor Storage Usage: Regularly monitor storage usage and set up alerts for capacity thresholds.

Secure Storage: Ensure that sensitive data is stored securely, using encryption and appropriate access controls.

Conclusion Persistent Volumes (PVs) and Persistent Volume Claims (PVCs) are foundational components for managing durable storage in Kubernetes. By understanding how to use and manage PVs and PVCs, you can effectively handle stateful applications, ensuring data persistence, security, and efficient storage utilization. Implementing best practices and leveraging dynamic provisioning further enhances the management of storage resources in your Kubernetes environment.

4.5 ConfigMaps and Secrets

ConfigMaps and Secrets are Kubernetes objects that provide a way to manage configuration data and sensitive information separately from the application code. This separation of configuration from the code allows for more secure and flexible management of applications in Kubernetes.

ConfigMaps ConfigMaps are used to store non-sensitive configuration data in key-value pairs. They allow you to decouple configuration artifacts from image content to keep containerized applications portable.

Key Features of ConfigMaps:

- **Decoupling Configuration:** Separates configuration data from application code.

- **Key-Value Storage:** Stores configuration as key-value pairs.

- **Flexible Injection:** Can be injected into pods as environment variables, command-line arguments, or mounted as configuration files.

Creating a ConfigMap ConfigMaps can be created using the 'kubectl' command or by defining them in a YAML manifest.

Example ConfigMap Configuration:

```
apiVersion: v1
kind: ConfigMap
metadata:
  name: example-configmap
data:
  config.json: |
    {
      "key": "value"
    }
  app.properties: |
    key1=value1
    key2=value2
```

Using ConfigMaps ConfigMaps can be used in pods in several ways, including as environment variables, command-line arguments, or mounted volumes.

Example Pod Using ConfigMap as Environment Variables:

```
apiVersion: v1
kind: Pod
metadata:
  name: example-pod
spec:
  containers:
  - name: example-container
    image: nginx:1.17.4
    env:
    - name: CONFIG_KEY
      valueFrom:
        configMapKeyRef:
          name: example-configmap
          key: config.json
```

Example Pod Using ConfigMap as a Volume:

```
apiVersion: v1
kind: Pod
metadata:
  name: example-pod
spec:
  containers:
  - name: example-container
    image: nginx:1.17.4
    volumeMounts:
    - mountPath: /etc/config
      name: config-volume
  volumes:
  - name: config-volume
    configMap:
      name: example-configmap
```

Secrets   Secrets are used to store sensitive information such as passwords, OAuth tokens, and SSH keys. They provide a way to manage sensitive data securely within Kubernetes.

Key Features of Secrets:

- **Secure Storage:** Stores sensitive data securely.

- **Base64 Encoding:** Data is encoded in base64 to avoid accidental exposure.

- **Flexible Injection:** Can be injected into pods as environment variables or mounted as files.

Creating a Secret   Secrets can be created using the 'kubectl' command or by defining them in a YAML manifest. Data in Secrets must be base64 encoded.

Example Secret Configuration:

```
apiVersion: v1
kind: Secret
```

```
metadata:
  name: example-secret
type: Opaque
data:
  username: dXNlcm5hbWU=
  password: cGFzc3dvcmQ=
```

Using Secrets   Secrets can be used in pods in several ways, including as
environment variables or mounted volumes.

Example Pod Using Secret as Environment Variables:

```
apiVersion: v1
kind: Pod
metadata:
  name: example-pod
spec:
  containers:
  - name: example-container
    image: nginx:1.17.4
    env:
    - name: USERNAME
      valueFrom:
        secretKeyRef:
          name: example-secret
          key: username
    - name: PASSWORD
      valueFrom:
        secretKeyRef:
          name: example-secret
          key: password
```

Example Pod Using Secret as a Volume:

```
apiVersion: v1
kind: Pod
metadata:
  name: example-pod
```

```
spec:
  containers:
  - name: example-container
    image: nginx:1.17.4
    volumeMounts:
    - mountPath: /etc/secret
      name: secret-volume
      readOnly: true
  volumes:
  - name: secret-volume
    secret:
      secretName: example-secret
```

Best Practices for Using ConfigMaps and Secrets   Implementing best practices ensures secure and efficient management of configuration data and sensitive information.

Separate Configuration and Code: Keep configuration data separate from application code to improve flexibility and portability.

Secure Sensitive Data: Use Secrets to manage sensitive data securely, and restrict access to Secrets to only those pods that need it.

Use Environment Variables for Simple Configurations: Inject configuration data into pods as environment variables for simple configurations.

Mount ConfigMaps and Secrets for Complex Configurations: Mount ConfigMaps and Secrets as volumes when dealing with complex configurations or large amounts of data.

Monitoring and Troubleshooting   Monitoring and troubleshooting ConfigMaps and Secrets ensure that they are used correctly and securely.

Monitoring Tools:

- **Kubernetes Dashboard:** Provides an overview of ConfigMaps and Secrets.

- **Logs:** Access logs to troubleshoot issues related to the injection of ConfigMaps and Secrets.

Common Issues and Solutions:

- **Data Not Injected:** Ensure that the ConfigMap or Secret exists and is correctly referenced in the pod specification.

- **Access Denied:** Verify that the pod has the necessary permissions to access the ConfigMap or Secret.

- **Incorrect Data:** Ensure that data in ConfigMaps and Secrets is correctly formatted and base64 encoded if necessary.

Conclusion ConfigMaps and Secrets are essential tools for managing configuration data and sensitive information in Kubernetes. By understanding how to use and manage ConfigMaps and Secrets, you can ensure secure and efficient configuration management for your applications. Implementing best practices and leveraging monitoring tools further enhances the reliability and security of your Kubernetes deployments.

4.6 Deployments

Deployments are one of the most fundamental resources in Kubernetes, providing a declarative way to manage the lifecycle of applications. They enable you to describe an application's desired state, and Kubernetes ensures that the current state matches this desired state. Deployments offer powerful features such as scaling, rolling updates, and rollbacks, making it easier to manage applications in a dynamic environment.

Key Features of Deployments Deployments offer several key features that make them essential for managing applications in Kubernetes:

Declarative Updates: Specify the desired state of your application, and Kubernetes will manage the process of bringing the current state to match the desired state.

Scaling: Easily scale applications up or down by adjusting the number of replicas.

Rolling Updates: Update applications to new versions without downtime, gradually replacing old pods with new ones.

Rollbacks: Quickly revert to a previous version if an update fails or introduces issues.

Self-Healing: Automatically replace failed or unhealthy pods to ensure that the desired number of replicas are always running.

Creating a Deployment A Deployment is defined using a YAML manifest, which specifies the desired state of the application, including the number of replicas, the container image to use, and any configuration details.

Example Deployment Configuration:

```yaml
apiVersion: apps/v1
kind: Deployment
metadata:
  name: example-deployment
spec:
  replicas: 3
  selector:
    matchLabels:
      app: example-app
  template:
    metadata:
      labels:
        app: example-app
    spec:
      containers:
      - name: example-container
        image: nginx:1.18.0
        ports:
```

```
    - containerPort: 80
```

Creating a Deployment: Apply the Deployment configuration using the 'kubectl apply' command.

```
kubectl apply -f example-deployment.yaml
```

Scaling Deployments   One of the primary benefits of Deployments is the ability to scale applications easily. You can scale the number of replicas up or down based on the load or other requirements.

Scaling Up: Increase the number of replicas to handle more traffic.

```
kubectl scale deployment example-deployment --replicas=5
```

Scaling Down: Decrease the number of replicas to conserve resources.

```
kubectl scale deployment example-deployment --replicas=2
```

Updating Deployments   Updating a Deployment involves changing the desired state, such as updating the container image. Kubernetes will then perform a rolling update to transition from the current state to the desired state.

Updating a Deployment: Modify the Deployment manifest and apply the changes.

```
kubectl apply -f updated-deployment.yaml
```

Monitoring and Managing Deployments   Kubernetes provides several commands to monitor and manage Deployments, ensuring that they are running as expected.

Checking Deployment Status: Monitor the status of the Deployment to ensure it is running correctly.

```
kubectl get deployments
kubectl describe deployment example-deployment
```

Viewing Rollout Status: Check the status of a rolling update or rollback.

```
kubectl rollout status deployment/example-deployment
```

Best Practices for Using Deployments Following best practices ensures that your applications are managed efficiently and reliably.

Use Declarative Configuration: Define Deployments using YAML manifests and manage them with version control.

Monitor Applications: Regularly monitor the health and performance of your applications to detect and address issues promptly.

Automate Deployments: Integrate Deployments with CI/CD pipelines to automate the deployment process.

Use Health Probes: Configure readiness and liveness probes to ensure that your applications are healthy and ready to serve traffic.

Conclusion Deployments are a powerful tool in Kubernetes for managing the lifecycle of applications. By understanding and leveraging their features, such as scaling, rolling updates, and rollbacks, you can ensure that your applications are resilient, scalable, and easy to manage. Implementing best practices further enhances the reliability and efficiency of your deployment processes, making it easier to maintain and update applications in a Kubernetes environment.

4.6.1 Rolling Updates and Rollbacks

Deployments in Kubernetes provide declarative updates to applications. They allow you to define the desired state of your application and manage the process of transitioning from the current state to the desired state. One of the key features of Deployments is the ability to perform rolling updates and rollbacks, ensuring minimal downtime and easy recovery from failures.

Rolling Updates   Rolling updates allow you to update your application to a new version without downtime. Kubernetes progressively replaces the existing pods with new ones, ensuring that some instances of the application remain available during the update process.

Key Features of Rolling Updates:

- **Zero Downtime:** Ensures continuous availability of the application.

- **Incremental Updates:** Updates pods incrementally, replacing old pods with new ones.

- **Controlled Rollout:** Provides control over the pace and conditions of the rollout.

Example Deployment Configuration for Rolling Updates:

```
apiVersion: apps/v1
kind: Deployment
metadata:
  name: example-deployment
spec:
  replicas: 3
  selector:
    matchLabels:
      app: example-app
  strategy:
    type: RollingUpdate
    rollingUpdate:
      maxUnavailable: 1
      maxSurge: 1
  template:
    metadata:
      labels:
        app: example-app
    spec:
      containers:
      - name: example-container
        image: nginx:1.18.0
```

```
    ports:
    - containerPort: 80
```

Initiating a Rolling Update: To initiate a rolling update, you simply update the Deployment's specification, such as the container image. Kubernetes automatically handles the rollout.

```
kubectl set image deployment/example-deployment
example-container=nginx:1.19.0
```

Monitoring Rolling Updates: Use 'kubectl rollout' commands to monitor the status of the update.

```
kubectl rollout status deployment/example-deployment
```

Rollbacks Rollbacks allow you to revert your application to a previous version if an update fails or introduces issues. Kubernetes keeps a history of previous deployments, making it easy to rollback to a known good state.

Key Features of Rollbacks:

- **Quick Recovery:** Quickly revert to a stable version in case of issues.

- **Version History:** Maintains a history of previous deployments.

- **Automated Process:** Easily revert to a previous state using simple commands.

Initiating a Rollback: Use the 'kubectl rollout undo' command to rollback to the previous version.

```
kubectl rollout undo deployment/example-deployment
```

Specifying a Revision: You can rollback to a specific revision by specifying the revision number.

```
kubectl rollout undo deployment/example-deployment
--to-revision=2
```

Monitoring Rollbacks: Use 'kubectl rollout' commands to monitor the status of the rollback.

```
kubectl rollout status deployment/example-deployment
```

Best Practices for Rolling Updates and Rollbacks Implementing best practices ensures smooth updates and quick recovery in case of issues.

Canary Deployments: Use canary deployments to test the new version with a small subset of users before a full rollout.

Automated Testing: Implement automated tests to validate the new version during the rollout process.

Monitor Metrics: Monitor application and system metrics to detect issues early during updates.

Maintain Version History: Keep a history of deployments to facilitate easy rollbacks.

Conclusion Rolling updates and rollbacks are essential features for managing application deployments in Kubernetes. By understanding and effectively using these features, you can ensure continuous availability, smooth transitions between application versions, and quick recovery from failures. Implementing best practices further enhances the reliability and efficiency of your deployment processes.

4.6.2 Probes: Readiness and Liveness

Probes are essential for managing the health and availability of containers in Kubernetes. They provide a mechanism for the Kubernetes control plane to check the status of containers and take appropriate actions based on their health. The two primary types of probes are readiness probes and liveness probes.

Readiness Probes   Readiness probes determine if a container is ready to start accepting traffic. If a readiness probe fails, the endpoints controller removes the pod's IP address from the endpoints of all services that match the pod, ensuring that traffic is not sent to a pod that is not ready.

Key Features of Readiness Probes:

- **Traffic Management:** Controls whether a pod should receive traffic.

- **Graceful Startup:** Ensures that a pod only starts receiving traffic once it is fully initialized and ready.

- **Dynamic Availability:** Can be used to dynamically control the availability of pods.

Example Readiness Probe Configuration:

```yaml
apiVersion: v1
kind: Pod
metadata:
  name: example-pod
spec:
  containers:
  - name: example-container
    image: nginx:1.17.4
    readinessProbe:
      httpGet:
        path: /ready
        port: 80
      initialDelaySeconds: 5
      periodSeconds: 10
```

Liveness Probes   Liveness probes determine if a container is still running. If a liveness probe fails, the kubelet kills the container, and the container is subjected to its restart policy. This helps in automatically recovering from situations where the container is in a bad state and cannot recover on its own.

Key Features of Liveness Probes:

- **Self-Healing:** Automatically restarts containers that are in a failed state.

- **Continuous Monitoring:** Regularly checks the health of the container during its lifecycle.

- **Improved Reliability:** Ensures that the application remains healthy and available.

Example Liveness Probe Configuration:

```yaml
apiVersion: v1
kind: Pod
metadata:
  name: example-pod
spec:
  containers:
  - name: example-container
    image: nginx:1.17.4
    livenessProbe:
      httpGet:
        path: /healthz
        port: 80
      initialDelaySeconds: 10
      periodSeconds: 10
```

Types of Probes Kubernetes supports three types of probes: HTTP, TCP, and Exec.

HTTP Probes: Perform an HTTP GET request to check the health of the container.

Example HTTP Probe:

```yaml
readinessProbe:
  httpGet:
    path: /ready
```

```
  port: 80
initialDelaySeconds: 5
periodSeconds: 10
```

TCP Probes: Perform a TCP check to ensure that the specified port is open and accepting connections.

Example TCP Probe:

```
livenessProbe:
  tcpSocket:
    port: 80
  initialDelaySeconds: 10
  periodSeconds: 10
```

Exec Probes: Execute a command inside the container to check its health.

Example Exec Probe:

```
livenessProbe:
  exec:
    command:
    - cat
    - /tmp/healthy
  initialDelaySeconds: 10
  periodSeconds: 10
```

Configuring Probes When configuring probes, it is important to set appropriate values for initial delay, period, timeout, success threshold, and failure threshold to ensure accurate health checks.

Key Configuration Parameters:

- **initialDelaySeconds:** Time to wait before starting the first probe.

- **periodSeconds:** Frequency of performing the probe.

- **timeoutSeconds:** Duration to wait for a probe to complete.

- **successThreshold:** Number of consecutive successes required to mark the pod as healthy.

- **failureThreshold:** Number of consecutive failures required to mark the pod as unhealthy.

Best Practices for Using Probes Implementing best practices for probes ensures reliable and accurate health checks for your containers.

Tailor Probes to Application Needs: Configure probes based on the specific needs and behavior of your application.

Monitor Probe Results: Regularly monitor the results of probes to detect and troubleshoot issues promptly.

Test Probes in Staging: Validate your probe configurations in a staging environment before deploying them to production.

Avoid Overly Aggressive Settings: Set reasonable thresholds for probe parameters to avoid unnecessary restarts or marking pods as unavailable.

Conclusion Readiness and liveness probes are critical tools for managing the health and availability of applications in Kubernetes. By configuring these probes appropriately and following best practices, you can ensure that your applications are resilient, self-healing, and always ready to serve traffic. Effective use of probes enhances the reliability and stability of your Kubernetes deployments.

4.7 StatefulSets

StatefulSets are a Kubernetes workload API object used to manage stateful applications. They are designed to manage the deployment and scaling of a set of pods, and provide guarantees about the ordering and uniqueness of these pods. StatefulSets are particularly useful for applications that require stable, persistent storage, ordered deployment, and consistent network identities.

What is a StatefulSet?   A StatefulSet is similar to a Deployment, but it is specifically designed for stateful applications.   Unlike Deployments, StatefulSets maintain a sticky identity for each of their pods. These pods are created from the same spec but are not interchangeable: each has a persistent identifier that it maintains across any rescheduling.

Key Features of StatefulSets:

- **Stable Network Identities:** Each pod in a StatefulSet gets a unique, stable network identity.

- **Ordered, Graceful Deployment and Scaling:** Pods are deployed and scaled in a specific order.

- **Persistent Storage:** Each pod is associated with a persistent volume that it retains across restarts.

- **Rolling Updates:** Supports rolling updates with the same ordering guarantees.

Components of StatefulSets StatefulSets consist of several key components that work together to manage stateful applications.

Service: A headless service is typically used to manage the network identities of the pods in the StatefulSet. This service does not provide load balancing, but instead returns the DNS records for the pods directly.

StatefulSet: The StatefulSet resource itself, which defines the desired state of the pods, including the number of replicas, the pod template, and the volume claims.

PersistentVolume Claims: PVCs are used to request persistent storage for each pod in the StatefulSet. Each pod gets its own PVC, ensuring that the storage is unique and stable.

Example StatefulSet Configuration:

```
apiVersion: apps/v1
kind: StatefulSet
metadata:
  name: example-statefulset
spec:
  serviceName: "example-service"
  replicas: 3
  selector:
    matchLabels:
      app: example-app
  template:
    metadata:
      labels:
        app: example-app
    spec:
      containers:
      - name: example-container
        image: nginx:1.17.4
        ports:
        - containerPort: 80
        volumeMounts:
        - name: example-volume
          mountPath: /usr/share/nginx/html
  volumeClaimTemplates:
  - metadata:
      name: example-volume
    spec:
      accessModes: [ "ReadWriteOnce" ]
      resources:
        requests:
          storage: 1Gi
```

Deploying a StatefulSet Deploying a StatefulSet involves creating the StatefulSet resource and the associated headless service.

Creating a Headless Service:

```
apiVersion: v1
kind: Service
metadata:
  name: example-service
spec:
  clusterIP: None
  selector:
    app: example-app
  ports:
  - port: 80
    name: web
```

Creating a StatefulSet:

```
kubectl apply -f example-statefulset.yaml
```

Scaling a StatefulSet Scaling a StatefulSet involves increasing or decreasing the number of replicas. Kubernetes ensures that scaling operations follow the correct order and maintain the uniqueness and ordering guarantees.

Scaling Up:

```
kubectl scale statefulset example-statefulset --replicas=5
```

Scaling Down:

```
kubectl scale statefulset example-statefulset --replicas=2
```

Rolling Updates with StatefulSets StatefulSets support rolling updates, allowing you to update the container image or other properties of the pods in a controlled manner. Updates are applied in reverse ordinal order, ensuring that each pod is updated and running successfully before moving on to the next.

Updating a StatefulSet: Modify the StatefulSet spec to update the container image or other properties, then apply the changes.

```
kubectl apply -f updated-statefulset.yaml
```

Monitoring Rolling Updates: Use the 'kubectl rollout' commands to monitor the status of the update.

```
kubectl rollout status statefulset/example-statefulset
```

Persistent Storage with StatefulSets Each pod in a StatefulSet can have one or more persistent volume claims. These claims ensure that each pod gets its own persistent storage, which is not shared with other pods.

Volume Claim Templates: Volume claim templates are used to automatically generate PVCs for each pod.

```
apiVersion: apps/v1
kind: StatefulSet
metadata:
  name: example-statefulset
spec:
  serviceName: "example-service"
  replicas: 3
  selector:
    matchLabels:
      app: example-app
  template:
    metadata:
      labels:
        app: example-app
    spec:
      containers:
      - name: example-container
        image: nginx:1.17.4
        ports:
        - containerPort: 80
        volumeMounts:
        - name: example-volume
          mountPath: /usr/share/nginx/html
  volumeClaimTemplates:
  - metadata:
      name: example-volume
```

```
spec:
  accessModes: [ "ReadWriteOnce" ]
  resources:
    requests:
      storage: 1Gi
```

Best Practices for Using StatefulSets Implementing best practices ensures the efficient and reliable operation of stateful applications using StatefulSets.

Use Headless Services: Use headless services to manage the network identities of the pods in the StatefulSet.

Define Appropriate Storage Classes: Use appropriate storage classes for the volume claim templates to ensure that the storage meets the performance and availability requirements.

Monitor StatefulSet Pods: Regularly monitor the health and performance of the pods in the StatefulSet to detect and address issues promptly.

Automate Backups: Implement automated backup strategies for the persistent storage associated with StatefulSet pods.

Conclusion StatefulSets are a powerful feature in Kubernetes for managing stateful applications that require stable identities, ordered deployment, and persistent storage. By understanding the key components and capabilities of StatefulSets, and implementing best practices, you can effectively manage complex stateful applications in your Kubernetes cluster. Leveraging StatefulSets ensures that your stateful applications are reliable, scalable, and maintain the necessary consistency and durability.

4.8   DaemonSets

DaemonSets are a special type of Kubernetes resource designed to ensure that a copy of a specified pod runs on all (or some) nodes in the cluster. They are particularly useful for deploying system-level and cluster-wide services such as log collectors, monitoring agents, and network plugins that need to run on every node.

What is a DaemonSet? A DaemonSet ensures that all nodes (or a specific subset of nodes) run a copy of a particular pod. As new nodes are added to the cluster, the DaemonSet controller automatically schedules the specified pod on the new nodes. Similarly, when nodes are removed from the cluster, the DaemonSet controller cleans up the pods that were running on those nodes.

Key Features of DaemonSets:

- **Node Coverage:** Ensures that a specified pod runs on all or selected nodes.

- **Automatic Updates:** Automatically schedules pods on new nodes and cleans up on node removal.

- **System-Level Services:** Ideal for running system-level services like log collection, monitoring, and network services.

Creating a DaemonSet A DaemonSet is defined using a YAML manifest, similar to other Kubernetes resources. The manifest specifies the pod template and the nodes on which the pods should be scheduled.

Example DaemonSet Configuration:

```
apiVersion: apps/v1
kind: DaemonSet
metadata:
  name: example-daemonset
spec:
  selector:
    matchLabels:
      app: example-daemon
  template:
    metadata:
```

```
    labels:
      app: example-daemon
  spec:
    containers:
    - name: example-container
      image: nginx:1.17.4
      ports:
      - containerPort: 80
```

Creating a DaemonSet: Apply the DaemonSet configuration using the 'kubectl apply' command.

```
kubectl apply -f example-daemonset.yaml
```

Controlling DaemonSet Pod Placement DaemonSets allow you to control pod placement using node selectors, node affinity, and tolerations. These mechanisms ensure that DaemonSet pods are only scheduled on appropriate nodes.

Node Selectors: Use node selectors to specify that DaemonSet pods should only be scheduled on nodes with certain labels.

Example Node Selector Configuration:

```
spec:
  template:
    spec:
      nodeSelector:
        disktype: ssd
```

Node Affinity: Use node affinity to create more complex rules for pod placement based on node labels.

Example Node Affinity Configuration:

```
spec:
  template:
    spec:
```

```
      affinity:
        nodeAffinity:
          requiredDuringSchedulingIgnoredDuringExecution:
            nodeSelectorTerms:
            - matchExpressions:
              - key: disktype
                operator: In
                values:
                - ssd
```

Tolerations: Use tolerations to allow DaemonSet pods to be scheduled on nodes with specific taints.

Example Tolerations Configuration:

```
spec:
  template:
    spec:
      tolerations:
      - key: "example-key"
        operator: "Exists"
        effect: "NoSchedule"
```

Updating DaemonSets   Updating a DaemonSet involves changing the pod template specification. Kubernetes supports two update strategies for DaemonSets: RollingUpdate and OnDelete.

RollingUpdate: In the RollingUpdate strategy, pods are updated in a controlled manner, ensuring that not all pods are updated simultaneously.

Example RollingUpdate Configuration:

```
spec:
  updateStrategy:
    type: RollingUpdate
    rollingUpdate:
      maxUnavailable: 1
```

OnDelete: In the OnDelete strategy, pods are only updated when they are manually deleted. This gives the administrator full control over the update process.

Example OnDelete Configuration:

```
spec:
  updateStrategy:
    type: OnDelete
```

Monitoring and Managing DaemonSets Kubernetes provides several commands to monitor and manage DaemonSets, ensuring that they are running as expected.

Checking DaemonSet Status: Monitor the status of the DaemonSet to ensure it is running correctly.

```
kubectl get daemonsets
kubectl describe daemonset example-daemonset
```

Viewing DaemonSet Pods: List the pods managed by a DaemonSet.

```
kubectl get pods -l app=example-daemon
```

Common Use Cases for DaemonSets DaemonSets are particularly useful for deploying system-level services that need to run on all or a subset of nodes.

Log Collection: Deploy log collection agents (e.g., Fluentd) on all nodes to collect and ship logs to a central logging service.

Monitoring: Deploy monitoring agents (e.g., Prometheus Node Exporter) on all nodes to collect metrics and monitor node health.

Network Services: Deploy network services (e.g., Calico, Weave) on all nodes to manage network policies and connectivity.

Best Practices for Using DaemonSets Implementing best practices ensures efficient and reliable operation of DaemonSets.

Use Node Selectors and Affinity: Use node selectors and affinity to control pod placement and ensure that DaemonSet pods are scheduled on appropriate nodes.

Monitor DaemonSet Health: Regularly monitor the health and performance of DaemonSet pods to detect and address issues promptly.

Automate Updates: Automate updates using the RollingUpdate strategy to ensure smooth and controlled updates of DaemonSet pods.

Limit Resource Usage: Define resource requests and limits for DaemonSet pods to prevent them from consuming excessive resources on nodes.

Conclusion DaemonSets are a powerful feature in Kubernetes for managing system-level and cluster-wide services. By understanding the key components and capabilities of DaemonSets, and implementing best practices, you can effectively manage services that need to run on all or specific nodes in your Kubernetes cluster. Leveraging DaemonSets ensures that your system-level services are reliably deployed, managed, and maintained across the entire cluster.

4.9 ReplicaSets

ReplicaSets are a fundamental Kubernetes resource designed to maintain a stable set of replica pods running at any given time. They ensure that a specified number of replicas of a pod are running at all times. ReplicaSets are often used as the underlying mechanism for Deployments, but they can also be used independently.

What is a ReplicaSet? A ReplicaSet ensures that a specified number of pod replicas are running at all times. If a pod fails or is deleted, the ReplicaSet controller automatically creates a new pod to replace it.

Conversely, if there are more pods running than desired, the ReplicaSet controller will delete the excess pods.

Key Features of ReplicaSets:

- **Stable Pod Counts:** Ensures a consistent number of pod replicas.

- **Self-Healing:** Automatically replaces failed or deleted pods.

- **Flexible Pod Management:** Can scale up or down based on specified replica counts.

Creating a ReplicaSet   A ReplicaSet is defined using a YAML manifest, which specifies the desired number of replicas, the pod template, and the selector for matching the pods.

Example ReplicaSet Configuration:

```
apiVersion: apps/v1
kind: ReplicaSet
metadata:
  name: example-replicaset
spec:
  replicas: 3
  selector:
    matchLabels:
      app: example-app
  template:
    metadata:
      labels:
        app: example-app
    spec:
      containers:
      - name: example-container
        image: nginx:1.18.0
        ports:
        - containerPort: 80
```

Creating a ReplicaSet: Apply the ReplicaSet configuration using the 'kubectl apply' command.

```
kubectl apply -f example-replicaset.yaml
```

Scaling ReplicaSets One of the primary benefits of ReplicaSets is the ability to scale the number of replicas up or down based on the application's needs.

Scaling Up: Increase the number of replicas to handle more traffic.

```
kubectl scale replicaset example-replicaset --replicas=5
```

Scaling Down: Decrease the number of replicas to conserve resources.

```
kubectl scale replicaset example-replicaset --replicas=2
```

Updating ReplicaSets Updating a ReplicaSet involves changing the pod template specification. Unlike Deployments, ReplicaSets do not support rolling updates natively. To update the pods managed by a ReplicaSet, you typically create a new ReplicaSet with the updated specification and delete the old one.

Example Update Process:

- Create a new ReplicaSet with the updated pod template.

- Delete the old ReplicaSet, ensuring that the new ReplicaSet takes over.

Creating a New ReplicaSet:

```
kubectl apply -f updated-replicaset.yaml
```

Deleting the Old ReplicaSet:

```
kubectl delete replicaset example-replicaset
```

Monitoring and Managing ReplicaSets   Kubernetes provides several commands to monitor and manage ReplicaSets, ensuring that they are running as expected.

Checking ReplicaSet Status: Monitor the status of the ReplicaSet to ensure it is running correctly.

```
kubectl get replicasets
kubectl describe replicaset example-replicaset
```

Viewing ReplicaSet Pods: List the pods managed by a ReplicaSet.

```
kubectl get pods -l app=example-app
```

Common Use Cases for ReplicaSets   ReplicaSets are useful for ensuring high availability and reliability of stateless applications that can run multiple instances independently.

Web Servers: Ensure that a specified number of web server instances are always running to handle incoming traffic.

API Servers: Maintain a stable set of API server instances to provide consistent access to backend services.

Batch Processing: Ensure that a certain number of worker instances are running to process jobs in a distributed manner.

Best Practices for Using ReplicaSets   Implementing best practices ensures efficient and reliable operation of ReplicaSets.

Use Labels and Selectors: Use clear and consistent labels and selectors to manage pod selection accurately.

Monitor ReplicaSet Health: Regularly monitor the health and performance of ReplicaSet pods to detect and address issues promptly.

Automate Scaling: Integrate ReplicaSets with Horizontal Pod Autoscalers (HPAs) to automate scaling based on resource usage.

Resource Requests and Limits: Define resource requests and limits for ReplicaSet pods to ensure they have sufficient resources to run efficiently.

Conclusion ReplicaSets are a foundational resource in Kubernetes for maintaining stable sets of stateless pod replicas. By understanding the key components and capabilities of ReplicaSets, and implementing best practices, you can effectively manage the availability and scalability of your applications in a Kubernetes cluster. Leveraging ReplicaSets ensures that your stateless applications are reliable, resilient, and capable of handling varying loads with ease.

4.10   Jobs and CronJobs

Jobs and CronJobs are Kubernetes resources used to manage batch and scheduled tasks. They ensure the completion of tasks, whether it's a one-time operation or recurring jobs, making them essential for running background processing, data cleanup, and other scheduled operations in a Kubernetes cluster.

Jobs Jobs are used to run a finite set of tasks to completion. Once a Job completes its execution successfully, it ensures that the specified number of pods terminate, even if some pods fail during execution. Jobs are ideal for tasks that need to be run to completion, such as data processing or batch tasks.

Key Features of Jobs:

- **Finite Execution:** Ensures that a set of pods run to completion.

- **Retry Mechanism:** Automatically retries failed pods to ensure successful task completion.

- **Parallelism:** Supports parallel execution of pods.

Creating a Job   A Job is defined using a YAML manifest, specifying the pod template and the desired completion criteria.

Example Job Configuration:

```yaml
apiVersion: batch/v1
kind: Job
metadata:
  name: example-job
spec:
  completions: 3
  parallelism: 2
  template:
    metadata:
      labels:
        app: example-job
    spec:
      containers:
      - name: example-container
        image: busybox
        command: ["sh", "-c", "echo Hello Kubernetes!
&& sleep 10"]
      restartPolicy: OnFailure
```

Creating a Job: Apply the Job configuration using the 'kubectl apply' command.

```
kubectl apply -f example-job.yaml
```

Managing Job Execution   Jobs can be configured to manage how pods are executed, including the number of completions, parallelism, and backoff limits.

Completions: Specifies the number of times the Job should be successfully completed.

```yaml
spec:
  completions: 3
```

Parallelism: Specifies the number of pods that can run in parallel.

```
spec:
  parallelism: 2
```

Backoff Limit: Specifies the number of retries before considering the Job as failed.

```
spec:
  backoffLimit: 4
```

Monitoring and Managing Jobs Kubernetes provides several commands to monitor and manage Jobs, ensuring that they run to completion.

Checking Job Status: Monitor the status of the Job to ensure it is running correctly.

```
kubectl get jobs
kubectl describe job example-job
```

Viewing Job Pods: List the pods managed by a Job.

```
kubectl get pods -l job-name=example-job
```

CronJobs CronJobs are used to run Jobs on a scheduled basis. They are similar to cron jobs in Unix-like operating systems, providing a way to schedule tasks at specified times or intervals. CronJobs are ideal for running periodic tasks such as backups, report generation, and maintenance activities.

Key Features of CronJobs:

- **Scheduled Execution:** Runs Jobs at specified times or intervals.

- **Flexible Scheduling:** Uses cron syntax to define schedules.

- **Job Management:** Creates and manages Jobs according to the schedule.

Creating a CronJob A CronJob is defined using a YAML manifest, specifying the schedule and the Job template.

Example CronJob Configuration:

```
apiVersion: batch/v1
kind: CronJob
metadata:
  name: example-cronjob
spec:
  schedule: "*/5 * * * *"
  jobTemplate:
    spec:
      template:
        metadata:
          labels:
            app: example-cronjob
        spec:
          containers:
          - name: example-container
            image: busybox
            command: ["sh", "-c", "echo Hello Kubernetes!
&& sleep 10"]
          restartPolicy: OnFailure
```

Creating a CronJob: Apply the CronJob configuration using the 'kubectl apply' command.

```
kubectl apply -f example-cronjob.yaml
```

Managing CronJobs CronJobs provide several options for managing how Jobs are scheduled and executed.

Schedule: Defines the schedule using cron syntax.

```
spec:
  schedule: "*/5 * * * *"
```

Concurrency Policy: Specifies how concurrent executions are handled. Options include 'Allow', 'Forbid', and 'Replace'.

```
spec:
  concurrencyPolicy: Forbid
```

Starting Deadline: Specifies the deadline for starting the Job if the schedule is missed.

```
spec:
  startingDeadlineSeconds: 60
```

Monitoring and Managing CronJobs Kubernetes provides several commands to monitor and manage CronJobs, ensuring that they run according to the specified schedule.

Checking CronJob Status: Monitor the status of the CronJob to ensure it is running correctly.

```
kubectl get cronjobs
kubectl describe cronjob example-cronjob
```

Viewing CronJob Jobs: List the Jobs created by a CronJob.

```
kubectl get jobs -l job-name=example-cronjob
```

Common Use Cases for Jobs and CronJobs Jobs and CronJobs are versatile tools for managing one-time and scheduled tasks in Kubernetes.

Data Processing: Use Jobs to run data processing tasks, such as ETL jobs, data cleanup, and batch processing.

Backups: Use CronJobs to schedule regular backups of databases and other persistent storage.

Maintenance Tasks: Use CronJobs to schedule periodic maintenance tasks, such as log rotation and system health checks.

Best Practices for Using Jobs and CronJobs Implementing best practices ensures efficient and reliable operation of Jobs and CronJobs.

Define Clear Schedules: Use clear and precise cron syntax to define schedules for CronJobs.

Monitor Job Execution: Regularly monitor the execution of Jobs and CronJobs to detect and address issues promptly.

Handle Failures Gracefully: Configure backoff limits and retry mechanisms to handle Job failures gracefully.

Resource Management: Define resource requests and limits for Job pods to ensure they have sufficient resources to run efficiently.

Conclusion Jobs and CronJobs are powerful features in Kubernetes for managing batch and scheduled tasks. By understanding their key components and capabilities, and implementing best practices, you can effectively manage one-time and recurring tasks in your Kubernetes cluster. Leveraging Jobs and CronJobs ensures that your background processing, data cleanup, and scheduled operations are reliable, efficient, and easy to manage.

Chapter 5

Controllers and Operators

5.1 Understanding Controllers

5.1.1 Lifecycle of Controllers

Controllers are a fundamental part of Kubernetes, responsible for ensuring that the current state of the cluster matches the desired state specified by users. They automate the management of various Kubernetes resources, such as pods, deployments, and services. Understanding the lifecycle of controllers is essential for effectively managing and extending Kubernetes functionality.

What is a Controller? A controller is a control loop that watches the state of the cluster, compares it to the desired state, and takes action to reconcile the two. Controllers operate continuously, making adjustments as needed to maintain the desired state.

Key Features of Controllers:

- **Reconciliation Loop:** Continuously watches the state of the cluster and makes adjustments to achieve the desired state.

- **Resource Management:** Manages the lifecycle of resources, ensuring that they are created, updated, and deleted as needed.

- **Automation:** Automates complex management tasks, reducing the need for manual intervention.

The Reconciliation Loop The reconciliation loop is the core mechanism of a controller. It involves continuously monitoring the cluster's state, detecting any deviations from the desired state, and taking corrective actions.

Steps in the Reconciliation Loop:

1. **Watch:** Monitor the current state of resources in the cluster using informers or watches.

2. **Compare:** Compare the current state to the desired state specified by the user.

3. **Act:** Take corrective actions to reconcile the current state with the desired state, such as creating, updating, or deleting resources.

Example of a Simple Reconciliation Loop:

```
for {
    desiredState := getDesiredState()
    currentState := getCurrentState()
    if !reflect.DeepEqual(desiredState, currentState) {
        reconcile(desiredState, currentState)
    }
    time.Sleep(reconciliationInterval)
}
```

Types of Controllers Kubernetes includes several built-in controllers that manage different types of resources. Additionally, custom controllers can be created to extend Kubernetes functionality.

Built-in Controllers:

- **ReplicationController:** Ensures that a specified number of pod replicas are running.

- **DeploymentController:** Manages deployments, ensuring that the desired state of deployments is maintained.

- **StatefulSetController:** Manages StatefulSets, ensuring stable identities and persistent storage for pods.

- **DaemonSetController:** Ensures that a pod runs on all or selected nodes.

- **JobController:** Manages Jobs, ensuring that tasks run to completion.

- **CronJobController:** Manages CronJobs, ensuring that jobs run on a scheduled basis.

Custom Controllers: Custom controllers can be created to manage new types of resources or to add custom behavior to existing resources. They use the same reconciliation loop pattern as built-in controllers.

Controller Lifecycle The lifecycle of a controller involves several stages, from creation and initialization to operation and eventual termination.

Stages of the Controller Lifecycle:

1. **Creation:** The controller is defined and created, either as a built-in component or a custom resource.

2. **Initialization:** The controller initializes its internal state and sets up watches or informers to monitor the cluster.

3. **Operation:** The controller enters the reconciliation loop, continuously monitoring and reconciling the state of resources.

4. **Termination:** The controller gracefully terminates, cleaning up any resources or state as needed.

Creating a Custom Controller Creating a custom controller involves defining the desired state, setting up watches or informers, and implementing the reconciliation logic. Tools like Kubebuilder and the Operator SDK can simplify this process.

Steps to Create a Custom Controller:

1. **Define the Custom Resource:** Define the custom resource that the controller will manage.

2. **Set Up Watches:** Set up watches or informers to monitor changes to the custom resource.

3. **Implement Reconciliation Logic:** Implement the reconciliation logic to manage the custom resource.

4. **Deploy the Controller:** Deploy the controller to the Kubernetes cluster.

Example Custom Controller Structure:

```
// Define the custom resource
type MyCustomResource struct {
    metav1.TypeMeta    'json:",inline"'
    metav1.ObjectMeta 'json:"metadata,omitempty"'
    Spec               MyCustomResourceSpec    'json:"spec,
omitempty"'
    Status             MyCustomResourceStatus 'json:"status,
omitempty"'
}

// Set up watches
func main() {
    mgr, err := ctrl.NewManager(ctrl.GetConfigOrDie(),
ctrl.Options{
        Scheme: scheme,
    })
    if err != nil {
        setupLog.Error(err, "unable to start manager")
        os.Exit(1)
    }

    if err = (&controllers.MyCustomResourceReconciler{
        Client: mgr.GetClient(),
```

```go
        Log:     ctrl.Log.WithName("controllers")
.WithName("MyCustomResource"),
        Scheme: mgr.GetScheme(),
    }).SetupWithManager(mgr); err != nil {
        setupLog.Error(err, "unable to create controller",
"controller", "MyCustomResource")
        os.Exit(1)
    }

    setupLog.Info("starting manager")
    if err := mgr.Start(ctrl.SetupSignalHandler());
err != nil {
        setupLog.Error(err, "problem running manager")
        os.Exit(1)
    }
}


// Implement reconciliation logic
func (r *MyCustomResourceReconciler) Reconcile(ctx
context.Context, req ctrl.Request) (ctrl.Result,
error) {
    log := r.Log.WithValues("mycustomresource",
req.NamespacedName)

    // Fetch the MyCustomResource instance
    myCustomResource := &examplev1.MyCustomResource{}
    err := r.Client.Get(ctx, req.NamespacedName,
myCustomResource)
    if err != nil {
        if errors.IsNotFound(err) {
            log.Info("MyCustomResource resource not found.
Ignoring since object must be deleted.")
            return ctrl.Result{}, nil
        }
        log.Error(err, "Failed to get MyCustomResource")
        return ctrl.Result{}, err
    }
```

```
// Implement your reconciliation logic here

return ctrl.Result{}, nil
}
```

Best Practices for Controllers   Implementing best practices ensures that controllers are efficient, reliable, and maintainable.

Use Informers: Use informers to efficiently watch and cache resource changes, reducing the load on the API server.

Handle Errors Gracefully: Ensure that controllers handle errors gracefully and implement retry mechanisms for transient failures.

Monitor Controller Health: Regularly monitor the health and performance of controllers to detect and address issues promptly.

Implement Metrics: Expose metrics for your controllers to facilitate monitoring and debugging.

Conclusion   Controllers are a vital component of Kubernetes, automating the management of resources and ensuring that the cluster operates as desired.   By understanding the lifecycle of controllers and following best practices, you can effectively manage and extend Kubernetes functionality, ensuring that your applications and services run smoothly and reliably. Custom controllers provide powerful tools for implementing custom behavior and managing new types of resources, making Kubernetes a highly flexible and extensible platform.

5.1.2   Implementing Custom Controllers

Custom controllers in Kubernetes provide a way to extend the platform's functionality by managing custom resources or adding specific behaviors to existing resources.   While all operators are custom controllers, not all custom controllers are operators.   Operators are a specialized subset of custom controllers that manage custom resources. This section focuses on the general implementation of custom controllers, whether they manage custom resources or existing resources.

Overview of Custom Controllers Custom controllers follow the same reconciliation loop pattern as built-in controllers. They watch the state of the cluster, compare it to the desired state, and take actions to reconcile the two. This involves setting up watches or informers, implementing reconciliation logic, and deploying the controller.

Key Components of Custom Controllers:

- **Watches/Informers:** Monitor changes to resources.

- **Controller Logic:** Implements the reconciliation logic.

Setting Up the Controller Setting up a custom controller involves writing the controller logic and setting up the necessary watches or informers to monitor the resources.

Using Kubebuilder: Kubebuilder is a framework for building Kubernetes APIs using CRDs and custom controllers. It provides scaffolding and libraries to simplify the development process.

Step-by-Step Process with Kubebuilder:

1. **Install Kubebuilder:** Follow the installation instructions from the Kubebuilder documentation.

2. **Initialize a Project:** Create a new Kubebuilder project.

   ```
   kubebuilder init --domain example.com --repo
   github.com/example/myproject
   ```

3. **Create an API:** Generate the API and controller code.

   ```
   kubebuilder create api --group example --version v1
   --kind MyCustomResource
   ```

4. **Define the API:** Edit the generated API definition files.

```go
// api/v1/mycustomresource_types.go
type MyCustomResourceSpec struct {
    Foo string `json:"foo,omitempty"`
}

type MyCustomResourceStatus struct {
    State string `json:"state,omitempty"`
}
```

5. **Implement the Controller:** Implement the reconciliation logic.

```go
// controllers/mycustomresource_controller.go
func (r *MyCustomResourceReconciler) Reconcile(ctx
context.Context, req ctrl.Request) (ctrl.Result,
error) {
    log := r.Log.WithValues("mycustomresource",
req.NamespacedName)

    // Fetch the MyCustomResource instance
    myCustomResource := &examplev1.MyCustomResource{}
    err := r.Client.Get(ctx, req.NamespacedName,
myCustomResource)
    if err != nil {
        if errors.IsNotFound(err) {
            log.Info("MyCustomResource resource not found.
Ignoring since object must be deleted.")
            return ctrl.Result{}, nil
        }
        log.Error(err, "Failed to get MyCustomResource")
        return ctrl.Result{}, err
    }

    // Implement your reconciliation logic here

    return ctrl.Result{}, nil
}
```

6. **Register the Controller with the Manager:** Ensure the controller is registered with the manager.

```go
// main.go
if err = (&controllers.MyCustomResourceReconciler{
    Client: mgr.GetClient(),
    Log:    ctrl.Log.WithName("controllers")
.WithName("MyCustomResource"),
    Scheme: mgr.GetScheme(),
}).SetupWithManager(mgr); err != nil {
    setupLog.Error(err, "unable to create controller",
"controller", "MyCustomResource")
    os.Exit(1)
}
```

7. **Deploy the Controller:** Build and deploy the controller to the Kubernetes cluster.

```
make install
make run
```

Implementing Custom Controllers Without CRDs Custom controllers can also manage existing Kubernetes resources without defining new CRDs. This involves setting up watches on the relevant resources and implementing the necessary logic to manage them.

Example: Managing Pods with a Custom Controller: Suppose you want to implement a custom controller that monitors and manages pods based on specific criteria.

```go
package main

import (
    "context"
    "log"

    corev1 "k8s.io/api/core/v1"
    metav1 "k8s.io/apimachinery/pkg/apis/meta/v1"
    "k8s.io/client-go/kubernetes"
    "k8s.io/client-go/rest"
)
```

```go
func main() {
    // Set up Kubernetes client
    config, err := rest.InClusterConfig()
    if err != nil {
        log.Fatalf("Error creating in-cluster config: %v", err)
    }
    clientset, err := kubernetes.NewForConfig(config)
    if err != nil {
        log.Fatalf("Error creating Kubernetes client: %v", err)
    }

    // Watch for changes to pods
    watch, err := clientset.CoreV1().Pods("").Watch(
context.TODO(), metav1.ListOptions{})
    if err != nil {
        log.Fatalf("Error setting up pod watch: %v", err)
    }

    // Process events from the watch
    for event := range watch.ResultChan() {
        pod, ok := event.Object.(*corev1.Pod)
        if !ok {
            log.Fatalf("Unexpected type")
        }

        // Implement your custom logic here
        log.Printf("Processing pod: %s", pod.Name)
        // For example, delete the pod if it meets
certain criteria
        if shouldDeletePod(pod) {
            err := clientset.CoreV1().Pods(pod.Namespace)
.Delete(context.TODO(), pod.Name, metav1.DeleteOptions{})
            if err != nil {
                log.Printf("Error deleting pod: %v", err)
            } else {
                log.Printf("Deleted pod: %s", pod.Name)
            }
```

```go
        }
    }
}

func shouldDeletePod(pod *corev1.Pod) bool {
    // Define your criteria for deleting the pod
    return pod.Status.Phase == corev1.PodFailed
}
```

Testing and Debugging Custom Controllers Proper testing and debugging are crucial for ensuring that custom controllers work as expected.

Unit Testing: Write unit tests for the reconciliation logic using frameworks like Go's testing package.

```go
func TestReconcile(t *testing.T) {
    // Initialize the fake client and other dependencies
    fakeClient := fake.NewFakeClient()
    reconciler := &MyCustomResourceReconciler{
        Client: fakeClient,
        Log:    ctrl.Log.WithName("controllers")
.WithName("MyCustomResource"),
    }

    // Define the test cases
    tests := []struct {
        name        string
        req         ctrl.Request
        expectError bool
    }{
        // Add test cases here
    }

    // Run the test cases
    for _, test := range tests {
        t.Run(test.name, func(t *testing.T) {
            _, err := reconciler.Reconcile(context
.Background(), test.req)
```

```
                if (err != nil) != test.expectError {
                    t.Errorf("expected error: %v, got: %v",
test.expectError, err)
                }
        })
    }
}
```

Integration Testing: Use integration tests to validate the behavior of the controller in a real Kubernetes cluster.

Logging and Metrics: Implement logging and metrics to facilitate debugging and monitoring of the controller's behavior.

Conclusion   Implementing custom controllers in Kubernetes allows you to extend the platform's capabilities to manage new types of resources and add specific behaviors tailored to your needs. By following the steps outlined and leveraging tools like Kubebuilder, you can efficiently create, test, and deploy custom controllers that ensure your Kubernetes clusters operate as desired. Proper testing, debugging, and monitoring are essential to ensure that your custom controllers are reliable and effective.

5.1.3   Reconciliation Loop

The reconciliation loop is the core mechanism of any Kubernetes controller, including custom controllers. It ensures that the current state of the cluster matches the desired state specified by the user. The reconciliation loop continuously monitors the state of resources, detects discrepancies, and takes corrective actions to reconcile the differences.

Overview of the Reconciliation Loop   The reconciliation loop operates in a continuous cycle, performing the following steps:

Steps in the Reconciliation Loop:

1. **Watch:**   Monitor the current state of resources using watches or informers.

2. **Get Desired State:** Retrieve the desired state from the user-defined specification.

3. **Get Current State:** Fetch the current state of the resources from the Kubernetes API server.

4. **Compare States:** Compare the desired state to the current state.

5. **Reconcile:** Take corrective actions to bring the current state in line with the desired state.

Watching and Informers   The reconciliation loop begins by setting up watches or informers to monitor changes to the resources of interest. Watches and informers are efficient ways to receive notifications about changes in the cluster state without continuously polling the API server.

Using Informers: Informers are higher-level abstractions that provide caching and event handling for resource changes.

```go
informerFactory := informers.NewSharedInformerFactory(
clientset, 0)
podInformer := informerFactory.Core().V1().Pods().Informer()

podInformer.AddEventHandler(cache.ResourceEventHandlerFuncs{
    AddFunc:    onAdd,
    UpdateFunc: onUpdate,
    DeleteFunc: onDelete,
})

stopCh := make(chan struct{})
defer close(stopCh)
go informerFactory.Start(stopCh)
cache.WaitForCacheSync(stopCh, podInformer.HasSynced)
```

Getting the Desired State   The desired state is specified by the user through resource manifests, such as YAML files. The controller fetches the desired state by reading the resource definitions.

Example Desired State:

```
apiVersion: v1
kind: Pod
metadata:
  name: example-pod
spec:
  containers:
  - name: nginx
    image: nginx:1.17.4
```

Getting the Current State   The current state is obtained by querying the Kubernetes API server to get the current status of the resources being managed by the controller.

Fetching the Current State:

```
pod := &corev1.Pod{}
err := client.Get(context.TODO(), types.NamespacedName{
    Namespace: req.Namespace,
    Name:      req.Name,
}, pod)
if err != nil {
    if errors.IsNotFound(err) {
        // Pod not found, handle accordingly
    } else {
        // Handle other errors
    }
}
```

Comparing Desired and Current States   The controller compares the desired state with the current state to identify any discrepancies. This comparison helps determine the actions needed to reconcile the two states.

Example State Comparison:

```
if desiredState.Spec.Containers[0].Image != currentState.Spec
.Containers[0].Image {
```

```
    // Image version mismatch, trigger an update
}
```

Reconciliation Actions Based on the comparison, the controller takes actions to reconcile the current state with the desired state. This may involve creating, updating, or deleting resources.

Example Reconciliation Logic:

```
if desiredState.Spec.Containers[0].Image != currentState.Spec
.Containers[0].Image {
    currentState.Spec.Containers[0].Image = desiredState.Spec
.Containers[0].Image
    err := client.Update(context.TODO(), currentState)
    if err != nil {
        log.Error(err, "Failed to update pod")
    }
}
```

Error Handling and Retries Controllers should implement error handling and retry mechanisms to manage transient failures and ensure eventual consistency.

Error Handling Example:

```
func (r *Reconciler) Reconcile(req ctrl.Request) (ctrl.Result,
error) {
    // Fetch resource
    err := r.client.Get(context.TODO(), req.NamespacedName,
resource)
    if err != nil {
        if errors.IsNotFound(err) {
            // Resource not found, could be deleted
            return ctrl.Result{}, nil
        }
        // Requeue the request for a retry
        return ctrl.Result{}, err
    }
```

```
    // Reconciliation logic
    ...

    // Requeue if needed
    return ctrl.Result{RequeueAfter: time.Minute}, nil
}
```

Idempotence in Controllers Controllers should be idempotent, meaning that applying the same operation multiple times has the same effect as applying it once. This ensures that the reconciliation loop can handle retries and duplicate events gracefully.

Ensuring Idempotence:

```
func (r *Reconciler) reconcile(req ctrl.Request) (ctrl.Result,
error) {
    // Fetch the resource
    err := r.client.Get(context.TODO(), req.NamespacedName,
resource)
    if err != nil {
        return ctrl.Result{}, err
    }

    // Determine the desired state
    desiredState := computeDesiredState(resource)

    // Compare current state with desired state
    if reflect.DeepEqual(currentState, desiredState) {
        return ctrl.Result{}, nil // No changes needed
    }

    // Apply changes to achieve desired state
    err = r.client.Update(context.TODO(), desiredState)
    if err != nil {
        return ctrl.Result{}, err
    }
```

```
    return ctrl.Result{}, nil
}
```

Best Practices for Reconciliation Loop Implementing best practices ensures that the reconciliation loop is efficient, reliable, and maintainable.

Minimize API Calls: Use informers and caches to minimize direct API server calls.

Rate Limiting: Implement rate limiting to avoid overwhelming the API server.

Graceful Handling of Failures: Implement retry mechanisms and handle transient errors gracefully.

Expose Metrics: Expose metrics to monitor the performance and behavior of the reconciliation loop.

Conclusion The reconciliation loop is the core mechanism that ensures Kubernetes controllers, including custom controllers, maintain the desired state of resources. By understanding and effectively implementing the reconciliation loop, you can create robust controllers that automate complex management tasks and ensure the consistency and reliability of your Kubernetes clusters. Following best practices further enhances the efficiency and reliability of your reconciliation logic.

5.2 Kubernetes Operators

Kubernetes Operators are a powerful concept that extends the functionality of custom controllers to manage complex, stateful applications. Operators encapsulate the operational knowledge required to manage applications and services, automating tasks that typically require human intervention. They follow the Operator Pattern, which involves using custom resources and custom controllers to manage the entire lifecycle of an application, including deployment, scaling, backups, upgrades, and more.

What is a Kubernetes Operator? A Kubernetes Operator is a method of packaging, deploying, and managing a Kubernetes application. It uses Custom Resource Definitions (CRDs) to define application-specific resources and implements custom controllers to manage these resources. The main goal of an Operator is to encode the operational knowledge of running and managing an application into code.

Key Features of Kubernetes Operators:

- **Custom Resources:** Define custom resources specific to the application being managed.

- **Automated Management:** Automate the management of the application lifecycle, including installation, updates, scaling, and recovery.

- **Application-specific Logic:** Embed domain-specific knowledge and operational logic for managing the application.

- **Declarative APIs:** Provide declarative APIs for managing the application, making it easier to integrate with other Kubernetes tools and workflows.

Advantages of Using Operators Operators provide several advantages over traditional methods of managing applications:

Automated Operations: Operators automate routine tasks such as scaling, backups, and updates, reducing the operational burden on administrators.

Consistency and Reliability: By encoding operational knowledge into code, Operators ensure that best practices are consistently applied, leading to more reliable and predictable application management.

Improved Efficiency: Operators enable self-managing applications, allowing teams to focus on higher-level tasks and innovations rather than repetitive operational tasks.

Declarative Management: Operators leverage Kubernetes' declarative model, making it easier to manage applications using familiar Kubernetes APIs and tools.

Operator Pattern in Kubernetes The Operator Pattern involves defining a custom resource that represents the application's desired state and implementing a custom controller that continuously monitors and manages this resource. The controller implements the operational logic necessary to reconcile the current state of the application with the desired state.

Operator SDKs and Frameworks Several SDKs and frameworks are available to simplify the development of Kubernetes Operators, such as the Operator SDK and Kubebuilder. These tools provide scaffolding, libraries, and best practices to streamline the development process.

Operator SDK: The Operator SDK provides a comprehensive toolkit for building, testing, and deploying Operators. It includes features like code scaffolding, CRD generation, and integration with Kubernetes APIs.

Kubebuilder: Kubebuilder is another popular framework for building Kubernetes APIs using CRDs. It provides scaffolding and libraries to simplify the development of custom controllers and Operators.

Use Cases for Kubernetes Operators Operators are particularly useful for managing complex, stateful applications that require domain-specific knowledge and operational procedures. Common use cases include:

Database Management: Operators can manage the lifecycle of database instances, including provisioning, scaling, backups, and recovery.

Middleware Management: Operators can manage middleware applications like message queues, caching systems, and application servers.

Application Lifecycle Management: Operators can manage the complete lifecycle of applications, including deployment, updates, and scaling.

Conclusion Kubernetes Operators provide a powerful and flexible way to manage complex applications in Kubernetes. By encapsulating operational knowledge into code, Operators automate routine tasks, ensure consistency, and improve the efficiency of application management. Leveraging tools like the Operator SDK and Kubebuilder can streamline the development and deployment of Operators, making it easier to extend Kubernetes' capabilities and manage stateful applications effectively.

5.2.1   Operator Pattern in Kubernetes

The Operator Pattern in Kubernetes is a design pattern used to manage complex, stateful applications and services by extending Kubernetes' declarative model. Operators encapsulate the operational knowledge needed to manage an application, automating tasks that would otherwise require human intervention. This pattern leverages Custom Resource Definitions (CRDs) and custom controllers to manage the entire lifecycle of an application, ensuring that it runs reliably and efficiently.

Understanding the Operator Pattern At the core of the Operator Pattern are two main components: Custom Resource Definitions (CRDs) and custom controllers. CRDs define the schema for custom resources, while custom controllers implement the logic required to manage these resources. Together, they enable the creation of custom APIs that encapsulate the desired state and operational logic for a specific application.

Key Components of the Operator Pattern:

- **Custom Resource Definitions (CRDs):** Define the custom resources that represent the desired state of the application.

- **Custom Controllers:** Implement the reconciliation logic to manage the custom resources and ensure the application reaches and maintains the desired state.

Defining Custom Resources   Custom resources are user-defined objects that extend the Kubernetes API. They represent the desired state of an application or service and are defined using CRDs. CRDs specify the structure and schema of the custom resources, including the fields and data types.

Example CRD Definition:

```
apiVersion: apiextensions.k8s.io/v1
kind: CustomResourceDefinition
metadata:
  name: mysqlclusters.example.com
spec:
  group: example.com
  versions:
    - name: v1
      served: true
      storage: true
      schema:
        openAPIV3Schema:
          type: object
          properties:
            spec:
              type: object
              properties:
                replicas:
                  type: integer
                version:
                  type: string
                storage:
                  type: string
            status:
              type: object
              properties:
                readyReplicas:
                  type: integer
  scope: Namespaced
  names:
```

```
plural: mysqlclusters
singular: mysqlcluster
kind: MySQLCluster
shortNames:
- mysql
```

Implementing Custom Controllers   Custom controllers are responsible for monitoring custom resources and taking actions to reconcile the current state with the desired state. They follow the reconciliation loop pattern, which involves watching for changes to custom resources, comparing the desired state to the current state, and making necessary adjustments.

Key Responsibilities of Custom Controllers:

- **Watch Custom Resources:** Monitor changes to custom resources using informers or watches.

- **Reconcile State:** Implement reconciliation logic to ensure the current state matches the desired state.

- **Manage Resource Lifecycle:** Handle the creation, update, and deletion of resources as needed.

Reconciliation Logic   The reconciliation logic in a custom controller is the core mechanism that ensures the custom resource's current state matches its desired state. This involves comparing the current state of the resource to its desired state and taking corrective actions when discrepancies are found.

Example Reconciliation Logic:

```go
func (r *MySQLClusterReconciler) Reconcile(ctx context.Context,
req ctrl.Request) (ctrl.Result, error) {
    log := r.Log.WithValues("mysqlcluster", req.NamespacedName)

    // Fetch the MySQLCluster instance
    mysqlCluster := &examplev1.MySQLCluster{}
    err := r.Client.Get(ctx, req.NamespacedName, mysqlCluster)
    if err != nil {
```

```go
        if errors.IsNotFound(err) {
            log.Info("MySQLCluster resource not found.
Ignoring since object must be deleted.")
            return ctrl.Result{}, nil
        }
        log.Error(err, "Failed to get MySQLCluster")
        return ctrl.Result{}, err
    }


    // Compare desired state with current state
    if mysqlCluster.Spec.Replicas != mysqlCluster.Status
.ReadyReplicas {
        // Update the number of replicas
        err = r.updateReplicas(ctx, mysqlCluster)
        if err != nil {
            log.Error(err, "Failed to update replicas")
            return ctrl.Result{}, err
        }
    }


    // Update status
    mysqlCluster.Status.ReadyReplicas = mysqlCluster.Spec
.Replicas
    err = r.Client.Status().Update(ctx, mysqlCluster)
    if err != nil {
        log.Error(err, "Failed to update MySQLCluster status")
        return ctrl.Result{}, err
    }

    return ctrl.Result{}, nil
}

func (r *MySQLClusterReconciler) updateReplicas(ctx
context.Context, mysqlCluster *examplev1.MySQLCluster) error {
    // Implement logic to update the number of replicas
    return nil
}
```

Lifecycle Management Operators manage the entire lifecycle of an application, from deployment to scaling, upgrades, and recovery. This involves implementing logic for handling various lifecycle events, such as scaling up or down, performing backups, and upgrading application versions.

Handling Lifecycle Events:

- **Scaling:** Adjust the number of replicas based on the desired state.

- **Upgrades:** Implement rolling updates or other upgrade strategies to update the application version.

- **Backups and Recovery:** Schedule and perform backups, and implement recovery procedures.

Advanced Operator Capabilities Operators can implement advanced capabilities to handle complex scenarios and provide enhanced functionality. This may include managing dependencies between resources, performing health checks, and integrating with external systems.

Managing Dependencies: Operators can manage dependencies between different resources, ensuring that they are created, updated, and deleted in the correct order.

Performing Health Checks: Operators can perform health checks on the managed application and take corrective actions if any issues are detected.

Integrating with External Systems: Operators can integrate with external systems, such as monitoring and alerting services, to provide a comprehensive management solution.

Best Practices for Implementing Operators Implementing best practices ensures that Operators are reliable, efficient, and maintainable.

Define Clear APIs: Define clear and consistent APIs for custom resources, making it easier for users to interact with the Operator.

Implement Robust Error Handling: Implement robust error handling and retry mechanisms to ensure that the Operator can recover from transient failures.

Expose Metrics and Logs: Expose metrics and logs to facilitate monitoring, debugging, and performance analysis.

Automate Testing: Automate testing of the Operator to ensure that it behaves correctly under various scenarios and edge cases.

Conclusion The Operator Pattern in Kubernetes provides a powerful framework for managing complex, stateful applications. By encapsulating operational knowledge into code, Operators automate routine tasks, ensure consistency, and improve the efficiency of application management. Understanding and implementing the Operator Pattern, along with best practices, allows you to extend Kubernetes' capabilities and manage sophisticated applications with ease.

5.2.2   Building Operators with the Operator SDK

The Operator SDK is a comprehensive toolkit designed to simplify the development, testing, and deployment of Kubernetes Operators. It provides scaffolding, libraries, and best practices to help developers build robust Operators that can manage complex, stateful applications. In this section, we will explore the steps involved in building an Operator using the Operator SDK, from setting up the development environment to deploying the Operator in a Kubernetes cluster.

Overview of the Operator SDK The Operator SDK streamlines the process of creating Kubernetes Operators by providing tools and libraries that handle common tasks. It supports three primary approaches for building Operators:

- **Go-based Operators:** Leverage the power of Go and Kubernetes client libraries to build custom Operators.

- **Ansible-based Operators:** Use Ansible playbooks to define the reconciliation logic for Operators.

- **Helm-based Operators:** Utilize Helm charts to manage the lifecycle of applications with Operators.

Setting Up the Development Environment To get started with the Operator SDK, you need to set up your development environment. This includes installing the necessary tools and dependencies.

Prerequisites:

- **Golang:** Install Go (version 1.16 or higher) if you are building a Go-based Operator.

- **Ansible:** Install Ansible if you are building an Ansible-based Operator.

- **Helm:** Install Helm if you are building a Helm-based Operator.

- **Kubectl:** Install kubectl to interact with your Kubernetes cluster.

- **Operator SDK:** Install the Operator SDK CLI tool.

Installing the Operator SDK CLI:

```
# Download and install the Operator SDK CLI
curl -LO https://github.com/operator-framework/operator-sdk/
releases/download/v1.12.0/operator-sdk_linux_amd64


chmod +x operator-sdk_linux_amd64


mv operator-sdk_linux_amd64 /usr/local/bin/operator-sdk
```

Creating a New Operator Project The Operator SDK provides a command to scaffold a new Operator project. This initializes the project structure and generates boilerplate code.

Creating a Go-based Operator:

```
# Initialize a new Go-based Operator project
operator-sdk init --domain example.com --repogithub.com/
example/myoperator
```

Creating an Ansible-based Operator:

```
# Initialize a new Ansible-based Operator project
operator-sdk init --plugins=ansible --domain example.com
```

Creating a Helm-based Operator:

```
# Initialize a new Helm-based Operator project
operator-sdk init --plugins=helm --domain example.com
```

Defining the Custom Resource   After initializing the project, the next step is to define the custom resource that the Operator will manage. This involves creating a Custom Resource Definition (CRD) and specifying the schema for the custom resource.

Generating the API and CRD:

```
# Generate the API and CRD for a Go-based Operator
operator-sdk create api --group apps --version v1 --kind MyApp
--resource --controller
```

Example CRD Definition:

```
// api/v1/myapp_types.go
type MyAppSpec struct {
    Size int32 `json:"size"`
}

type MyAppStatus struct {
    Nodes []string `json:"nodes"`
}
```

Implementing the Controller   The core of the Operator is the controller, which implements the reconciliation logic. The Operator SDK provides a scaffolded controller implementation that you can customize to meet the specific needs of your application.

Example Reconciliation Logic:

```go
// controllers/myapp_controller.go
func (r *MyAppReconciler) Reconcile(ctx context.Context,
req ctrl.Request) (ctrl.Result, error) {
    log := r.Log.WithValues("myapp", req.NamespacedName)

    // Fetch the MyApp instance
    myApp := &appsv1.MyApp{}
    err := r.Client.Get(ctx, req.NamespacedName, myApp)
    if err != nil {
        if errors.IsNotFound(err) {
            log.Info("MyApp resource not found. Ignoring
since object must be deleted.")
            return ctrl.Result{}, nil
        }
        log.Error(err, "Failed to get MyApp")
        return ctrl.Result{}, err
    }

    // Compare desired state with current state and reconcile
    desiredSize := myApp.Spec.Size
    currentSize := getCurrentSize(myApp)
    if desiredSize != currentSize {
        err = r.updateSize(ctx, myApp, desiredSize)
        if err != nil {
            log.Error(err, "Failed to update size")
            return ctrl.Result{}, err
        }
    }

    // Update status
    myApp.Status.Nodes = getNodes(myApp)
    err = r.Client.Status().Update(ctx, myApp)
    if err != nil {
        log.Error(err, "Failed to update MyApp status")
        return ctrl.Result{}, err
    }
```

```go
    return ctrl.Result{}, nil
}

func getCurrentSize(myApp *appsv1.MyApp) int32 {
    // Implement logic to get the current size of
the application
    return 0
}

func (r *MyAppReconciler) updateSize(ctx context.Context,
myApp *appsv1.MyApp, size int32) error {
    // Implement logic to update the size of the application
    return nil
}

func getNodes(myApp *appsv1.MyApp) []string {
    // Implement logic to get the list of nodes
    return []string{}
}
```

Deploying the Operator   Once the Operator is implemented, it needs to be deployed to a Kubernetes cluster. The Operator SDK provides tools to build, deploy, and manage the Operator.

Building the Operator:

```
# Build the Operator image
make docker-build docker-push IMG=<your-operator-image>
```

Deploying the Operator:

```
# Deploy the Operator to the cluster
make deploy IMG=<your-operator-image>
```

Testing the Operator   Testing is a crucial part of the development process to ensure the Operator behaves as expected. The Operator SDK supports unit testing, integration testing, and end-to-end testing.

Running Unit Tests:

```
# Run unit tests
make test
```

Running End-to-End Tests:

```
# Run end-to-end tests
make test-e2e
```

Best Practices for Building Operators   Following best practices ensures that the Operators you build are reliable, maintainable, and efficient.

Use Clear and Consistent APIs: Define clear and consistent APIs for custom resources to make them easy to use and understand.

Implement Robust Error Handling: Implement robust error handling and retry mechanisms to ensure that the Operator can recover from transient failures.

Expose Metrics and Logs: Expose metrics and logs to facilitate monitoring, debugging, and performance analysis.

Automate Testing: Automate testing to ensure that the Operator behaves correctly under various scenarios and edge cases.

Conclusion   Building Operators with the Operator SDK simplifies the process of developing, testing, and deploying Kubernetes Operators. By leveraging the tools and libraries provided by the SDK, you can create robust Operators that automate the management of complex, stateful applications.   Following best practices and thoroughly testing your Operators ensures that they are reliable and maintainable, providing a solid foundation for managing applications in Kubernetes.

5.2.3 Managing Application State with Operators

Managing the state of applications is a critical aspect of Kubernetes Operators. Operators are designed to automate complex operational tasks for stateful applications, ensuring that they are always running in the desired state. This involves managing the entire lifecycle of the application, including deployment, scaling, updates, backups, and recovery.

Understanding Application State In the context of Operators, application state refers to the configuration, status, and data of an application that must be managed to ensure its proper functioning. This includes the number of instances, configuration settings, version information, and persistent data.

Types of Application State:

- **Configuration State:** Settings and parameters that define the behavior of the application.

- **Operational State:** The current status and health of the application instances.

- **Persistent State:** Data that needs to be retained across restarts, such as databases and user data.

Defining Desired State The desired state of an application is defined through custom resources managed by the Operator. These custom resources specify the desired configuration, number of instances, version, and other relevant parameters.

Example Custom Resource for Desired State:

```
apiVersion: apps.example.com/v1
kind: MyApp
metadata:
  name: myapp
spec:
  replicas: 3
  version: "1.0.0"
```

```
config:
  setting1: "value1"
  setting2: "value2"
```

Monitoring Current State Operators continuously monitor the current state of the application by querying the Kubernetes API and other relevant sources. This involves fetching the status of the application instances, configuration settings, and persistent data.

Fetching Current State:

```go
func (r *MyAppReconciler) getCurrentState(ctx context.Context,
req ctrl.Request) (*MyApp, error) {
    myApp := &appsv1.MyApp{}
    err := r.Client.Get(ctx, req.NamespacedName, myApp)
    if err != nil {
        return nil, err
    }
    return myApp, nil
}
```

Reconciliation Logic The core of managing application state with Operators lies in the reconciliation logic. This logic compares the current state with the desired state and takes actions to reconcile any differences. This may involve creating, updating, or deleting resources, as well as performing application-specific operations.

Example Reconciliation Logic:

```go
func (r *MyAppReconciler) Reconcile(ctx context.Context,
req ctrl.Request) (ctrl.Result, error) {
    log := r.Log.WithValues("myapp", req.NamespacedName)

    // Fetch the current state
    myApp, err := r.getCurrentState(ctx, req)
    if err != nil {
        if errors.IsNotFound(err) {
            log.Info("MyApp resource not found. Ignoring since
```

```
object must be deleted.")
            return ctrl.Result{}, nil
        }
        log.Error(err, "Failed to get MyApp")
        return ctrl.Result{}, err
    }

    // Compare desired state with current state
    if myApp.Spec.Replicas != myApp.Status.Replicas {
        err = r.updateReplicas(ctx, myApp)
        if err != nil {
            log.Error(err, "Failed to update replicas")
            return ctrl.Result{}, err
        }
    }

    // Update status
    myApp.Status.Replicas = myApp.Spec.Replicas
    err = r.Client.Status().Update(ctx, myApp)
    if err != nil {
        log.Error(err, "Failed to update MyApp status")
        return ctrl.Result{}, err
    }

    return ctrl.Result{}, nil
}

func (r *MyAppReconciler) updateReplicas(ctx context.Context,
myApp *appsv1.MyApp) error {
    // Implement logic to update the number of replicas
    return nil
}
```

Handling Application Updates   Operators are responsible for managing
application updates, including rolling updates and version upgrades. This
involves orchestrating the update process to ensure minimal downtime and
maintaining application availability.

Rolling Updates: Rolling updates involve gradually updating instances of the application to a new version, ensuring that some instances remain available during the update process.

```go
func (r *MyAppReconciler) updateVersion(ctx context.Context,
myApp *appsv1.MyApp, newVersion string) error {
    // Implement logic for rolling update to the new version
    return nil
}
```

Backup and Recovery Managing stateful applications often involves handling backups and recovery. Operators can automate the backup process, ensuring that application data is regularly backed up and can be restored in case of failures.

Automating Backups: Operators can schedule and perform backups of application data, storing them in a safe location.

```go
func (r *MyAppReconciler) backupData(ctx context.Context,
myApp *appsv1.MyApp) error {
    // Implement logic to backup application data
    return nil
}
```

Implementing Recovery: In the event of a failure, Operators can automate the recovery process, restoring data from backups and ensuring that the application returns to its desired state.

```go
func (r *MyAppReconciler) restoreData(ctx context.Context,
myApp *appsv1.MyApp) error {
    // Implement logic to restore application data from backup
    return nil
}
```

Scaling Applications Operators can manage the scaling of applications, adjusting the number of instances based on demand or predefined criteria. This involves monitoring resource usage and scaling the application up or down as needed.

Horizontal Scaling:　Adjust the number of replicas to handle changes in load.

```go
func (r *MyAppReconciler) scaleApplication(ctx context.Context,
myApp *appsv1.MyApp, replicas int32) error {
    // Implement logic to scale the application
    return nil
}
```

Best Practices for Managing Application State with Operators
Following best practices ensures that Operators manage application state efficiently and reliably.

Ensure Idempotence: Reconciliation logic should be idempotent, meaning that applying the same changes multiple times has the same effect as applying them once.

Handle Errors Gracefully:　Implement robust error handling and retry mechanisms to manage transient failures and ensure consistency.

Monitor and Log:　Continuously monitor the application state and log significant events to facilitate debugging and performance analysis.

Automate Testing:　Automate the testing of Operators to ensure that they handle various scenarios and edge cases correctly.

Conclusion Managing application state with Kubernetes Operators involves defining the desired state, continuously monitoring the current state, and implementing reconciliation logic to ensure that the application remains in the desired state.　By automating tasks such as updates, backups, recovery, and scaling, Operators reduce the operational burden on administrators and ensure the reliable and efficient management of stateful applications. Following best practices further enhances the reliability and maintainability of Operators, making them a powerful tool for managing complex applications in Kubernetes.

5.2.4   Real-world Examples and Use Cases

Kubernetes Operators have been widely adopted across various industries to manage complex, stateful applications. This section provides detailed real-world examples and use cases that highlight the power and flexibility of Operators. These examples demonstrate how Operators can automate operational tasks, improve reliability, and streamline application management.

Example 1: MySQL Operator The MySQL Operator is designed to manage MySQL clusters, handling tasks such as deployment, scaling, backups, and recovery. This Operator ensures that MySQL instances are always running in the desired state, providing a robust and scalable database solution.

Custom Resource Definition:

```
apiVersion: mysql.example.com/v1
kind: MySQLCluster
metadata:
  name: my-mysql-cluster
spec:
  replicas: 3
  version: "5.7"
  storage:
    size: 10Gi
```

Reconciliation Logic: The MySQL Operator monitors the MySQLCluster custom resource and reconciles the current state with the desired state.

```
func (r *MySQLClusterReconciler) Reconcile(ctx context.Context,
req ctrl.Request) (ctrl.Result, error) {
    log := r.Log.WithValues("mysqlcluster", req.NamespacedName)

    // Fetch the MySQLCluster instance
    mysqlCluster := &mysqlv1.MySQLCluster{}
    err := r.Client.Get(ctx, req.NamespacedName, mysqlCluster)
```

```go
    if err != nil {
        if errors.IsNotFound(err) {
            log.Info("MySQLCluster resource not found.
Ignoring since object must be deleted.")
            return ctrl.Result{}, nil
        }
        log.Error(err, "Failed to get MySQLCluster")
        return ctrl.Result{}, err
    }

    // Ensure the desired number of replicas are running
    err = r.reconcileReplicas(ctx, mysqlCluster)
    if err != nil {
        log.Error(err, "Failed to reconcile replicas")
        return ctrl.Result{}, err
    }

    // Ensure backups are scheduled
    err = r.reconcileBackups(ctx, mysqlCluster)
    if err != nil {
        log.Error(err, "Failed to reconcile backups")
        return ctrl.Result{}, err
    }

    // Update status
    mysqlCluster.Status.ReadyReplicas = mysqlCluster.Spec
.Replicas
    err = r.Client.Status().Update(ctx, mysqlCluster)
    if err != nil {
        log.Error(err, "Failed to update MySQLCluster status")
        return ctrl.Result{}, err
    }

    return ctrl.Result{}, nil
}

func (r *MySQLClusterReconciler) reconcileReplicas(ctx
context.Context, mysqlCluster *mysqlv1.MySQLCluster) error {
```

```go
    // Get the current statefulset
    statefulSet := &appsv1.StatefulSet{}
    err := r.Client.Get(ctx, types.NamespacedName{Name:
mysqlCluster.Name, Namespace: mysqlCluster.Namespace},
statefulSet)
    if err != nil && !errors.IsNotFound(err) {
        return err
    }

    // Update the replicas if needed
    if *statefulSet.Spec.Replicas != mysqlCluster.Spec
.Replicas {
        statefulSet.Spec.Replicas = &mysqlCluster.Spec.Replicas
        err = r.Client.Update(ctx, statefulSet)
        if err != nil {
            return err
        }
    }

    return nil
}

func (r *MySQLClusterReconciler) reconcileBackups(ctx
context.Context, mysqlCluster *mysqlv1.MySQLCluster) error {
    // Implement backup reconciliation logic
    // For example, create a CronJob to schedule backups
    cronJob := &batchv1.CronJob{
        ObjectMeta: metav1.ObjectMeta{
            Name:        fmt.Sprintf("%s-backup", mysqlCluster
.Name),
            Namespace: mysqlCluster.Namespace,
        },
        Spec: batchv1.CronJobSpec{
            Schedule: "0 3 * * *", // Daily at 3 AM
            JobTemplate: batchv1.JobTemplateSpec{
                Spec: batchv1.JobSpec{
                    Template: corev1.PodTemplateSpec{
                        Spec: corev1.PodSpec{
```

```go
                                Containers: []corev1.Container{
                                    {
                                        Name:  "backup",
                                        Image: "mysql-backup
:latest",

                                        Env: []corev1.EnvVar{
                                            {
                                                Name:
"MYSQL_HOST",

                                                Value:
mysqlCluster.Status.Host,

                                            },
                                        },
                                        VolumeMounts:
[]corev1.VolumeMount{

                                            {
                                                Name:
"backup-storage",

                                                MountPath:
"/backup",

                                            },
                                        },
                                    },
                                },
                                RestartPolicy:
corev1.RestartPolicyOnFailure,
                            },
                        },
                    },
                },
        }

        // Create or update the CronJob
        err := r.Client.Create(ctx, cronJob)
        if err != nil && !errors.IsAlreadyExists(err) {
            return err
        }
```

```
    if errors.IsAlreadyExists(err) {
        err = r.Client.Update(ctx, cronJob)
        if err != nil {
            return err
        }
    }

    return nil
}
```

Example 2:   Prometheus Operator The Prometheus Operator simplifies the deployment and management of Prometheus monitoring systems.   It automates tasks such as setting up Prometheus instances, configuring alerting rules, and managing service discovery.

Custom Resource Definition:

```yaml
apiVersion: monitoring.coreos.com/v1
kind: Prometheus
metadata:
  name: prometheus
spec:
  replicas: 2
  version: "v2.22.2"
  alerting:
    alertmanagers:
      - namespace: monitoring
        name: alertmanager
  storage:
    volumeClaimTemplate:
      spec:
        resources:
          requests:
            storage: 10Gi
```

Reconciliation   Logic: The   Prometheus   Operator   ensures   that Prometheus instances are configured and running as specified in the custom resource.

```go
func (r *PrometheusReconciler) Reconcile(ctx context.Context,
req ctrl.Request) (ctrl.Result, error) {
    log := r.Log.WithValues("prometheus", req.NamespacedName)

    // Fetch the Prometheus instance
    prometheus := &monitoringv1.Prometheus{}
    err := r.Client.Get(ctx, req.NamespacedName, prometheus)
    if err != nil {
        if errors.IsNotFound(err) {
            log.Info("Prometheus resource not found. Ignoring
since object must be deleted.")
            return ctrl.Result{}, nil
        }
        log.Error(err, "Failed to get Prometheus")
        return ctrl.Result{}, err
    }

    // Ensure the Prometheus StatefulSet is updated
    err = r.reconcileStatefulSet(ctx, prometheus)
    if err != nil {
        log.Error(err, "Failed to reconcile StatefulSet")
        return ctrl.Result{}, err
    }

    // Ensure Alertmanager configuration is updated
    err = r.reconcileAlertmanagerConfig(ctx, prometheus)
    if err != nil {
        log.Error(err, "Failed to reconcile Alertmanager
configuration")
        return ctrl.Result{}, err
    }

    // Update status
    prometheus.Status.AvailableReplicas = prometheus.Spec
.Replicas
    err = r.Client.Status().Update(ctx, prometheus)
    if err != nil {
        log.Error(err, "Failed to update Prometheus status")
```

```go
        return ctrl.Result{}, err
    }

    return ctrl.Result{}, nil
}

func (r *PrometheusReconciler) reconcileStatefulSet(ctx
context.Context, prometheus *monitoringv1.Prometheus) error {
    // Get the current StatefulSet
    statefulSet := &appsv1.StatefulSet{}
    err := r.Client.Get(ctx, types.NamespacedName{Name:
prometheus.Name, Namespace: prometheus.Namespace}, statefulSet)
    if err != nil && !errors.IsNotFound(err) {
        return err
    }

    // Update the StatefulSet if needed
    if *statefulSet.Spec.Replicas != prometheus.Spec
.Replicas {
        statefulSet.Spec.Replicas = &prometheus.Spec.Replicas
        err = r.Client.Update(ctx, statefulSet)
        if err != nil {
            return err
        }
    }

    return nil
}

func (r *PrometheusReconciler) reconcileAlertmanagerConfig(
ctx context.Context, prometheus *monitoringv1.Prometheus)
error {
    // Implement logic to update Alertmanager configuration
    // For example, update a ConfigMap with alerting rules
    configMap := &corev1.ConfigMap{
        ObjectMeta: metav1.ObjectMeta{
            Name:       fmt.Sprintf("%s-alertmanager-config",
prometheus.Name),
```

```go
            Namespace: prometheus.Namespace,
        },
        Data: map[string]string{
            "alertmanager.yaml": `
global:
  resolve_timeout: 5m
route:
  receiver: 'team-X-mails'
  group_by: ['alertname', 'job']
  group_wait: 30s
  group_interval: 5m
  repeat_interval: 12h
receivers:
  - name: 'team-X-mails'
    email_configs:
      - to: 'team-x@example.com'
        from: 'alertmanager@example.com'
        smarthost: 'smtp.example.com:587'
        auth_username: 'alertmanager@example.com'
        auth_identity: 'alertmanager@example.com'
        auth_password: 'password'
`,
        },
    }

    // Create or update the ConfigMap
    err := r.Client.Create(ctx, configMap)
    if err != nil && !errors.IsAlreadyExists(err) {
        return err
    }
    if errors.IsAlreadyExists(err) {
        err = r.Client.Update(ctx, configMap)
        if err != nil {
            return err
        }
    }

    return nil
```

```
}
```

Example 3: Elasticsearch Operator The Elasticsearch Operator manages Elasticsearch clusters, automating tasks such as node provisioning, scaling, and backups. This Operator ensures that Elasticsearch clusters are always running in the desired state, providing a scalable and reliable search and analytics solution.

Custom Resource Definition:

```yaml
apiVersion: elasticsearch.k8s.elastic.co/v1
kind: Elasticsearch
metadata:
  name: my-elasticsearch
spec:
  version: "7.10.1"
  nodeSets:
    - name: master
      count: 3
      config:
        node.master: true
        node.data: false
        node.ingest: false
      volumeClaimTemplates:
        - metadata:
            name: data
          spec:
            accessModes: [ "ReadWriteOnce" ]
            resources:
              requests:
                storage: 50Gi
    - name: data
      count: 3
      config:
        node.master: false
        node.data: true
        node.ingest: false
      volumeClaimTemplates:
```

```
    - metadata:
        name: data
      spec:
        accessModes: [ "ReadWriteOnce" ]
        resources:
          requests:
            storage: 200Gi
```

Reconciliation Logic: The Elasticsearch Operator ensures that the Elasticsearch cluster is configured and running as specified in the custom resource.

```go
func (r *ElasticsearchReconciler) Reconcile(
ctx context.Context, req ctrl.Request) (ctrl.Result, error) {
    log := r.Log.WithValues("elasticsearch",
req.NamespacedName)

    // Fetch the Elasticsearch instance
    es := &elasticsearchv1.Elasticsearch{}
    err := r.Client.Get(ctx, req.NamespacedName, es)
    if err != nil {
        if errors.IsNotFound(err) {
            log.Info("Elasticsearch resource not found.
Ignoring since object must be deleted.")
            return ctrl.Result{}, nil
        }
        log.Error(err, "Failed to get Elasticsearch")
        return ctrl.Result{}, err
    }

    // Ensure the Elasticsearch StatefulSets are updated
    for _, nodeSet := range es.Spec.NodeSets {
        err = r.reconcileNodeSet(ctx, es, nodeSet)
        if err != nil {
            log.Error(err, "Failed to reconcile NodeSet",
"NodeSet", nodeSet.Name)
            return ctrl.Result{}, err
        }
```

```go
    }

    // Update status
    es.Status.Phase = "Running"
    err = r.Client.Status().Update(ctx, es)
    if err != nil {
        log.Error(err, "Failed to update Elasticsearch status")
        return ctrl.Result{}, err
    }

    return ctrl.Result{}, nil
}

func (r *ElasticsearchReconciler) reconcileNodeSet(ctx
context.Context, es *elasticsearchv1.Elasticsearch,
nodeSet elasticsearchv1.NodeSet) error {
    // Get the current StatefulSet
    statefulSet := &appsv1.StatefulSet{}
    err := r.Client.Get(ctx, types.NamespacedName{Name:
nodeSet.Name, Namespace: es.Namespace}, statefulSet)
    if err != nil && !errors.IsNotFound(err) {
        return err
    }

    // Create or update the StatefulSet
    if errors.IsNotFound(err) {
        // Create a new StatefulSet
        newStatefulSet := &appsv1.StatefulSet{
            ObjectMeta: metav1.ObjectMeta{
                Name:      nodeSet.Name,
                Namespace: es.Namespace,
            },
            Spec: appsv1.StatefulSetSpec{
                Replicas: &nodeSet.Count,
                Selector: &metav1.LabelSelector{
                    MatchLabels: map[string]string{"nodeSet":
nodeSet.Name},
                },
```

```go
                    Template: corev1.PodTemplateSpec{
                        ObjectMeta: metav1.ObjectMeta{
                            Labels: map[string]string{"nodeSet":
nodeSet.Name},
                        },
                        Spec: corev1.PodSpec{
                            Containers: []corev1.Container{
                                {
                                    Name:  "elasticsearch",
                                    Image: fmt.Sprintf(
"docker.elastic.co/elasticsearch/elasticsearch:%s", es.Spec
.Version),
                                    Ports: []corev1.ContainerPort{
                                        {Name: "http",
ContainerPort: 9200},
                                        {Name: "transport",
ContainerPort: 9300},
                                    },
                                    VolumeMounts:
[]corev1.VolumeMount{
                                        {
                                            Name:      "data",
                                            MountPath: "/usr/share
/elasticsearch/data",
                                        },
                                    },
                                },
                            },
                        },
                    },
                    VolumeClaimTemplates:
nodeSet.VolumeClaimTemplates,
                },
            }
            err = r.Client.Create(ctx, newStatefulSet)
            if err != nil {
                return err
            }
```

```
    } else {
        // Update the existing StatefulSet
        if *statefulSet.Spec.Replicas != nodeSet.Count {
            statefulSet.Spec.Replicas = &nodeSet.Count
            err = r.Client.Update(ctx, statefulSet)
            if err != nil {
                return err
            }
        }
    }

    return nil
}
```

Conclusion These real-world examples and use cases demonstrate the power and flexibility of Kubernetes Operators in managing complex, stateful applications. By automating operational tasks such as deployment, scaling, updates, and backups, Operators ensure that applications are always running in the desired state, improving reliability and reducing the operational burden on administrators. Implementing detailed reconciliation logic and following best practices enables you to create robust and efficient Operators tailored to the specific needs of your applications.

Chapter 6

Networking in Kubernetes

6.1 Introduction to Kubernetes Networking

Kubernetes networking is a fundamental aspect of the platform, providing the connectivity required for communication between various components, including pods, services, and external resources. It encompasses a range of networking functionalities such as service discovery, load balancing, network policies, and ingress management. Understanding Kubernetes networking is essential for deploying and managing applications effectively within a cluster.

6.1.1 Pod-to-Pod Communication

Pod-to-Pod communication is a core aspect of Kubernetes networking, enabling direct communication between pods within a cluster. Each pod in Kubernetes is assigned a unique IP address, allowing pods to communicate with each other without the need for Network Address Translation (NAT). This direct communication model simplifies the development and deployment of distributed applications.

Kubernetes Networking Model Kubernetes adopts a flat networking model where every pod can communicate with every other pod within the cluster without the need for NAT. This model assumes that:

- All pods can communicate with all other pods on all nodes.

- The IP address of a pod is routable within the cluster.

- No NAT is required for pod-to-pod communication.

Pod Network Implementation The implementation of the pod network is achieved through the Container Network Interface (CNI), which provides a standardized way to configure network interfaces in Linux containers. Various CNI plugins can be used to implement the networking model, such as Flannel, Calico, Weave, and Cilium.

Example CNI Plugin Configuration:

```
# Example Flannel configuration
apiVersion: v1
kind: ConfigMap
metadata:
  name: kube-flannel-cfg
  namespace: kube-system
data:
  net-conf.json: |
    {
      "Network": "10.244.0.0/16",
      "Backend": {
        "Type": "vxlan"
      }
    }
```

Pod IP Addressing Each pod in Kubernetes is assigned a unique IP address from the pod network CIDR (Classless Inter-Domain Routing) range. This IP address is used for communication with other pods within the cluster.

Example Pod Network CIDR:

```
# Example kubeadm configuration with pod network CIDR
apiVersion: kubeadm.k8s.io/v1beta2
kind: ClusterConfiguration
networking:
  podSubnet: "10.244.0.0/16"
```

Pod Communication Mechanisms Pods can communicate with each other through the following mechanisms:

- **Direct IP Addressing:** Pods can communicate directly using their IP addresses.

- **DNS:** Kubernetes provides a built-in DNS service that allows pods to communicate using DNS names.

Direct IP Addressing: In Kubernetes, each pod has an IP address that other pods can use to communicate directly. For example, if pod A needs to communicate with pod B, it can send requests to pod B's IP address.

Example Direct Communication:

```
# Example of a pod communicating directly with another pod
apiVersion: v1
kind: Pod
metadata:
  name: busybox
spec:
  containers:
  - name: busybox
    image: busybox
    command: ["sh", "-c", "ping <pod-IP-address>"]
```

DNS: Kubernetes includes a DNS server that automatically creates DNS records for Kubernetes services. Pods can use these DNS names to communicate with each other without needing to know the IP addresses.

Example DNS Communication:

```
# Example of a pod using DNS to communicate with another pod
apiVersion: v1
kind: Pod
metadata:
  name: dns-test
spec:
  containers:
```

```
  - name: dns-test
    image: busybox
    command: ["sh", "-c", "nslookup <service-name>"]
```

Network Policies Network policies are used to control the communication between pods. They provide fine-grained control over which pods can communicate with each other and can be used to enforce security policies.

Example Network Policy:

```
apiVersion: networking.k8s.io/v1
kind: NetworkPolicy
metadata:
  name: allow-specific-pod
  namespace: default
spec:
  podSelector:
    matchLabels:
      app: myapp
  ingress:
  - from:
    - podSelector:
        matchLabels:
          app: otherapp
    ports:
    - protocol: TCP
      port: 80
```

Service Discovery and Load Balancing Kubernetes services provide a stable endpoint for accessing pods. Services can be used for service discovery and load balancing, ensuring that requests are distributed evenly across the available pods.

Example Service Configuration:

```
apiVersion: v1
kind: Service
```

```
metadata:
  name: my-service
spec:
  selector:
    app: myapp
  ports:
  - protocol: TCP
    port: 80
    targetPort: 8080
```

Conclusion Pod-to-pod communication is a fundamental aspect of Kubernetes networking, enabling seamless connectivity between pods within a cluster. By leveraging direct IP addressing, DNS, network policies, and services, Kubernetes ensures that pods can communicate efficiently and securely. Understanding these concepts is essential for effectively deploying and managing applications in a Kubernetes environment.

6.1.2 Service Networking

Service networking in Kubernetes is a fundamental concept that enables reliable communication between different services running within the cluster. Services provide stable IP addresses and DNS names to abstract and balance traffic across a set of pods. This section focuses on the key aspects of service networking, including service discovery, service types, and load balancing mechanisms.

Service Discovery Service discovery is the process through which services in a Kubernetes cluster find and communicate with each other. Kubernetes provides built-in service discovery mechanisms that allow pods to locate services using DNS and environment variables.

DNS-Based Service Discovery: Kubernetes includes a DNS server that automatically creates DNS records for services. This allows pods to use DNS names to communicate with services instead of hardcoding IP addresses.

```
# Example of a pod using DNS to access a service
apiVersion: v1
```

```
kind: Pod
metadata:
  name: dns-test
spec:
  containers:
  - name: dns-test
    image: busybox
    command: ["sh", "-c", "nslookup my-service"]
```

Environment Variables: Kubernetes injects environment variables into pods that contain information about the services. These environment variables can be used by applications to discover and access services.

```
# Example of a pod accessing service information through
environment variables

apiVersion: v1
kind: Pod
metadata:
  name: env-var-test
spec:
  containers:
  - name: env-var-test
    image: busybox
    command: ["sh", "-c", "printenv | grep MY_SERVICE"]
```

Service Types Kubernetes supports several types of services, each serving a specific purpose in terms of network exposure and accessibility. The main types are ClusterIP, NodePort, LoadBalancer, and ExternalName.

ClusterIP: The default service type, ClusterIP, exposes the service on a cluster-internal IP. This type of service is only accessible within the cluster and is used for internal communication between microservices.

```
apiVersion: v1
kind: Service
metadata:
  name: example-clusterip-service
```

```
spec:
  selector:
    app: example-app
  ports:
  - protocol: TCP
    port: 80
    targetPort: 8080
  type: ClusterIP
```

NodePort: NodePort exposes the service on each node's IP at a static port. This makes the service accessible externally using `<NodeIP>:<NodePort>`. NodePort is useful for development and testing or when a simple external access mechanism is needed.

```
apiVersion: v1
kind: Service
metadata:
  name: example-nodeport-service
spec:
  selector:
    app: example-app
  ports:
  - protocol: TCP
    port: 80
    targetPort: 8080
    nodePort: 30007
  type: NodePort
```

LoadBalancer: LoadBalancer exposes the service externally using a cloud provider's load balancer. This type automatically provisions a load balancer and assigns a public IP address to the service. It is ideal for services that need to be accessible from the internet.

```
apiVersion: v1
kind: Service
metadata:
  name: example-loadbalancer-service
spec:
```

```
selector:
  app: example-app
ports:
- protocol: TCP
  port: 80
  targetPort: 8080
type: LoadBalancer
```

ExternalName: ExternalName maps the service to an external DNS name by returning a CNAME record with the external name. This type does not proxy traffic but instead allows Kubernetes services to refer to external resources using a consistent DNS name.

```
apiVersion: v1
kind: Service
metadata:
  name: example-externalname-service
spec:
  type: ExternalName
  externalName: example.com
```

Load Balancing Load balancing is a critical aspect of service networking in Kubernetes, ensuring that traffic is evenly distributed across the available pods. Kubernetes services inherently provide load balancing capabilities.

Internal Load Balancing: ClusterIP services automatically balance traffic between the pods matching the service selector. Kubernetes uses iptables or IPVS to achieve this internal load balancing.

External Load Balancing: LoadBalancer services utilize the cloud provider's load balancing mechanisms to distribute external traffic to the pods. This ensures high availability and scalability for internet-facing services.

Session Affinity Session affinity, also known as sticky sessions, directs requests from a client to the same pod. This can be configured for services that require session persistence.

```
apiVersion: v1
kind: Service
metadata:
  name: example-session-affinity-service
spec:
  selector:
    app: example-app
  ports:
  - protocol: TCP
    port: 80
    targetPort: 8080
  sessionAffinity: ClientIP
```

Network Policies   Network policies define rules that control the traffic between pods and services. They are used to enhance security by restricting which pods can communicate with each other.

```
apiVersion: networking.k8s.io/v1
kind: NetworkPolicy
metadata:
  name: allow-frontend-to-backend
spec:
  podSelector:
    matchLabels:
      role: backend
  ingress:
  - from:
    - podSelector:
        matchLabels:
          role: frontend
    ports:
    - protocol: TCP
      port: 8080
```

Conclusion   Service networking in Kubernetes provides a robust and flexible mechanism for discovering and accessing services within a cluster. By leveraging various service types, load balancing, session affinity, and network policies, Kubernetes ensures that applications can communicate reliably and securely. Understanding these concepts is crucial for deploying and managing services effectively in a Kubernetes environment.

6.1.3 DNS in Kubernetes

DNS (Domain Name System) is a critical component of Kubernetes networking, providing a reliable mechanism for service discovery and name resolution within a cluster. Kubernetes includes an internal DNS service that automatically creates DNS records for services and pods, enabling seamless communication between different components.

Kubernetes DNS Overview   Kubernetes DNS provides name resolution for all services and pods in the cluster. It ensures that services can be accessed using consistent and human-readable names, rather than IP addresses, which may change as pods are recreated or scaled.

CoreDNS: CoreDNS is the default DNS server in Kubernetes. It is a flexible and extensible DNS server that can be configured to handle various DNS-related tasks within the cluster.

Service Discovery with DNS   When a service is created in Kubernetes, the DNS server automatically assigns it a DNS name. This name can be used by other services and pods to locate and communicate with the service.

Example Service DNS Name:

```
# Service definition
apiVersion: v1
kind: Service
metadata:
  name: my-service
spec:
  selector:
    app: myapp
  ports:
  - protocol: TCP
    port: 80
```

```
   targetPort: 8080
```

```
# DNS name for the service
my-service.default.svc.cluster.local
```

In the example above, the service named 'my-service' in the 'default' namespace can be accessed using the DNS name 'my-service.default.svc.cluster.local'.

Pod DNS Names   Kubernetes also assigns DNS names to individual pods. However, these names are not as commonly used as service names, since pods are more ephemeral and their IP addresses can change frequently.

Example Pod DNS Name:

```
# Pod definition
apiVersion: v1
kind: Pod
metadata:
  name: my-pod
  namespace: default
spec:
  containers:
  - name: my-container
    image: my-image
```

```
# DNS name for the pod
my-pod.default.pod.cluster.local
```

In the example above, the pod named 'my-pod' in the 'default' namespace can be accessed using the DNS name 'my-pod.default.pod.cluster.local'.

Configuring CoreDNS   CoreDNS can be configured to customize DNS behavior within the Kubernetes cluster. The configuration is managed through a ConfigMap.

Example CoreDNS ConfigMap:

```
apiVersion: v1
kind: ConfigMap
metadata:
  name: coredns
  namespace: kube-system
data:
  Corefile: |
    .:53 {
        errors
        health
        kubernetes cluster.local in-addr.arpa ip6.arpa {
            pods insecure
            fallthrough in-addr.arpa ip6.arpa
            ttl 30
        }
        prometheus :9153
        forward . /etc/resolv.conf
        cache 30
        loop
        reload
        loadbalance
    }
```

Custom DNS Entries In some cases, you might need to add custom DNS entries for services or external resources. CoreDNS allows you to create custom entries by modifying its configuration.

Example Custom DNS Entry:

```
apiVersion: v1
kind: ConfigMap
metadata:
  name: coredns
  namespace: kube-system
data:
  Corefile: |
    .:53 {
        errors
```

```
health
kubernetes cluster.local in-addr.arpa ip6.arpa {
    pods insecure
    fallthrough in-addr.arpa ip6.arpa
    ttl 30
}
hosts {
    10.0.0.1 my-custom-service.local
    fallthrough
}
prometheus :9153
forward . /etc/resolv.conf
cache 30
loop
reload
loadbalance
}
```

In the example above, the IP address '10.0.0.1' is mapped to the DNS name 'my-custom-service.local'.

DNS Policies Kubernetes allows you to specify DNS policies for pods to control how DNS resolution is handled. The 'dnsPolicy' field in the pod specification can be set to one of the following values:

- **Default:** The pod inherits the DNS settings of the node it is running on.

- **ClusterFirst:** The pod uses the cluster's DNS server for name resolution.

- **ClusterFirstWithHostNet:** The pod uses the cluster's DNS server, but falls back to the host's DNS settings if the pod uses host networking.

- **None:** The pod does not inherit DNS settings from the cluster or node, and custom DNS settings must be specified.

Example DNS Policy Configuration:

```
apiVersion: v1
kind: Pod
metadata:
  name: custom-dns-policy-pod
spec:
  containers:
  - name: my-container
    image: my-image
  dnsPolicy: ClusterFirstWithHostNet
```

Troubleshooting DNS Issues   DNS issues can affect service discovery and communication within the cluster. Common troubleshooting steps include:

- **Check CoreDNS Pods:** Ensure that CoreDNS pods are running and healthy.

- **Validate DNS Configurations:** Verify the CoreDNS configuration in the ConfigMap.

- **Test DNS Resolution:** Use tools like 'nslookup' or 'dig' to test DNS resolution from within a pod.

- **Review Logs:** Check the logs of CoreDNS pods for any error messages or warnings.

Example DNS Resolution Test:

```
# Launch a pod to test DNS resolution
apiVersion: v1
kind: Pod
metadata:
  name: dns-test
spec:
  containers:
  - name: dns-test
    image: busybox
    command: ["sh", "-c", "nslookup my-service"]
```

Conclusion   DNS in Kubernetes is a powerful tool for service discovery and name resolution, ensuring that services and pods can communicate reliably within the cluster. By leveraging CoreDNS and configuring DNS settings appropriately, you can enhance the networking capabilities of your Kubernetes environment. Understanding DNS in Kubernetes is crucial for managing and troubleshooting networking issues effectively.

6.2   Container Network Interfaces (CNIs)

6.2.1   Understanding CNI

The Container Network Interface (CNI) is a specification and a set of libraries for configuring network interfaces in Linux containers. In Kubernetes, CNI is crucial for implementing the networking model, enabling pods to communicate with each other seamlessly. The CNI project provides a standardized way to configure network interfaces and is essential for ensuring network connectivity within a Kubernetes cluster.

Overview of CNI   CNI defines a standardized interface for configuring network interfaces and managing the lifecycle of these configurations. It is designed to be a lightweight, efficient, and flexible solution that can work with different networking technologies and environments.

Key Components of CNI:

- **CNI Plugins:** Executables that implement the CNI specification and perform the actual network configuration tasks.

- **CNI Configuration:** JSON files that describe how the network interfaces should be configured.

- **CNI Library:** A set of libraries that handle the communication between Kubernetes and the CNI plugins.

CNI Plugins   CNI plugins are responsible for setting up the network interfaces in containers. Each plugin implements the CNI specification and can support various networking backends such as VXLAN, IPsec, and

GRE. There are numerous CNI plugins available, each offering different features and use cases.

Types of CNI Plugins:

- **Flannel:** A simple and easy-to-configure CNI plugin that provides basic network connectivity.

- **Calico:** A robust CNI plugin that offers advanced features such as network policies, security, and scalability.

- **Weave:** A CNI plugin that focuses on simplicity and ease of use, providing automatic network discovery and encryption.

- **Cilium:** A CNI plugin designed for security and observability, leveraging eBPF for high-performance networking.

CNI Configuration Files CNI configuration files are JSON files that specify how the network interfaces should be configured. These files are typically located in the '/etc/cni/net.d/' directory and are read by the CNI plugins during the container lifecycle.

Example CNI Configuration File:

```
{
  "cniVersion": "0.3.1",
  "name": "my-network",
  "type": "bridge",
  "bridge": "cni0",
  "isGateway": true,
  "ipMasq": true,
  "ipam": {
    "type": "host-local",
    "subnet": "10.22.0.0/16",
    "routes": [
      { "dst": "0.0.0.0/0" }
    ]
  }
}
```

CNI Lifecycle   The CNI lifecycle involves the following stages:

ADD: The ADD operation is invoked when a container is created. The CNI plugin configures the network interface for the container, assigns an IP address, and sets up any necessary routes.

```
# Example ADD operation
{
  "cniVersion": "0.3.1",
  "name": "my-network",
  "type": "bridge",
  "bridge": "cni0",
  "isGateway": true,
  "ipMasq": true,
  "ipam": {
    "type": "host-local",
    "subnet": "10.22.0.0/16",
    "routes": [
      { "dst": "0.0.0.0/0" }
    ]
  }
}
```

DEL: The DEL operation is invoked when a container is deleted. The CNI plugin cleans up the network interface, releases the IP address, and removes any routes associated with the container.

```
# Example DEL operation
{
  "cniVersion": "0.3.1",
  "name": "my-network",
  "type": "bridge",
  "bridge": "cni0",
  "isGateway": true,
  "ipMasq": true,
  "ipam": {
    "type": "host-local",
    "subnet": "10.22.0.0/16",
```

```
  "routes": [
    { "dst": "0.0.0.0/0" }
  ]
 }
}
```

Integrating CNI with Kubernetes   Kubernetes uses the CNI plugin to manage the network interfaces of pods. When a pod is created, Kubernetes invokes the CNI plugin to configure the network interface according to the specified CNI configuration.

Conclusion   Understanding CNI is essential for managing network connectivity in Kubernetes. By leveraging CNI plugins, Kubernetes can provide flexible and scalable networking solutions for containerized applications. CNI's standardized interface and extensible architecture make it a powerful tool for configuring network interfaces and ensuring seamless communication within a Kubernetes cluster. In the following sections, we will dive deeper into specific CNI plugins and explore their unique features and use cases.

6.2.2   Calico: Secure Network Connectivity with Network Policies

Calico is a popular CNI plugin that provides highly scalable and secure networking for Kubernetes clusters. It offers advanced network policy capabilities, allowing administrators to enforce fine-grained security controls and ensure secure communication between pods. Calico supports a range of networking modes, including pure Layer 3 routing and IP-in-IP encapsulation, making it a versatile choice for various deployment scenarios.

Overview of Calico   Calico uses a pure Layer 3 approach to networking, which means that it routes packets directly between hosts without requiring an overlay network. This approach provides high performance and scalability. Calico can also integrate with Kubernetes network policies to provide comprehensive security controls.

Key Features of Calico:

- **Scalability:** Calico's pure Layer 3 approach ensures that it scales efficiently with the size of the cluster.

- **Network Policies:** Advanced network policy capabilities allow for granular control over pod-to-pod communication.

- **Flexibility:** Supports various networking modes, including BGP, IP-in-IP, and VXLAN.

- **Security:** Provides strong security controls to protect against unauthorized access and network attacks.

Installing Calico Installing Calico in a Kubernetes cluster involves deploying the necessary components using Kubernetes manifests. The installation process sets up the Calico controllers, agents, and configuration files.

Example Installation Steps:

```
# Apply the Calico manifest to install Calico components
kubectl apply -f https://docs.projectcalico.org/manifests/
calico.yaml
```

Configuring Calico Networking Calico provides several configuration options to tailor the networking setup to your specific needs. This includes configuring IP pools, BGP settings, and encapsulation modes.

Example Configuration:

```
# Calico IP pool configuration
apiVersion: crd.projectcalico.org/v1
kind: IPPool
metadata:
  name: default-ipv4-ippool
spec:
  cidr: 192.168.0.0/16
  ipipMode: Always
  natOutgoing: true
```

Calico Network Policies   One of the standout features of Calico is its support for Kubernetes network policies. These policies allow administrators to define rules that control the traffic flow between pods, providing a powerful mechanism for enforcing security requirements.

Creating a Network Policy: A network policy in Calico can be defined using a YAML manifest. This policy specifies the allowed and denied traffic based on labels, namespaces, and other criteria.

Example Network Policy:

```yaml
apiVersion: networking.k8s.io/v1
kind: NetworkPolicy
metadata:
  name: allow-frontend-to-backend
  namespace: default
spec:
  podSelector:
    matchLabels:
      role: backend
  ingress:
  - from:
    - podSelector:
        matchLabels:
          role: frontend
    ports:
    - protocol: TCP
      port: 8080
```

In the example above, the policy allows traffic from pods with the label 'role=frontend' to pods with the label 'role=backend' on port 8080.

Monitoring and Troubleshooting Calico   Calico provides several tools for monitoring and troubleshooting network issues within a Kubernetes cluster. These tools help ensure that the network is operating correctly and securely.

Calicoctl: Calicoctl is a command-line tool for managing and troubleshooting Calico configurations and components.

```
# Check the status of Calico components
calicoctl node status
```

Calico Metrics: Calico exposes various metrics that can be collected and monitored using Prometheus or other monitoring tools.

```
# Example Prometheus configuration for Calico metrics
scrape_configs:
  - job_name: 'calico'
    static_configs:
      - targets: ['<calico-node-ip>:9091']
```

Best Practices for Using Calico Implementing best practices when using Calico helps ensure a secure and efficient network environment in your Kubernetes cluster.

Define Clear Network Policies: Use network policies to enforce security controls and minimize the attack surface.

Monitor Network Traffic: Regularly monitor network traffic and metrics to detect and respond to potential issues.

Regular Updates: Keep Calico components up to date to benefit from the latest features and security patches.

Conclusion Calico provides a powerful and flexible solution for secure network connectivity in Kubernetes. By leveraging its advanced network policy capabilities and scalable architecture, administrators can ensure that their Kubernetes clusters are both secure and efficient. Understanding how to install, configure, and manage Calico is essential for maintaining a robust networking environment in Kubernetes.

6.2.3　Cilium: API-aware Networking and Security

Cilium is a sophisticated CNI (Container Network Interface) that provides advanced networking, security, and observability for Kubernetes clusters. Leveraging the power of eBPF (Extended Berkeley Packet Filter), Cilium enables high-performance networking, fine-grained security policies, and deep visibility into network traffic. This section will delve into the details of Cilium's features, its integration with eBPF, and its capabilities for API-aware networking and security.

Overview of Cilium　Cilium stands out due to its use of eBPF, a revolutionary Linux kernel technology that allows the dynamic insertion of bytecode into the kernel at various integration points, such as network IO, application sockets, and tracepoints. This capability enables Cilium to implement complex networking, security, and visibility logic with high efficiency and flexibility.

Key Features of Cilium:

- **eBPF-based Networking:** Cilium uses eBPF to provide efficient and scalable networking, replacing traditional iptables-based approaches.

- **API-aware Security:** Cilium can enforce security policies at the API layer, supporting protocols like HTTP, gRPC, and Kafka.

- **Transparent Encryption:** Provides encryption for both internal and external traffic using IPsec, WireGuard, and TLS.

- **Observability:** Offers deep visibility into network traffic with Hubble, capturing metrics and flow logs.

- **Multi-cluster and Multi-cloud Support:** Enables seamless networking across multiple clusters and cloud environments with Cluster Mesh.

eBPF Integration　eBPF is central to Cilium's functionality. It allows Cilium to perform high-speed packet processing and apply complex security policies directly in the kernel, bypassing the limitations of user-space processing. This results in significant performance improvements and reduced latency.

eBPF Use Cases in Cilium:

- **Load Balancing:** Cilium uses eBPF for efficient Layer 4 load balancing, replacing kube-proxy with a more performant solution.

- **Network Policies:** Implements identity-based and API-aware network policies using eBPF, providing granular control over traffic.

- **Observability:** Leverages eBPF for capturing detailed metrics and flow logs, enabling comprehensive monitoring and troubleshooting.

System Requirements To leverage Cilium's full capabilities, ensure that your Kubernetes cluster meets the following requirements:

- **Kernel Version:** Linux kernel version 4.9.17 or higher is required. However, for advanced features such as BPF-based bandwidth manager, 5.2 or later is recommended.

- **Kubernetes:** Cilium supports Kubernetes versions 1.12 and later.

Installing Cilium Installing Cilium in a Kubernetes cluster involves deploying the necessary components using the Cilium CLI or Helm. The installation process sets up the Cilium agents, operators, and configuration files.

Using Cilium CLI:

```
# Install the Cilium CLI
CILIUM_CLI_VERSION=$(curl -s https://raw.githubusercontent.com/
cilium/cilium-cli/main/stable.txt)


CLI_ARCH=amd64


if [ "$(uname -m)" = "aarch64" ]; then CLI_ARCH=arm64; fi


curl -L --fail --remote-name-all https://github.com/cilium/
cilium-cli/releases/download/${CILIUM_CLI_VERSION}/
cilium-linux-${CLI_ARCH}.tar.gz{,.sha256sum}
```

```
sha256sum --check cilium-linux-${CLI_ARCH}.tar.gz.sha256sum

sudo tar xzvfC cilium-linux-${CLI_ARCH}.tar.gz /usr/local/bin

rm cilium-linux-${CLI_ARCH}.tar.gz{,.sha256sum}

# Install Cilium in the cluster
cilium install --version 1.15.6
```

Using Helm:

```
# Add the Cilium Helm repository
helm repo add cilium https://helm.cilium.io/

# Install Cilium using Helm
helm install cilium cilium/cilium --version 1.15.6
--namespace kube-system
```

Configuring Cilium Networking Cilium provides several configuration options to tailor the networking setup to your specific needs. This includes configuring IP pools, BGP settings, and encapsulation modes.

Example Configuration:

```
# Example IP pool configuration
apiVersion: cilium.io/v2
kind: CiliumNetworkPolicy
metadata:
  name: default-ipv4-ippool
spec:
  ipam:
    pool:
      cidr: 192.168.0.0/16
  encapsulation:
    type: ipip
  natOutgoing: true
```

API-aware Networking and Security Cilium enhances traditional network policies by enabling API-aware filtering. This means that security policies can be defined not only based on IP addresses and ports but also at the application protocol level, such as specific HTTP methods and paths.

Example API-aware Policy:

```
apiVersion: "cilium.io/v2"
kind: CiliumNetworkPolicy
metadata:
  name: api-aware-policy
spec:
  endpointSelector:
    matchLabels:
      app: myapp
  ingress:
  - fromEndpoints:
    - matchLabels:
        app: frontend
    toPorts:
    - ports:
      - port: "80"
        protocol: TCP
      rules:
        http:
        - method: "GET"
          path: "/public/.*"
```

Transparent Encryption Cilium provides transparent encryption for both intra-cluster and inter-cluster traffic using technologies like IPsec and WireGuard. This ensures that all data in transit is protected without requiring changes to application code.

Enabling Transparent Encryption:

```
# Enable IPsec encryption in Cilium
apiVersion: cilium.io/v2
kind: CiliumEncryptionConfiguration
```

```
metadata:
  name: encryption-config
spec:
  encryption:
    enable: true
    backend: ipsec
```

Observability with Hubble Hubble is the observability component of Cilium, built on top of eBPF. It provides real-time visibility into network traffic, capturing detailed flow logs, metrics, and policy enforcement events. Hubble integrates with monitoring tools like Prometheus and Grafana for advanced visualization.

Enabling Hubble:

```
# Enable Hubble with the Cilium CLI
cilium hubble enable --ui

# Install the Hubble CLI for accessing observability data
curl -L --remote-name-all https://github.com/cilium/hubble/
releases/download/$HUBBLE_VERSION/
hubble-linux-amd64.tar.gz{,.sha256sum}

shasum -a 256 -c hubble-linux-amd64.tar.gz.sha256sum

sudo tar xzvfC hubble-linux-amd64.tar.gz /usr/local/bin

rm hubble-linux-amd

# Access Hubble UI
cilium hubble port-forward --ui
```

Using Hubble for Observability: Hubble provides various tools for observing and troubleshooting network traffic within the cluster. Here are some common commands:

```
# View network flows in real-time
hubble observe
```

```
# Get a summary of network flows
hubble status

# View service map
hubble service list
```

Hubble also integrates seamlessly with Grafana and Prometheus, providing a rich set of dashboards for visualizing network traffic and policy enforcement. You can set up Grafana to use Hubble as a data source and explore predefined dashboards for detailed insights.

Grafana Integration Example:

```
# Example Grafana configuration to integrate with Hubble
datasources:
  - name: Hubble
    type: prometheus
    url: http://hubble-relay:80
    access: proxy
    isDefault: true

# Import Hubble dashboards into Grafana
kubectl apply -f https://raw.githubusercontent.com/cilium/
hubble/v0.8.0/examples/grafana/dashboards.yaml
```

Multi-cluster and Multi-cloud Networking Cilium's Cluster Mesh feature allows seamless networking across multiple Kubernetes clusters, whether on-premises or in the cloud. This is crucial for high-availability setups, disaster recovery, and geo-distributed applications.

Setting up Cluster Mesh: Cluster Mesh connects multiple clusters by enabling inter-cluster communication and service discovery. It uses Cilium's eBPF-based datapath to establish secure and efficient connectivity between clusters.

```
# Example configuration for Cluster Mesh
apiVersion: cilium.io/v2
```

```
kind: CiliumClusterwideNetworkPolicy
metadata:
  name: cluster-mesh
spec:
  description: "Cluster mesh configuration"
  clusterMesh:
    enable: true
    peeringPolicy:
      bgp:
        enable: true
```

To set up Cluster Mesh, you need to configure each cluster to recognize and communicate with the other clusters in the mesh. This involves setting up BGP peering or leveraging other peering methods supported by Cilium.

Complex Network Policies Cilium supports complex network policies that go beyond basic ingress and egress rules. These policies can be defined based on identity, labels, and even specific application protocols. For example, you can create policies that allow HTTP traffic only to specific endpoints or block access to certain parts of your API.

Example Complex Policy:

```
apiVersion: cilium.io/v2
kind: CiliumNetworkPolicy
metadata:
  name: complex-policy
spec:
  endpointSelector:
    matchLabels:
      app: myapp
  ingress:
  - fromEndpoints:
    - matchLabels:
        app: frontend
    toPorts:
    - ports:
      - port: "80"
```

```
    protocol: TCP
  rules:
    http:
    - method: "POST"
      path: "/api/v1/secure/.*"
```

Kernel Version Requirements Cilium leverages eBPF, which requires a compatible kernel version to function correctly. While the minimum required kernel version is 4.9.17, certain advanced features like the BPF-based bandwidth manager require a kernel version of 5.2 or higher.

Kernel Compatibility:

- **Basic eBPF Functionality:** Requires kernel 4.9.17 or later.

- **Advanced Features (e.g., Bandwidth Manager):** Requires kernel 5.2 or later.

To check your kernel version, use the following command:

```
uname -r
```

Ensure that your environment meets these requirements before deploying Cilium to leverage its full capabilities.

Troubleshooting Cilium Effective troubleshooting is critical for maintaining a healthy Cilium deployment. Common troubleshooting steps include checking the status of Cilium components, validating network policies, and inspecting logs for errors.

Common Troubleshooting Commands:

```
# Check the status of Cilium components
kubectl -n kube-system get pods -l k8s-app=cilium

# Describe a Cilium pod to check for issues
kubectl -n kube-system describe pod <cilium-pod-name>

# View Cilium logs for error messages
kubectl -n kube-system logs <cilium-pod-name>
```

Debugging Network Policies: To debug network policies, use the Cilium CLI to inspect the current state of policies and flow logs.

```
# List all Cilium network policies
cilium policy get

# Observe network flows to verify policy enforcement
hubble observe
```

Best Practices for Using Cilium   Implementing best practices when using Cilium helps ensure a secure and efficient network environment in your Kubernetes cluster.

Define Clear Network Policies: Use network policies to enforce security controls and minimize the attack surface.

Monitor Network Traffic: Regularly monitor network traffic and metrics to detect and respond to potential issues.

Regular Updates: Keep Cilium components up to date to benefit from the latest features and security patches.

Resource Requests and Limits: Define resource requests and limits for Cilium components to ensure they have sufficient resources to operate efficiently.

Case Study: Using Cilium in Production   To illustrate the real-world application of Cilium, let's consider a case study of a large enterprise that implemented Cilium for secure and scalable networking.

Background: A financial services company needed a robust solution to manage network traffic and enforce security policies in a multi-cluster Kubernetes environment.   They chose Cilium for its eBPF-based performance and advanced security features.

Implementation: The company deployed Cilium across their clusters, enabling Cluster Mesh to facilitate inter-cluster communication. They defined detailed network policies to restrict access to sensitive services and used Hubble for real-time observability.

Outcomes: By implementing Cilium, the company achieved:

- Improved network performance and reduced latency.

- Enhanced security through API-aware policies.

- Comprehensive visibility into network traffic with Hubble.

- Seamless connectivity across multiple clusters.

Conclusion Cilium, with its integration of eBPF, offers a powerful and flexible solution for networking, security, and observability in Kubernetes. By enabling API-aware security policies, transparent encryption, and comprehensive observability, Cilium addresses the complex requirements of modern cloud-native environments. Its multi-cluster capabilities further enhance its utility in large-scale, distributed deployments. Understanding and leveraging Cilium can significantly improve the performance, security, and manageability of your Kubernetes clusters.

6.2.4   Weave, Flannel, and Other CNIs

Container Network Interfaces (CNIs) are essential for networking within Kubernetes clusters, enabling communication between pods and services. This section will cover Weave, Flannel, and other notable CNIs, highlighting their features, installation processes, configurations, and use cases. These CNIs offer different approaches to networking, each with unique advantages and considerations.

Weave: Simple and Secure Networking Weave is a popular CNI that focuses on simplicity and security. It provides a seamless way to connect containers across multiple hosts, ensuring that they can communicate securely. Weave uses an overlay network that encapsulates traffic, making it possible to create a virtual network that spans multiple hosts.

Key Features of Weave:

- **Simplicity:** Easy to install and configure, with minimal setup required.

- **Security:** Supports encryption for all network traffic, ensuring data security.

- **Automatic Discovery:** Automatically discovers and connects new nodes in the cluster.

- **Flexible Networking:** Supports both Layer 2 and Layer 3 networking.

Installing Weave   Installing Weave involves running a simple command to deploy the Weave Net DaemonSet, which sets up the necessary components on each node in the cluster.

Installation Command:

```
# Deploy Weave Net
kubectl apply -f "https://cloud.weave.works/k8s/
net?k8s-version=$(kubectl version | base64 | tr -d '\n')"
```

Configuring Weave   Weave can be configured using environment variables and configuration files. Common configuration options include setting IP address ranges, enabling encryption, and adjusting performance settings.

Example Configuration:

```
# Enable encryption in Weave
kubectl set env daemonset/weave-net
-n kube-system WEAVE_PASSWORD=mysecretpassword
```

Flannel: Simple Overlay Networking   Flannel is a straightforward CNI that provides basic overlay networking for Kubernetes clusters. It is designed to be easy to deploy and manage, making it a popular choice for small to medium-sized clusters.

Key Features of Flannel:

- **Simplicity:** Easy to install and configure, with minimal setup required.

- **Overlay Networking:** Uses VXLAN or other backend options for creating an overlay network.

- **Flexibility:** Supports multiple backend options, including VXLAN, host-gw, and AWS VPC.

- **Performance:** Optimized for low overhead and high performance.

Installing Flannel Installing Flannel involves applying a Kubernetes manifest that deploys the Flannel DaemonSet, which sets up the necessary components on each node in the cluster.

Installation Command:

```
# Deploy Flannel
kubectl apply -f https://raw.githubusercontent.com/coreos/
flannel/master/Documentation/kube-flannel.yml
```

Configuring Flannel Flannel configuration is managed through a ConfigMap, where you can specify the desired backend and other network settings.

Example Configuration:

```
# Example Flannel ConfigMap
apiVersion: v1
kind: ConfigMap
metadata:
  name: kube-flannel-cfg
  namespace: kube-system
data:
  net-conf.json: |
    {
      "Network": "10.244.0.0/16",
```

```
  "Backend": {
    "Type": "vxlan"
  }
}
```

Other CNIs: Canal and Romana Beyond the advanced CNIs like Cilium and Calico, other options such as Canal and Romana offer unique features and benefits tailored to specific needs. This section provides an overview of Canal and Romana, detailing their key features, installation processes, and use cases.

Canal: Combined Flannel and Calico Canal combines Flannel's simple overlay networking with Calico's advanced network policy enforcement. It provides a balanced solution for clusters that need both easy networking setup and robust security.

Key Features of Canal:

- **Combined Benefits:** Offers the simplicity of Flannel with the security of Calico.

- **Network Policies:** Supports advanced network policies via Calico.

- **Easy Deployment:** Simple to install and configure.

Installing Canal:

```
# Deploy Canal
kubectl apply -f https://docs.projectcalico.org/v3.14/
manifests/canal.yaml
```

Romana: Simplified Network and Security Management Romana focuses on simplifying network and security management in Kubernetes clusters. It provides native Layer 3 networking and integrates seamlessly with Kubernetes network policies.

Key Features of Romana:

- **Layer 3 Networking:** Provides native Layer 3 networking without overlays.

- **Network Policies:** Supports Kubernetes network policies.

- **Scalability:** Scales efficiently with cluster size.

Installing Romana:

```
# Deploy Romana
kubectl apply -f https://raw.githubusercontent.com/romana/
romana/master/docs/kubernetes/romana-kubeadm.yml
```

Conclusion Weave, Flannel, Canal, and Romana each provide unique features and benefits that cater to different networking and security requirements in Kubernetes clusters. By understanding the specific capabilities and use cases of each CNI, administrators can select the most appropriate solution to meet their cluster's needs. Whether you require the simplicity and ease of use offered by Weave and Flannel, or the advanced policy enforcement provided by Canal and Romana, these CNIs contribute significantly to the robustness and efficiency of Kubernetes networking.

6.2.5 Comparing CNI Solutions: Use Cases and Performance

When selecting a Container Network Interface (CNI) for a Kubernetes cluster, understanding the strengths, use cases, and performance characteristics of different CNIs is essential. This section provides a comparative analysis of Calico, Cilium, Weave, Flannel, Canal, and Romana to help you make an informed decision based on your specific requirements.

Calico vs. Cilium: Feature Comparison Both Calico and Cilium are advanced CNIs, but they differ in their approach and features:

Calico:

- **Network Policies:** Offers robust, label-based network policies with support for Layer 3 and Layer 7 rules.

- **Performance:** High performance with a focus on Layer 3 routing and efficient IP routing.

- **Scalability:** Designed to scale efficiently with large clusters.

- **Security:** Strong security features, including support for network segmentation and IPsec encryption.

Cilium:

- **eBPF-based Networking:** Utilizes eBPF for high-performance, programmable networking and security policies.

- **API-aware Security:** Enables security policies at the application layer, supporting protocols like HTTP and gRPC.

- **Observability:** Provides deep observability with Hubble, capturing detailed flow logs and metrics.

- **Multi-cluster Support:** Offers advanced multi-cluster networking with Cluster Mesh.

Use Case Comparison: Calico and Cilium

Calico Use Cases:

- **Enterprise Deployments:** Ideal for large-scale enterprise environments requiring robust network policies and scalability.

- **Security-Focused Clusters:** Suitable for clusters where security is a top priority, with features like IPsec and BGP routing.

Cilium Use Cases:

- **High-Performance Workloads:** Best for workloads that require high performance and low latency networking.

- **API-centric Applications:** Perfect for microservices architectures with strict API security requirements.

Weave vs. Flannel: Simplicity and Performance

Weave:

- **Simplicity:** Easy to install and configure with minimal setup.

- **Security:** Provides encryption for network traffic, ensuring data security.

- **Flexibility:** Supports both Layer 2 and Layer 3 networking, suitable for various network setups.

Flannel:

- **Simplicity:** Simple and lightweight, designed for easy deployment and management.

- **Overlay Networking:** Uses VXLAN for creating overlay networks, making it easy to set up.

- **Performance:** Optimized for low overhead and high performance, suitable for smaller to medium-sized clusters.

Use Case Comparison: Weave and Flannel

Weave Use Cases:

- **Small to Medium Clusters:** Ideal for smaller clusters where ease of use and security are key.

- **Flexible Networking Needs:** Suitable for scenarios requiring both Layer 2 and Layer 3 networking.

Flannel Use Cases:

- **Simple Deployments:** Great for environments where simplicity and ease of setup are prioritized.

- **Low Overhead Networking:** Perfect for clusters that require minimal network overhead and high performance.

Canal vs. Romana: Combining Simplicity with Advanced Features

Canal:

- **Integration of Flannel and Calico:** Combines Flannel's simplicity with Calico's advanced network policies.

- **Easy to Deploy:** Simple installation process, making it an excellent choice for straightforward network setups.

- **Robust Security:** Leverages Calico's security features, providing strong network segmentation and policy enforcement.

Romana:

- **Layer 3 Networking:** Focuses on native Layer 3 networking, avoiding the complexities of overlay networks.

- **Scalability:** Designed to scale efficiently with the cluster size, suitable for large deployments.

- **Kubernetes Integration:** Seamlessly integrates with Kubernetes network policies, simplifying network management.

Use Case Comparison: Canal and Romana

Canal Use Cases:

- **Balanced Approach:** Ideal for clusters needing a balance between simplicity and advanced security features.

- **Security and Flexibility:** Suitable for environments requiring robust network policies with minimal configuration.

Romana Use Cases:

- **Large Scale Deployments:** Best for large clusters where native Layer 3 networking is advantageous.

- **Simplified Management:** Perfect for scenarios where straightforward network management and scalability are crucial.

Performance Benchmarks and Considerations

Calico Performance:

- **Scalability Tests:** Demonstrates strong performance in large clusters with thousands of nodes and pods.

- **Network Policy Evaluation:** Efficiently evaluates and enforces network policies, maintaining low latency and high throughput.

Cilium Performance:

- **eBPF Processing:** Utilizes eBPF for high-speed packet processing, reducing CPU overhead and latency.

- **Real-Time Observability:** Provides detailed traffic visibility with Hubble, enhancing monitoring and troubleshooting capabilities.

Weave Performance:

- **Simplicity vs. Overhead:** While easy to use, it may introduce more overhead compared to other CNIs, particularly in large clusters.

- **Encryption Overhead:** Encryption features may impact performance, especially in high-throughput environments.

Flannel Performance:

- **Low Overhead:** Designed for minimal network overhead, making it suitable for performance-sensitive applications.

- **VXLAN Efficiency:** Utilizes VXLAN for overlay networking, providing a balance between simplicity and performance.

Canal Performance:

- **Combined Performance:** Leverages Flannel's simplicity and Calico's policy enforcement, providing a balanced performance profile.

- **Deployment Simplicity:** Easy to deploy and maintain, ensuring efficient network operations without complex configurations.

Romana Performance:

- **Native Layer 3:** Avoids overlay network complexities, enhancing performance and reducing latency.

- **Scalability:** Optimized for large-scale deployments, maintaining high performance and reliability across nodes and pods.

Conclusion Choosing the right CNI depends on your cluster's specific needs, including performance requirements, security considerations, and ease of management. Calico and Cilium are well-suited for environments requiring advanced security and high performance, with Cilium offering additional observability and API-aware features. Weave and Flannel excel in simplicity and ease of use, with Flannel providing a lightweight option for low-overhead networking. Canal offers a hybrid solution combining Flannel's simplicity with Calico's security, while Romana focuses on straightforward Layer 3 networking for scalable deployments.
By understanding these differences, you can select the CNI that best aligns with your Kubernetes cluster's goals and operational requirements.

6.2.6 Customizing and Extending CNI

Customizing and extending a Container Network Interface (CNI) is essential for tailoring Kubernetes networking to specific use cases and enhancing cluster performance, security, and observability. This section explores how to customize CNIs, integrate additional features, and extend their functionality to meet specialized requirements.

Understanding CNI Customization Customization involves configuring the CNI to meet specific networking needs, such as adjusting IP address ranges, enabling specific features, or integrating with existing network infrastructure. Most CNIs provide configuration options through ConfigMaps, environment variables, and command-line parameters.

General Customization Steps:

- **Configuration Files:** Modify configuration files such as ConfigMaps to adjust settings like IP ranges, backend types, and policy options.

- **Environment Variables:** Set environment variables to enable or disable specific features during CNI initialization.

- **Command-line Parameters:** Use command-line parameters when deploying CNI components to customize behavior.

Customizing Calico Calico provides extensive customization options through its configuration files and command-line tools. Key customization areas include IP address management, network policies, and BGP settings.

IP Address Management:

```
# Calico IP pool configuration
apiVersion: crd.projectcalico.org/v1
kind: IPPool
metadata:
  name: custom-ipv4-ippool
spec:
  cidr: 10.0.0.0/16
  ipipMode: Never
  natOutgoing: true
```

Network Policies: Customize network policies to enforce specific traffic rules between pods.

```
apiVersion: networking.k8s.io/v1
kind: NetworkPolicy
metadata:
  name: custom-network-policy
  namespace: default
spec:
  podSelector:
    matchLabels:
      role: backend
  ingress:
  - from:
    - podSelector:
        matchLabels:
```

```
        role: frontend
  ports:
  - protocol: TCP
    port: 8080
```

BGP Settings: Configure BGP peering for advanced routing scenarios.

```
apiVersion: projectcalico.org/v3
kind: BGPPeer
metadata:
  name: bgp-peer
spec:
  peerIP: 192.168.0.1
  asNumber: 64512
```

Customizing Cilium Cilium's customization leverages eBPF, allowing for highly programmable networking. Key areas of customization include IP allocation, network policies, and Hubble observability.

IP Allocation: Adjust IP allocation settings to fit your network requirements.

```
# Cilium IPAM configuration
apiVersion: cilium.io/v2
kind: CiliumNode
metadata:
  name: node1
spec:
  ipam:
    podCIDR: 10.0.0.0/16
```

Network Policies: Define granular, API-aware network policies.

```
apiVersion: cilium.io/v2
kind: CiliumNetworkPolicy
metadata:
  name: api-policy
spec:
```

```
endpointSelector:
  matchLabels:
    app: myapp
ingress:
- fromEndpoints:
  - matchLabels:
      app: frontend
  toPorts:
  - ports:
    - port: "80"
      protocol: TCP
    rules:
      http:
      - method: "GET"
        path: "/api/v1/.*"
```

Hubble Observability: Customize Hubble for detailed traffic observability.

```
# Enable Hubble metrics
cilium hubble enable
```

Extending CNIs with Additional Features Extending CNIs involves integrating additional tools and features to enhance functionality. This can include adding support for service meshes, leveraging external monitoring tools, or implementing custom plugins.

Service Mesh Integration: Integrate CNIs with service meshes like Istio or Linkerd for advanced traffic management and observability.

```
# Example of integrating Istio with CNI
kubectl label namespace default istio-injection=enabled
kubectl apply -f istio-manifest.yaml
```

Monitoring and Logging: Extend CNIs with external monitoring and logging tools such as Prometheus, Grafana, and ELK stack.

```
# Example Prometheus configuration for monitoring CNI
scrape_configs:
  - job_name: 'cni-metrics'
    static_configs:
      - targets: ['<cni-metrics-endpoint>:9090']
```

Custom Plugins: Develop and deploy custom plugins to add specialized networking functionality.

```
# Example of deploying a custom CNI plugin
kubectl apply -f custom-cni-plugin.yaml
```

Conclusion Customizing and extending CNIs in Kubernetes allows administrators to tailor the networking stack to their specific requirements, enhancing performance, security, and functionality. By leveraging the customization options and extension capabilities of CNIs like Calico and Cilium, clusters can achieve optimal networking configurations suited to their operational needs. Whether through fine-tuning configurations, integrating with service meshes, or adding custom plugins, these modifications can significantly improve the effectiveness and efficiency of Kubernetes networking.

6.3   Service Mesh

6.3.1   Introduction to Service Mesh

A service mesh is a dedicated infrastructure layer that controls service-to-service communication within a microservices architecture. It provides a way to manage a large number of microservices with various features like load balancing, service discovery, traffic management, security, and observability. This section introduces the core concepts of service meshes, their benefits, and how they integrate with Kubernetes.

Core Concepts of Service Mesh At its core, a service mesh consists of a data plane and a control plane. The data plane is responsible for handling the communication between services, while the control plane manages and configures the proxies that handle this communication.

Data Plane: The data plane consists of lightweight proxies deployed alongside each service instance. These proxies intercept all incoming and outgoing network traffic between services, applying various policies such as load balancing, retries, and circuit breaking.

Control Plane: The control plane manages the configuration of the proxies. It provides APIs to define and enforce policies, monitor traffic, and gather telemetry data. The control plane ensures that the proxies in the data plane are consistently configured and updated.

Benefits of a Service Mesh A service mesh provides several key benefits that are particularly valuable in microservices architectures:

Traffic Management: Service meshes offer advanced traffic management capabilities, including load balancing, traffic splitting, retries, and circuit breaking. This ensures reliable and efficient communication between services.

Security: By managing service-to-service communication, a service mesh can enforce security policies such as mutual TLS (mTLS) for encrypting traffic, authentication, and authorization. This enhances the security of inter-service communication.

Observability: Service meshes provide deep observability into the interactions between services. They collect telemetry data such as metrics, logs, and traces, which can be used for monitoring and debugging. This data is critical for understanding the behavior and performance of microservices.

Reliability: Features like retries, timeouts, and circuit breaking improve the reliability and resilience of services. These mechanisms help to gracefully handle failures and ensure that services remain available and responsive.

Service Discovery: Service meshes facilitate service discovery by dynamically maintaining an up-to-date map of available services and their endpoints. This allows services to find and communicate with each other without hardcoding service locations.

Service Mesh Architecture   A typical service mesh architecture includes the following components:

Sidecar Proxies: Each microservice instance is paired with a sidecar proxy, which handles all network traffic to and from the service. The sidecar proxy enforces the policies defined in the control plane.

Ingress and Egress Proxies: In addition to sidecar proxies, a service mesh may include ingress and egress proxies to manage traffic entering and leaving the mesh. These proxies enforce policies at the boundaries of the service mesh.

Control Plane Components: The control plane consists of several components that manage configuration, policy enforcement, and telemetry collection. These components ensure that the data plane proxies are properly configured and functioning correctly.

Popular Service Mesh Implementations   Several service mesh implementations are widely used in the Kubernetes ecosystem, each offering unique features and capabilities:

Istio: Istio is a feature-rich service mesh that provides comprehensive traffic management, security, and observability. It integrates seamlessly with Kubernetes and offers a robust set of tools for managing microservices.

Linkerd: Linkerd is a lightweight and performance-focused service mesh designed for simplicity and ease of use. It offers essential features like mTLS, observability, and traffic management with minimal configuration overhead.

Consul: Consul is a service mesh that focuses on service discovery, configuration, and segmentation. It provides a powerful control plane for managing microservices across diverse environments.

Conclusion   A service mesh is a critical component for managing microservices in Kubernetes. By providing advanced traffic management, security, and observability, service meshes help ensure that microservices can communicate reliably and securely. Understanding the core concepts and benefits of service meshes is essential for effectively deploying and managing microservices in Kubernetes environments.

6.3.2 Istio: Features and Components

Istio is one of the most comprehensive and widely adopted service mesh implementations in the Kubernetes ecosystem. It provides a robust set of features designed to manage the complexities of microservice-based architectures, offering advanced traffic management, security, and observability. This section delves into the various features and components of Istio, providing a detailed overview of its capabilities and how it integrates with Kubernetes.

Overview of Istio Istio enhances the microservices architecture by abstracting the service-to-service communication, making it more manageable and secure. It decouples the network concerns from the application logic, enabling developers to focus on core functionalities while Istio handles the networking aspects.

Key Features of Istio Istio's feature set includes traffic management, security, observability, and extensibility. Each feature area is supported by specific components and configurations, allowing for fine-grained control over the service mesh.

Traffic Management Traffic management in Istio provides tools to control the flow of traffic between services, ensuring reliability and flexibility in handling requests.

Routing: Istio allows for advanced routing rules to manage traffic flow based on various attributes such as HTTP headers, URI paths, and weights. This enables canary deployments, A/B testing, and traffic splitting.

```
# Example of Istio VirtualService for routing traffic
apiVersion: networking.istio.io/v1alpha3
kind: VirtualService
metadata:
```

```
  name: my-service
spec:
  hosts:
  - my-service
  http:
  - match:
    - uri:
        prefix: /test
    route:
    - destination:
        host: my-service
        subset: v2
  - route:
    - destination:
        host: my-service
        subset: v1
```

Load Balancing: Istio supports various load balancing strategies, including round-robin, least connections, and random. It ensures efficient distribution of traffic across service instances.

Fault Injection: Fault injection allows for the simulation of failures to test the resilience of services. This includes introducing delays, aborts, and other errors into the network path.

Traffic Shifting: Traffic shifting enables gradual rollout of new versions by directing a percentage of traffic to the new version while keeping the rest on the old version. This is critical for safe and controlled deployments.

Security Istio provides robust security features to protect service-to-service communication and ensure secure operations within the service mesh.

Mutual TLS (mTLS): Istio supports mutual TLS to encrypt traffic between services and authenticate service identities. This ensures that communication is secure and trusted.

```
# Example of enabling mTLS in Istio
apiVersion: security.istio.io/v1beta1
kind: PeerAuthentication
metadata:
  name: default
  namespace: istio-system
spec:
  mtls:
    mode: STRICT
```

Authentication and Authorization: Istio integrates with external identity providers to enforce authentication and authorization policies. This includes role-based access control (RBAC) and JWT token validation.

Security Policies: Istio allows the definition of security policies to enforce who can communicate with whom. This is crucial for ensuring compliance with security standards and protecting sensitive data.

Observability Istio enhances observability by providing detailed insights into the behavior and performance of services within the mesh.

Telemetry Collection: Istio collects telemetry data such as metrics, logs, and traces from the services within the mesh. This data is essential for monitoring and troubleshooting.

Distributed Tracing: Distributed tracing allows for the tracking of requests as they flow through various services. This helps in identifying bottlenecks and understanding the dependencies between services.

Logging: Istio integrates with logging systems to capture and store logs from services, making it easier to diagnose issues and understand application behavior.

Extensibility Istio's architecture is designed to be extensible, allowing for the addition of custom policies and plugins.

Envoy Proxy: Istio uses Envoy as the default data plane proxy. Envoy is highly extensible and supports a wide range of filters and plugins to enhance its capabilities.

Mixer: Mixer is the component responsible for enforcing policies and collecting telemetry data. It can be extended with custom adapters to integrate with external systems.

WebAssembly (Wasm): Istio supports WebAssembly for extending the functionality of the Envoy proxy. This enables the development of custom filters and plugins using a portable and safe runtime.

Istio Components Istio's architecture consists of several key components that work together to provide its powerful features. Understanding these components is essential for effectively deploying and managing Istio.

Pilot: Pilot provides service discovery, configuration, and certificate management. It translates high-level routing rules into configurations that Envoy proxies can understand.

Citadel: Citadel handles security and identity management within the mesh. It issues and rotates certificates for service identities, enabling mutual TLS and secure communication.

Galley: Galley is responsible for validating and distributing configuration to the other components. It ensures that configurations are correct and consistent across the mesh.

Envoy: Envoy is the default data plane proxy used by Istio. It intercepts and routes all traffic between services, applying the policies and configurations defined in the control plane.

Deploying Istio Deploying Istio involves installing its components and configuring the mesh to manage traffic, enforce security, and collect telemetry. The installation can be done using the Istio CLI or Helm charts.

Installation Steps:

```
# Install Istio using Istioctl
istioctl install --set profile=demo

# Verify the installation
kubectl get pods -n istio-system
```

Configuring Istio   After installation, Istio can be configured to manage traffic, enforce security, and collect telemetry.   This involves defining resources such as VirtualServices, DestinationRules, and Gateway objects.

Example Configuration:

```
# Define a VirtualService for routing traffic
apiVersion: networking.istio.io/v1alpha3
kind: VirtualService
metadata:
  name: my-service
spec:
  hosts:
  - my-service
  http:
  - route:
    - destination:
        host: my-service
        subset: v1
```

Monitoring and Managing Istio   Istio provides tools for monitoring and managing the service mesh.   This includes the Kiali dashboard for visualizing the mesh, Prometheus for metrics collection, and Grafana for metrics visualization.

Kiali: Kiali provides an interactive dashboard for visualizing the service mesh, showing the relationships between services and their health status.

Prometheus and Grafana: Prometheus collects metrics from Istio components and services, while Grafana provides dashboards for visualizing these metrics.

Jaeger: Jaeger is used for distributed tracing, allowing you to trace the flow of requests through the services in the mesh.

Conclusion Istio is a powerful service mesh that offers comprehensive features for traffic management, security, and observability. Its robust architecture and rich set of tools make it an excellent choice for managing microservices in Kubernetes. By understanding its features and components, administrators can effectively deploy and manage Istio to enhance the reliability, security, and performance of their applications.

6.3.3   Linkerd and Other Alternatives

While Istio is one of the most comprehensive service meshes, several other alternatives offer unique features and benefits. This section explores Linkerd and other notable service mesh solutions, including Cilium's service mesh capabilities. Each service mesh has its own strengths and use cases, providing a range of options for managing service-to-service communication in Kubernetes.

Linkerd: Lightweight and Performance-focused Linkerd is a lightweight, open-source service mesh designed to be simple and performance-oriented. It provides essential features for observability, security, and reliability, making it a popular choice for organizations seeking an easy-to-use service mesh.

Key Features of Linkerd:

- **Simplicity:** Designed for ease of installation and use, with minimal configuration required.

- **Performance:** Optimized for low latency and high throughput, making it suitable for performance-sensitive applications.

- **Security:** Provides mutual TLS (mTLS) for secure communication between services.

- **Observability:** Includes built-in tools for monitoring and diagnostics, such as Tap and Top for real-time data.

Components of Linkerd Linkerd's architecture consists of a control plane and a data plane, similar to other service meshes. The control plane manages configuration and policy enforcement, while the data plane handles the actual traffic between services.

Control Plane: The control plane components include the controller, proxy injector, and identity service. These components manage the configuration of the data plane proxies and ensure secure communication.

Data Plane: The data plane consists of lightweight proxies deployed alongside each service instance. These proxies intercept and route traffic, applying policies and collecting telemetry data.

Installing Linkerd Installing Linkerd is straightforward, typically done using the Linkerd CLI. The installation process sets up the control plane components and injects the data plane proxies into the service pods.

Installation Steps:

```
# Install the Linkerd CLI
curl -sL https://run.linkerd.io/install | sh

# Install the Linkerd control plane
linkerd install | kubectl apply -f -

# Verify the installation
linkerd check
```

Configuring Linkerd After installation, Linkerd can be configured to manage traffic, enforce security policies, and collect telemetry. Configuration is typically done through Kubernetes manifests and the Linkerd CLI.

Example Configuration:

```
# Inject Linkerd proxy into a deployment
kubectl get -n default deploy/my-deployment -o yaml |
linkerdinject - | kubectl apply -f -
```

Observability with Linkerd Linkerd includes several tools for monitoring and diagnostics, providing real-time visibility into the service mesh.

Linkerd Dashboard: The Linkerd dashboard offers a web-based interface for visualizing the health and performance of services within the mesh.

Linkerd CLI Tools: Tools like Tap and Top provide real-time data on service communication and performance, helping administrators troubleshoot issues quickly.

Cilium's Service Mesh Capabilities Cilium, primarily known for its advanced networking and security features, also offers service mesh capabilities. Leveraging eBPF, Cilium provides high-performance, transparent service mesh functionality integrated directly into the Linux kernel.

Key Features of Cilium's Service Mesh:

- **eBPF-based Performance:** Utilizes eBPF for efficient packet processing and policy enforcement.

- **API-aware Security:** Supports API-aware security policies, enhancing traditional network policies.

- **Transparent Encryption:** Provides transparent encryption for service-to-service communication.

- **Observability:** Integrates with Hubble for detailed observability and monitoring.

Installing and Configuring Cilium Service Mesh Cilium's service mesh capabilities can be enabled as part of its standard installation process. Configuration is typically done through Kubernetes manifests and the Cilium CLI.

Installation Steps:

```
# Install Cilium with service mesh enabled
cilium install --config enable-envoy-config=true

# Verify the installation
cilium status
```

Other Service Mesh Alternatives In addition to Istio, Linkerd, and Cilium, several other service mesh solutions are worth considering:

Consul: Consul by HashiCorp provides service discovery, configuration, and segmentation. It integrates seamlessly with Kubernetes and supports advanced traffic management and security features.

AWS App Mesh: AWS App Mesh is a managed service mesh offering by Amazon Web Services. It provides seamless integration with AWS services and simplifies the management of microservices on AWS.

Kuma: Kuma, developed by Kong, is a universal control plane for service meshes. It supports both Kubernetes and non-Kubernetes environments, offering a flexible and scalable solution for service mesh management.

Conclusion Choosing the right service mesh involves evaluating the specific needs of your application and environment. Istio provides comprehensive features and flexibility, making it suitable for complex environments. Linkerd offers simplicity and performance, ideal for those seeking an easy-to-use solution. Cilium brings advanced networking and security capabilities to the service mesh, leveraging eBPF for high performance. Other alternatives like Consul, AWS App Mesh, and Kuma provide additional options tailored to various use cases and cloud environments.

By understanding the strengths and capabilities of each service mesh, you can select the solution that best fits your operational requirements and enhances the reliability, security, and observability of your microservices architecture.

6.3.4 Integrating Service Mesh in Kubernetes

Integrating a service mesh into a Kubernetes environment involves deploying the service mesh components, configuring the mesh, and adapting existing applications to leverage the mesh's features. This section outlines the general steps and considerations for integrating a service mesh like Istio, Linkerd, or Cilium into a Kubernetes cluster.

Prerequisites for Integration Before integrating a service mesh, ensure that your Kubernetes cluster meets the following prerequisites:

- **Kubernetes Version:** Verify that your Kubernetes cluster is running a version compatible with the service mesh you intend to use.

- **Cluster Access:** Ensure you have administrative access to the Kubernetes cluster to deploy and configure the service mesh components.

- **Resources:** Confirm that your cluster has sufficient resources (CPU, memory, and storage) to accommodate the service mesh components.

Installing the Service Mesh The first step in integrating a service mesh is to install its control plane and data plane components. This process varies slightly depending on the service mesh chosen. Here, we provide examples for Istio, Linkerd, and Cilium.

Installing Istio:

```
# Download and install Istio CLI
curl -L https://istio.io/downloadIstio |
ISTIO_VERSION=1.9.0 sh -

# Change to the Istio package directory
cd istio-1.9.0

# Install Istio with the demo profile
istioctl install --set profile=demo

# Verify the installation
kubectl get pods -n istio-system
```

Installing Linkerd:

```
# Install the Linkerd CLI
curl -sL https://run.linkerd.io/install | sh

# Install the Linkerd control plane
linkerd install | kubectl apply -f -

# Verify the installation
linkerd check
```

Installing Cilium with Service Mesh:

```
# Install Cilium with service mesh capabilities
cilium install --config enable-envoy-config=true

# Verify the installation
cilium status
```

Configuring the Service Mesh After installation, the service mesh needs to be configured to manage traffic, enforce security, and collect telemetry. Configuration typically involves defining resources like VirtualServices, DestinationRules, and NetworkPolicies.

Configuring Istio:

```
# Define a VirtualService for routing traffic
apiVersion: networking.istio.io/v1alpha3
kind: VirtualService
metadata:
  name: my-service
spec:
  hosts:
  - my-service
  http:
  - route:
    - destination:
        host: my-service
        subset: v1
```

Configuring Linkerd:

```
# Inject Linkerd proxy into a deployment
kubectl get -n default deploy/my-deployment -o yaml |
linkerd inject - | kubectl apply -f -
```

Configuring Cilium:

```
# Example of Cilium NetworkPolicy
apiVersion: cilium.io/v2
kind: CiliumNetworkPolicy
metadata:
  name: allow-frontend-to-backend
  namespace: default
spec:
  endpointSelector:
    matchLabels:
      app: backend
  ingress:
  - fromEndpoints:
    - matchLabels:
        app: frontend
    toPorts:
    - ports:
      - port: "80"
        protocol: TCP
```

Adapting Applications   Integrating a service mesh often requires changes to existing applications. This includes modifying deployment manifests to include sidecar proxies and configuring applications to take advantage of service mesh features.

Injecting Sidecar Proxies: Most service meshes use sidecar proxies to handle traffic to and from services. Injecting these proxies can be done manually or automatically.

Manual Injection:

```
# Manually inject an Istio sidecar proxy
istioctl kube-inject -f deployment.yaml | kubectl apply -f -
```

Automatic Injection:

```
# Enable automatic sidecar injection for a namespace in Linkerd
kubectl label namespace default linkerd.io/inject=enabled
```

Managing Traffic and Security   Once integrated, the service mesh can manage traffic routing, load balancing, retries, and security policies. Configurations are typically defined in Kubernetes custom resources specific to the service mesh.

Traffic Management in Istio:

```
# Define traffic routing rules
apiVersion: networking.istio.io/v1alpha3
kind: VirtualService
metadata:
  name: my-service
spec:
  hosts:
  - my-service
  http:
  - match:
    - uri:
        prefix: /v2
    route:
    - destination:
        host: my-service
        subset: v2
  - route:
    - destination:
        host: my-service
        subset: v1
```

Security Policies in Linkerd:

```
# Define a Linkerd policy for mTLS
apiVersion: policy.linkerd.io/v1alpha1
kind: MeshTLS
metadata:
  name: default
  namespace: default
spec:
  mtls:
    mode: STRICT
```

Observability and Monitoring   Integrating a service mesh also enhances observability. Most service meshes provide built-in tools and integrations with monitoring systems.

Observability in Istio: Istio integrates with tools like Prometheus, Grafana, and Jaeger to provide metrics, logs, and traces.

Prometheus and Grafana:

```
# Add Istio metrics to Prometheus
kubectl apply -f prometheus-istio.yaml

# Add Grafana dashboards for Istio
kubectl apply -f grafana-istio.yaml
```

Observability in Linkerd: Linkerd provides its own dashboard and CLI tools for real-time observability.

Linkerd Dashboard:

```
# Launch the Linkerd dashboard
linkerd dashboard
```

Conclusion   Integrating a service mesh into a Kubernetes environment involves installing the service mesh components, configuring the mesh, and adapting existing applications. Service meshes like Istio, Linkerd, and Cilium provide powerful tools for managing traffic, enhancing security, and improving observability. By following the steps outlined in this section, you can successfully integrate a service mesh into your Kubernetes cluster, leveraging its features to improve the reliability, security, and performance of your microservices architecture.

6.3.5 Monitoring and Tracing with Service Mesh

Monitoring and tracing are critical components of maintaining a healthy and performant microservices architecture. Service meshes provide robust observability tools that offer deep insights into the behavior and performance of services within the mesh. This section explores the monitoring and tracing capabilities provided by service meshes like Istio, Linkerd, and Cilium, detailing how to leverage these features to gain comprehensive visibility into your applications.

Overview of Monitoring and Tracing in Service Meshes Service meshes enhance observability by collecting and exposing metrics, logs, and traces from the services they manage. These observability tools help administrators monitor the health of the services, understand traffic patterns, and diagnose issues.

Metrics Collection Metrics provide quantitative data about the performance and health of services. Service meshes typically collect metrics such as request rates, error rates, and latency, and integrate with monitoring tools like Prometheus and Grafana.

Metrics in Istio: Istio collects a wide range of metrics using Envoy proxies, which are then exposed to Prometheus for scraping. These metrics include HTTP request and response counts, latency, and gRPC metrics.

```
# Example Prometheus configuration for scraping Istio metrics
scrape_configs:
  - job_name: 'istio'
    static_configs:
      - targets: ['<istio-metrics-endpoint>']
```

Grafana Dashboards: Grafana can be configured to visualize the metrics collected by Prometheus, providing a comprehensive view of service performance.

```
# Deploy Grafana with Istio dashboards
kubectl apply -f https://raw.githubusercontent.com/istio/istio/
release-1.9/samples/addons/grafana.yaml
```

Metrics in Linkerd: Linkerd collects similar metrics using its own proxies and provides a built-in Prometheus instance for metrics collection.

```
# Access Linkerd metrics
linkerd stat deploy --namespace default
```

Tracing Tracing allows for the tracking of individual requests as they propagate through various services. This is crucial for understanding the flow of requests, identifying bottlenecks, and diagnosing performance issues.

Distributed Tracing in Istio: Istio integrates with tracing systems like Jaeger and Zipkin to provide detailed traces of requests. Traces capture the path of a request, including each service it interacts with and the latency at each hop.

```
# Deploy Jaeger for tracing
kubectl apply -f https://raw.githubusercontent.com/istio/
istio/release-1.9/samples/addons/jaeger.yaml
```

Using Jaeger: Jaeger provides a web-based interface for viewing and analyzing traces. It allows you to search for traces, view the service call graph, and analyze the latency of each span.

Distributed Tracing in Linkerd: Linkerd also supports distributed tracing and integrates with systems like Jaeger. Linkerd's proxies automatically generate trace spans for requests passing through the mesh.

```
# Enable tracing in Linkerd
linkerd install --set tracing.enabled=true | kubectl apply -f -
```

Log Collection and Analysis   Logs provide detailed records of events and errors that occur within services. Service meshes capture logs from proxies and services, which can be integrated with logging systems like the ELK stack (Elasticsearch, Logstash, Kibana) or Fluentd.

Log Collection in Istio: Istio proxies (Envoy) generate access logs that can be shipped to logging systems for analysis.

```
# Example Fluentd configuration for collecting Istio logs
<source>
  @type tail
  path /var/log/istio/*.log
  pos_file /var/log/td-agent/istio.pos
  tag istio.access
  format none
</source>
```

Log Analysis with Kibana: Kibana can be used to visualize and search through logs collected by Elasticsearch, providing insights into the behavior and errors within the mesh.

Advanced Observability with Cilium and Hubble   Cilium leverages eBPF for advanced observability, with Hubble providing real-time monitoring and visibility into network traffic and service interactions.

Hubble Metrics and Logs: Hubble captures detailed flow logs, metrics, and trace data, offering deep insights into the network behavior of services.

```
# Enable Hubble observability
cilium hubble enable --ui
```

```
# Access Hubble UI
cilium hubble port-forward --ui
```

Using Hubble for Observability: Hubble provides various tools for observing and troubleshooting network traffic within the cluster. Common commands include:

```
# View network flows in real-time
hubble observe

# Get a summary of network flows
hubble status

# View service map
hubble service list
```

Best Practices for Monitoring and Tracing Implementing best practices for monitoring and tracing helps ensure comprehensive observability and effective troubleshooting.

Define Clear Metrics: Identify and define key performance indicators (KPIs) for your services. Collect metrics that provide insights into these KPIs.

Regular Monitoring: Continuously monitor the health and performance of services using dashboards and alerts. Regularly review logs and traces to detect and address issues promptly.

Integrate with CI/CD: Integrate monitoring and tracing into your CI/CD pipeline to ensure that new deployments do not introduce performance regressions or errors.

Leverage Automation: Use automation tools to deploy and configure observability components, ensuring consistent and repeatable setups across environments.

Conclusion Monitoring and tracing are essential for maintaining the health and performance of microservices in a Kubernetes environment. Service meshes like Istio, Linkerd, and Cilium provide robust tools for collecting and analyzing metrics, logs, and traces. By leveraging these capabilities, administrators can gain comprehensive visibility into their services, quickly diagnose issues, and ensure that their applications run smoothly and efficiently.

6.4 Network Policies

6.4.1 Basics of Network Policies

Network policies in Kubernetes provide a way to control the communication between pods within a cluster. By defining rules that specify how pods are allowed to communicate with each other and with external endpoints, network policies enhance the security and manageability of Kubernetes clusters. This section covers the basics of network policies, including their components, creation, and enforcement.

What are Network Policies? Network policies are Kubernetes resources that use labels to select pods and define rules about how those pods can communicate with each other and with other network endpoints. They are implemented by network plugins, such as Calico, Cilium, and others, which enforce the policies across the network.

Components of a Network Policy A network policy in Kubernetes consists of several key components:

Pod Selector: The pod selector specifies the pods to which the network policy applies. It uses labels to select the targeted pods.

Ingress and Egress Rules: Network policies can define ingress (incoming) and egress (outgoing) rules. These rules specify the allowed or denied traffic based on criteria such as pod labels, namespaces, IP blocks, and ports.

Policy Types: The policy types indicate whether the network policy applies to ingress, egress, or both. By default, a network policy applies to ingress traffic if no policy type is specified.

Creating a Basic Network Policy Creating a network policy involves defining a YAML manifest that specifies the pod selector, ingress and/or egress rules, and other relevant parameters.

Example Network Policy: The following example demonstrates a simple network policy that allows traffic to a set of pods labeled 'role=db' only from pods labeled 'role=frontend' within the same namespace.

```
apiVersion: networking.k8s.io/v1
kind: NetworkPolicy
metadata:
  name: allow-frontend-to-db
  namespace: default
spec:
  podSelector:
    matchLabels:
      role: db
  policyTypes:
  - Ingress
  ingress:
  - from:
    - podSelector:
        matchLabels:
          role: frontend
    ports:
    - protocol: TCP
      port: 5432
```

In this example, the 'podSelector' selects pods with the label 'role=db'. The 'policyTypes' field specifies that the policy applies to ingress traffic. The 'ingress' rule allows traffic from pods labeled 'role=frontend' on port 5432.

Enforcing Network Policies Network policies are enforced by the network plugin used in the Kubernetes cluster. Different plugins offer varying levels of support and features for network policies.

Calico: Calico provides robust support for Kubernetes network policies, including advanced features like global network policies and policy tiers.

Cilium: Cilium enhances network policies with API-aware capabilities and supports advanced features like DNS-based policies and L7 filtering.

Weave Net: Weave Net supports basic Kubernetes network policies and integrates seamlessly with the Kubernetes network policy API.

Default Behavior and Policy Application   By default, if no network policies are applied to a pod, it can communicate with any other pod in the cluster. Once a network policy is applied to a pod, the default behavior changes to deny all traffic that is not explicitly allowed by the policy.

Default Deny Policy: To ensure a secure baseline, it is common to create a "default deny" policy that denies all traffic except that which is explicitly allowed by other network policies.

```
apiVersion: networking.k8s.io/v1
kind: NetworkPolicy
metadata:
  name: default-deny
  namespace: default
spec:
  podSelector: {}
  policyTypes:
  - Ingress
  - Egress
```

In this example, the 'podSelector' selects all pods in the namespace, and the 'policyTypes' field specifies that both ingress and egress traffic are denied by default.

Best Practices for Using Network Policies   Implementing best practices for network policies helps ensure a secure and well-managed Kubernetes environment.

Start with Least Privilege: Begin with a "default deny" policy and then add specific policies to allow necessary traffic. This approach minimizes the attack surface by denying all unnecessary traffic.

Use Namespaces for Isolation: Leverage namespaces to isolate different environments (e.g., development, staging, production) and apply network policies to enforce strict communication boundaries.

Monitor and Audit Policies: Regularly monitor and audit network policies to ensure they are effective and up-to-date. Use tools and logs provided by the network plugin to verify that policies are being enforced as intended.

Document and Version Control Policies: Document network policies and manage them using version control to track changes and facilitate collaboration among team members.

Conclusion Network policies are a powerful tool for controlling communication between pods in a Kubernetes cluster. By understanding and implementing network policies, administrators can enhance the security and manageability of their clusters. Leveraging best practices and regularly reviewing policies ensures that the network remains secure and efficient.

6.4.2 Policy Types and their Use Cases

Kubernetes network policies define how pods communicate with each other and with other network endpoints. There are two main types of network policies: ingress and egress. Each policy type has specific use cases and configurations, which help secure and manage network traffic within a Kubernetes cluster.

Ingress Policies Ingress policies control incoming traffic to pods. They define which sources are allowed to send traffic to the selected pods, specifying rules based on pod labels, namespaces, IP blocks, and ports.

Key Features of Ingress Policies:

- Control incoming traffic to pods.

- Define rules based on sources (pods, namespaces, IP blocks).

- Specify allowed ports and protocols.

Use Cases for Ingress Policies:

- **Restricting Access:** Limit access to sensitive applications or databases to only specific frontend services or namespaces.

- **Enforcing Security Boundaries:** Create boundaries between different application tiers, such as allowing traffic from web servers to application servers but not directly to databases.

- **Isolating Environments:** Ensure that traffic between development, staging, and production environments is strictly controlled.

Example Ingress Policy: The following example from the previous section shows an ingress policy that allows traffic to pods labeled 'role=db' only from pods labeled 'role=frontend' within the same namespace.

```
apiVersion: networking.k8s.io/v1
kind: NetworkPolicy
metadata:
  name: allow-frontend-to-db
  namespace: default
spec:
  podSelector:
    matchLabels:
      role: db
  policyTypes:
  - Ingress
  ingress:
  - from:
    - podSelector:
        matchLabels:
          role: frontend
    ports:
    - protocol: TCP
      port: 5432
```

Egress Policies Egress policies control outgoing traffic from pods. They define which destinations the selected pods are allowed to send traffic to, specifying rules based on destination pod labels, namespaces, IP blocks, and ports.

Key Features of Egress Policies:

- Control outgoing traffic from pods.

- Define rules based on destinations (pods, namespaces, IP blocks).

- Specify allowed ports and protocols.

Use Cases for Egress Policies:

- **Restricting External Access:** Limit pods' access to external networks to prevent unauthorized data exfiltration.

- **Controlling Service Dependencies:** Ensure that services only communicate with approved external APIs or services.

- **Enforcing Compliance:** Maintain compliance with security policies by restricting pods' ability to send data outside the cluster.

Example Egress Policy: The following example shows an egress policy that allows pods to communicate only with an external database server at a specific IP address.

```
apiVersion: networking.k8s.io/v1
kind: NetworkPolicy
metadata:
  name: allow-to-external-db
  namespace: default
spec:
  podSelector: {}
  policyTypes:
  - Egress
  egress:
  - to:
    - ipBlock:
        cidr: 192.168.1.100/32
    ports:
    - protocol: TCP
      port: 3306
```

Combining Ingress and Egress Policies   Network policies can combine both ingress and egress rules to define comprehensive security controls for pods. This ensures that traffic is tightly controlled in both directions, enhancing overall security.

Use Cases for Combined Policies:

- **Isolating Critical Applications:** Ensure that critical applications can only communicate with specific internal and external services.

- **Implementing Zero Trust Networks:** Apply zero trust principles by strictly controlling all ingress and egress traffic to and from pods.

- **Enhancing Defense in Depth:** Create layered security controls by combining ingress and egress policies with other security mechanisms.

Example Combined Policy: The following example demonstrates a network policy that allows ingress traffic from specific pods and egress traffic to a specific external IP.

```
apiVersion: networking.k8s.io/v1
kind: NetworkPolicy
metadata:
  name: allow-specific-traffic
  namespace: default
spec:
  podSelector:
    matchLabels:
      role: app
  policyTypes:
  - Ingress
  - Egress
  ingress:
  - from:
    - podSelector:
        matchLabels:
          role: frontend
    ports:
    - protocol: TCP
```

```
    port: 80
egress:
- to:
  - ipBlock:
      cidr: 192.168.1.100/32
  ports:
  - protocol: TCP
    port: 8080
```

Best Practices for Using Network Policies   To effectively implement and manage network policies, consider the following best practices:

Define Clear Policies: Clearly define and document the network policies to ensure they align with your security requirements and operational goals.

Start with Least Privilege: Begin with restrictive policies and gradually open up access as needed. This minimizes the attack surface and helps enforce security best practices.

Regularly Review and Update Policies: Continuously monitor and review network policies to ensure they remain effective and up-to-date with changing security needs.

Test Policies Thoroughly: Test network policies in a controlled environment before applying them to production clusters to avoid unintended disruptions.

Conclusion   Understanding the different types of network policies and their use cases is essential for securing Kubernetes clusters. Ingress and egress policies provide granular control over traffic, helping to enforce security boundaries and manage communication between pods effectively. By following best practices and carefully defining policies, administrators can enhance the security and reliability of their Kubernetes environments.

6.4.3   Best Practices in Defining Policies

Defining effective network policies in Kubernetes is crucial for ensuring the security, reliability, and manageability of your cluster. Adhering to best practices when creating and managing these policies can help mitigate risks and optimize network performance. This section provides detailed best practices for defining network policies, covering principles, implementation strategies, and maintenance tips.

Principles of Network Policy Design   The design of network policies should be guided by fundamental security principles that ensure robust protection and efficient network management.

Principle of Least Privilege: The principle of least privilege states that components should only have the access necessary to perform their functions. This minimizes the potential attack surface and limits the impact of any security breaches.

Separation of Concerns: Separate different types of traffic (e.g., internal, external, management) and apply appropriate policies to each category. This separation enhances security and simplifies policy management.

Defense in Depth: Implement multiple layers of security controls to protect against potential threats. Network policies are one layer, complemented by other measures such as authentication, encryption, and monitoring.

Implementation Strategies   Implementing network policies effectively involves careful planning, consistent application, and thorough testing.

Start with Default Deny Policies: Begin with a default deny policy to block all traffic by default. This creates a secure baseline and ensures that only explicitly allowed traffic can flow between pods.

```yaml
apiVersion: networking.k8s.io/v1
kind: NetworkPolicy
metadata:
```

```
  name: default-deny
  namespace: default
spec:
  podSelector: {}
  policyTypes:
  - Ingress
  - Egress
```

Gradually Open Up Access: After establishing a default deny policy, gradually open up access by defining specific network policies that allow necessary traffic. This approach helps to minimize exposure and ensure tight control over network communications.

Use Labels and Selectors Effectively: Utilize pod labels and selectors to define precise policies. Labels should be well-organized and consistently applied across the cluster to ensure that policies target the correct pods.

```
# Example of using labels for precise policy targeting
apiVersion: networking.k8s.io/v1
kind: NetworkPolicy
metadata:
  name: allow-frontend-to-backend
  namespace: default
spec:
  podSelector:
    matchLabels:
      role: backend
  ingress:
  - from:
    - podSelector:
        matchLabels:
          role: frontend
    ports:
    - protocol: TCP
      port: 8080
```

Implement Layered Policies: Create layered policies that address different levels of network traffic. For instance, you can define policies for internal pod-to-pod communication, external access, and inter-namespace traffic.

Regularly Update Policies: As your application evolves, regularly review and update network policies to ensure they remain relevant and effective. Changes in the application architecture, deployment patterns, or security requirements may necessitate policy adjustments.

Testing and Validation Thorough testing and validation of network policies are essential to avoid disruptions and ensure they work as intended.

Test in a Staging Environment: Before applying network policies to production, test them in a staging or development environment that mirrors the production setup. This helps identify and resolve any issues without impacting live services.

Use Policy Simulation Tools: Leverage tools and features that simulate the effects of network policies without enforcing them. This allows you to verify the policies' impact on network traffic and adjust them if necessary.

Monitor Policy Enforcement: Continuously monitor the enforcement of network policies to detect any anomalies or unintended traffic patterns. Use monitoring tools and logs provided by your network plugin to track policy effectiveness.

Conduct Security Audits: Periodically conduct security audits to review the network policies and ensure they comply with security best practices and organizational policies.

Documentation and Version Control Proper documentation and version control of network policies are crucial for maintaining clarity and facilitating collaboration.

Document Policies Clearly: Maintain clear and detailed documentation for each network policy, including its purpose, scope, and rules. This documentation helps team members understand and manage the policies effectively.

Use Version Control: Store network policy definitions in a version control system (e.g., Git) to track changes, facilitate collaboration, and maintain a history of policy modifications.

Leveraging Advanced Features Advanced network policy features provided by some network plugins can enhance the flexibility and security of your policies.

Global Network Policies: Tools like Calico support global network policies that apply across the entire cluster, providing a way to enforce consistent security standards.

```
# Example of a global network policy in Calico
apiVersion: projectcalico.org/v3
kind: GlobalNetworkPolicy
metadata:
  name: allow-dns
spec:
  selector: all()
  egress:
  - action: Allow
    protocol: UDP
    destination:
      nets:
      - 10.96.0.10/32
      ports:
      - 53
```

API-aware Policies: Cilium supports API-aware network policies, allowing you to define rules based on API endpoints and methods. This provides granular control over API traffic.

```
# Example of an API-aware network policy in Cilium
apiVersion: "cilium.io/v2"
kind: CiliumNetworkPolicy
metadata:
  name: api-policy
spec:
```

```
endpointSelector:
  matchLabels:
    app: myapp
ingress:
- fromEndpoints:
  - matchLabels:
      app: frontend
  toPorts:
  - ports:
    - port: "80"
      protocol: TCP
    rules:
      http:
      - method: "GET"
        path: "/api/v1/.*"
```

Conclusion Defining and managing network policies in Kubernetes is a critical aspect of securing and optimizing your cluster. By following best practices, leveraging advanced features, and maintaining thorough documentation, administrators can create effective network policies that enhance security and performance. Regular testing, monitoring, and updates ensure that these policies remain relevant and effective in dynamic environments.

Chapter 7

Advanced Storage Solutions

7.1 CSI: Container Storage Interface

7.1.1 Introduction to CSI

The Container Storage Interface (CSI) is a standardized mechanism for exposing storage systems to containerized workloads running on orchestration platforms like Kubernetes. Introduced to overcome the limitations of in-tree storage plugins, CSI allows for more maintainable, flexible, and secure storage integration. This section introduces CSI, its architecture, benefits, and its role in the evolving Kubernetes ecosystem.

Overview of CSI CSI was developed to address the challenges associated with in-tree storage plugins in Kubernetes. In-tree plugins were built into the core Kubernetes codebase, which meant that any updates or new features required changes to Kubernetes itself. This coupling led to slower innovation and increased complexity for both Kubernetes maintainers and storage vendors.

Key Goals of CSI:

- **Decoupling Storage from Kubernetes:** CSI separates storage concerns from Kubernetes core, allowing storage providers to develop and update their plugins independently.

- **Standardization:** Provides a uniform API that can be implemented by storage providers, ensuring compatibility across various container orchestration platforms.

- **Flexibility:** Facilitates rapid innovation in storage solutions without waiting for Kubernetes release cycles.

- **Enhanced Security:** Reduces the attack surface by minimizing the storage-related code within Kubernetes core.

CSI Architecture The CSI architecture consists of several key components that work together to manage storage for containerized applications. These components include the CSI driver, the CSI controller, and Kubernetes sidecar containers.

CSI Driver: The CSI driver is a storage provider-specific plugin that implements the CSI specification. It runs on the nodes where the containers are running and handles operations required to provision, attach, mount, and format the storage.

CSI Controller: The CSI controller is responsible for operations that require interaction with the storage backend, such as provisioning and attaching volumes. It runs as a separate service and communicates with the CSI driver on the nodes.

Kubernetes Sidecars: Kubernetes uses sidecar containers to extend the functionality of the CSI driver. Common sidecars include:

- **External Provisioner:** Handles volume provisioning requests from Kubernetes.

- **External Attacher:** Manages volume attachment operations.

- **External Resizer:** Supports dynamic volume resizing.

- **External Snapshotter:** Manages volume snapshots and restores.

Benefits of CSI CSI brings numerous benefits to the Kubernetes storage ecosystem, making it easier for both developers and storage providers to manage and use storage resources.

Modularity: CSI's modular design allows storage providers to develop and release their plugins independently of Kubernetes. This modularity speeds up the development cycle and enables rapid innovation in storage solutions.

Ecosystem Support: CSI is supported by a wide range of storage vendors, providing a rich ecosystem of plugins that cater to various storage needs. This broad support ensures that Kubernetes users have access to a diverse set of storage solutions.

Advanced Features: CSI supports advanced storage features such as snapshots, cloning, and dynamic provisioning. These features enhance the flexibility and capabilities of storage management in Kubernetes.

Scalability: CSI improves the scalability of storage management in Kubernetes by offloading storage operations to the CSI plugins. This offloading reduces the burden on the Kubernetes control plane and enhances overall cluster performance.

How CSI Works in Kubernetes Kubernetes interacts with CSI drivers through the CSI API. When a storage request is made (e.g., provisioning a new volume), Kubernetes sends the request to the appropriate CSI plugin via the CSI controller and sidecar containers.

Provisioning a Volume: When a PersistentVolumeClaim (PVC) is created, the external provisioner sidecar communicates with the CSI controller to provision the required storage. The CSI driver then handles the actual creation of the volume on the storage backend.

```
# Example PersistentVolumeClaim (PVC) manifest
apiVersion: v1
kind: PersistentVolumeClaim
metadata:
  name: example-pvc
spec:
  accessModes:
  - ReadWriteOnce
  resources:
```

```
    requests:
      storage: 10Gi
  storageClassName: csi-example-sc
```

Attaching and Mounting a Volume: Once the volume is provisioned, the external attacher and CSI driver work together to attach the volume to the appropriate node and mount it to the container's filesystem.

Transition from In-Tree Plugins to CSI Kubernetes has been moving away from in-tree plugins to CSI drivers to allow for better maintainability, flexibility, and security. In-tree plugins were tightly integrated with Kubernetes core, requiring updates to Kubernetes for every change in the storage plugin. This integration slowed down innovation and made it difficult to maintain and secure the storage codebase.

Advantages of CSI over In-Tree Plugins:

- **Independent Updates:** Storage vendors can update their CSI drivers independently of Kubernetes releases, enabling faster delivery of new features and bug fixes.

- **Reduced Complexity:** Decoupling storage plugins from Kubernetes core reduces the complexity of the Kubernetes codebase and minimizes the risk of bugs and security vulnerabilities.

- **Enhanced Security:** By reducing the amount of storage-related code in Kubernetes core, the attack surface is minimized, enhancing the overall security of the cluster.

Deprecation of In-Tree Plugins: Kubernetes has been deprecating in-tree storage plugins in favor of CSI drivers. This transition requires users to migrate their existing storage configurations to CSI-based solutions. The Kubernetes community provides tools and documentation to facilitate this migration.

CSI in Production Deploying CSI in a production environment requires careful planning and consideration. It is essential to ensure that the chosen CSI plugin is compatible with the Kubernetes version in use and that it supports the required storage features.

Selecting a CSI Plugin: Choose a CSI plugin that meets your storage requirements and is well-supported by the community or vendor. Consider factors such as performance, scalability, and support for advanced features.

Monitoring and Troubleshooting: Implement monitoring and logging for CSI components to track their performance and identify potential issues. Use tools like Prometheus and Grafana for monitoring and centralized logging solutions to collect and analyze logs from CSI components.

Conclusion The Container Storage Interface (CSI) is a pivotal advancement in the Kubernetes ecosystem, providing a standardized way for storage providers to integrate with Kubernetes. By decoupling storage management from the core Kubernetes codebase, CSI enables rapid innovation and a richer ecosystem of storage solutions. Understanding the basics of CSI, its architecture, and its benefits is essential for effectively managing storage in Kubernetes environments.

7.1.2   Integrating External Storage Solutions

Integrating external storage solutions in a Kubernetes environment using the Container Storage Interface (CSI) allows users to leverage a wide range of storage systems, from cloud-based solutions to on-premises enterprise storage arrays. This section provides detailed steps and considerations for integrating these external storage solutions, covering installation, configuration, and best practices.

Selecting an External Storage Solution The first step in integrating an external storage solution is selecting the right storage provider that meets your requirements. Consider factors such as performance, scalability, cost, and the specific features offered by the storage solution. Popular external storage solutions include:

- **AWS EBS (Elastic Block Store):** Provides high-performance block storage for use with Amazon EC2 instances.

- **Google Persistent Disks:** Offers durable and high-performance block storage for Google Cloud VMs.

- **Azure Disks:** Provides persistent, durable, and high-performance block storage for Azure VMs.

- **NetApp ONTAP:** Enterprise-grade storage offering advanced features such as snapshots, replication, and cloning.

- **Ceph:** Open-source distributed storage system providing object, block, and file storage.

Installing the CSI Driver Each external storage solution typically provides a CSI driver that you need to install on your Kubernetes cluster. This driver acts as an interface between Kubernetes and the storage backend. Below are examples of how to install CSI drivers for different storage providers.

Installing AWS EBS CSI Driver:

```
# Add the AWS EBS CSI Driver Helm repository
helm repo add aws-ebs-csi-driver https://kubernetes-sigs.
github.io/aws-ebs-csi-driver

# Install the AWS EBS CSI Driver
helm install aws-ebs-csi-driver aws-ebs-csi-driver/
aws-ebs-csi-driver --namespace kube-system
```

Installing Google Persistent Disk CSI Driver:

```
# Apply the Google Persistent Disk CSI Driver manifest
kubectl apply -k "github.com/kubernetes-sigs/
gcp-compute-persistent-disk-csi-driver/deploy/
kubernetes/overlays/stable?ref=release-1.5"
```

Installing Azure Disk CSI Driver:

```
# Add the Azure Disk CSI Driver Helm repository
helm repo add azuredisk-csi-driver https://raw.
githubusercontent.com/kubernetes-sigs/azuredisk-csi-driver/
master/charts
```

```
# Install the Azure Disk CSI Driver
helm install azuredisk-csi-driver azuredisk-csi-driver/
azuredisk-csi-driver --namespace kube-system
```

Configuring Storage Classes After installing the CSI driver, you need to configure StorageClasses that define the parameters for dynamically provisioning storage. A StorageClass specifies the CSI driver to use, parameters for the storage backend, and reclaim policies.

Example StorageClass for AWS EBS:

```
apiVersion: storage.k8s.io/v1
kind: StorageClass
metadata:
  name: ebs-sc
provisioner: ebs.csi.aws.com
parameters:
  type: gp2
  fsType: ext4
reclaimPolicy: Delete
volumeBindingMode: WaitForFirstConsumer
```

Example StorageClass for Google Persistent Disk:

```
apiVersion: storage.k8s.io/v1
kind: StorageClass
metadata:
  name: gpd-sc
provisioner: pd.csi.storage.gke.io
parameters:
  type: pd-standard
  fsType: ext4
reclaimPolicy: Retain
volumeBindingMode: Immediate
```

Example StorageClass for Azure Disk:

```
apiVersion: storage.k8s.io/v1
kind: StorageClass
metadata:
  name: azure-disk-sc
provisioner: disk.csi.azure.com
parameters:
  skuname: StandardSSD_LRS
  kind: Managed
  cachingmode: ReadOnly
reclaimPolicy: Delete
volumeBindingMode: WaitForFirstConsumer
```

Provisioning Persistent Volumes   With the StorageClass configured, you can now create PersistentVolumeClaims (PVCs) to request storage. Kubernetes uses the specified StorageClass to dynamically provision the storage volume.

Example PersistentVolumeClaim:

```
apiVersion: v1
kind: PersistentVolumeClaim
metadata:
  name: example-pvc
spec:
  accessModes:
  - ReadWriteOnce
  resources:
    requests:
      storage: 10Gi
  storageClassName: ebs-sc
```

When this PVC is created, the CSI driver provisions a new storage volume according to the parameters defined in the StorageClass and binds it to the PVC.

Best Practices for Integrating External Storage   To ensure efficient and reliable integration of external storage solutions, follow these best practices:

Ensure Compatibility: Verify that the CSI driver and storage solution are compatible with your Kubernetes version. Check the documentation for supported features and versions.

Monitor Storage Performance: Use monitoring tools to track the performance and health of your storage volumes. Tools like Prometheus and Grafana can be configured to monitor storage metrics.

Implement Backup and Recovery: Ensure that you have a robust backup and recovery strategy in place for your storage volumes. Use tools like Velero for backup and restore operations.

Security Considerations: Implement security best practices, such as encryption at rest and in transit, access controls, and regular security audits.

Regularly Update Drivers: Keep your CSI drivers up to date to benefit from the latest features, performance improvements, and security patches. Follow the release notes and upgrade instructions provided by the storage vendor.

Conclusion Integrating external storage solutions in Kubernetes using CSI provides a flexible and powerful way to manage storage for containerized applications. By carefully selecting the appropriate storage solution, installing and configuring the CSI driver, and following best practices, you can ensure reliable and efficient storage management in your Kubernetes environment. Understanding the detailed steps and considerations for integration helps you leverage the full potential of external storage systems in Kubernetes.

7.1.3 Dynamic Volume Provisioning

Dynamic volume provisioning is a powerful feature in Kubernetes that allows for the automatic creation and management of storage volumes based on user-defined specifications. This eliminates the need for pre-provisioning storage, providing flexibility and efficiency in managing storage resources.

This section delves into the mechanisms of dynamic volume provisioning, its configuration, and best practices for its implementation.

Overview of Dynamic Volume Provisioning Dynamic volume provisioning enables Kubernetes to automatically create storage volumes when a PersistentVolumeClaim (PVC) is submitted. This is accomplished through the use of StorageClasses, which define the parameters for the storage volumes, such as performance characteristics and reclaim policies.

Key Benefits:

- **Efficiency:** Eliminates the need to manually provision storage, reducing administrative overhead.

- **Scalability:** Automatically scales storage resources based on application demands.

- **Flexibility:** Supports a wide range of storage backends and configurations.

How Dynamic Volume Provisioning Works The process of dynamic volume provisioning involves several key components and steps:

StorageClass: A StorageClass is a Kubernetes resource that defines the type of storage to be provisioned. It specifies the provisioner (the CSI driver), parameters for the storage backend, and policies for reclaiming resources.

PersistentVolumeClaim (PVC): A PVC is a user request for storage. When a PVC is created, Kubernetes uses the StorageClass to dynamically provision a PersistentVolume (PV) that matches the request.

Provisioner: The provisioner is part of the CSI driver that interacts with the storage backend to create and manage volumes. It is specified in the StorageClass.

Configuring StorageClass for Dynamic Provisioning To enable dynamic volume provisioning, you need to define a StorageClass that specifies the provisioner and the desired parameters for the storage volumes.

Example StorageClass: Below is an example StorageClass for AWS EBS:

```
apiVersion: storage.k8s.io/v1
kind: StorageClass
metadata:
  name: ebs-sc
provisioner: ebs.csi.aws.com
parameters:
  type: gp2
  fsType: ext4
reclaimPolicy: Delete
volumeBindingMode: WaitForFirstConsumer
```

Parameters Explained:

- **provisioner:** Specifies the CSI driver to use (e.g., ebs.csi.aws.com for AWS EBS).

- **parameters:** Defines the storage backend-specific parameters (e.g., type: gp2 for General Purpose SSD).

- **reclaimPolicy:** Determines what happens to the volume when the PVC is deleted (e.g., Delete or Retain).

- **volumeBindingMode:** Controls when the volume binding and dynamic provisioning should occur (e.g., WaitForFirstConsumer).

Creating a PersistentVolumeClaim   Once the StorageClass is defined, users can create PersistentVolumeClaims to request storage dynamically. Kubernetes will use the specified StorageClass to provision a volume that meets the claim's requirements.

Example PersistentVolumeClaim:

```
apiVersion: v1
kind: PersistentVolumeClaim
metadata:
  name: example-pvc
spec:
```

```
accessModes:
- ReadWriteOnce
resources:
  requests:
    storage: 10Gi
storageClassName: ebs-sc
```

Access Modes: Access modes define how the volume can be mounted. Common access modes include:

- **ReadWriteOnce (RWO):** The volume can be mounted as read-write by a single node.

- **ReadOnlyMany (ROX):** The volume can be mounted as read-only by many nodes.

- **ReadWriteMany (RWX):** The volume can be mounted as read-write by many nodes.

Provisioning Process When a PVC is created, the Kubernetes control plane processes the request as follows:

- The PVC is submitted and detected by the Kubernetes API server.

- The external provisioner, specified in the StorageClass, handles the request by creating a corresponding PV.

- The PV is created and bound to the PVC, making the storage available to the requesting pod.

Best Practices for Dynamic Volume Provisioning Implementing dynamic volume provisioning effectively requires adherence to several best practices:

Select Appropriate StorageClass Parameters: Choose parameters that align with your application's performance and durability requirements. For example, use SSDs for high-performance databases and magnetic disks for archival storage.

Use Namespaces and ResourceQuotas: Apply namespaces and resource quotas to control and limit storage resource consumption, ensuring fair usage and avoiding resource exhaustion.

Monitor Storage Usage: Implement monitoring tools like Prometheus and Grafana to track storage usage, performance, and health. This helps in proactively managing storage resources and identifying issues.

Implement Backup and Recovery: Ensure a robust backup and recovery strategy is in place for dynamically provisioned volumes. Tools like Velero can automate backup and restore processes.

Regularly Update CSI Drivers: Keep CSI drivers up to date to benefit from the latest features, performance improvements, and security patches. Follow the storage provider's documentation for upgrade procedures.

Troubleshooting Dynamic Provisioning Issues Effective troubleshooting is essential for maintaining a healthy storage environment. Common issues include misconfigured StorageClasses, insufficient permissions, and storage backend limitations.

Common Issues and Solutions:

- **PVC Stuck in Pending State:** Verify that the StorageClass exists and is correctly configured. Check for available storage capacity and ensure the provisioner has sufficient permissions.

- **Volume Provisioning Failures:** Inspect the CSI driver and provisioner logs for errors. Ensure that the storage backend is operational and accessible.

- **Performance Issues:** Monitor storage performance metrics and adjust parameters such as IOPS and throughput settings to meet application requirements.

Conclusion Dynamic volume provisioning streamlines the management of storage resources in Kubernetes by automating the creation and configuration of storage volumes. By defining StorageClasses and using PersistentVolumeClaims, administrators can efficiently manage storage based on application demands. Adhering to best practices and effectively troubleshooting issues ensures a robust and scalable storage environment in Kubernetes.

7.1.4 Storage Migration

Storage migration in Kubernetes involves transferring data from one storage system to another without disrupting running applications. This is crucial for various scenarios, such as upgrading to a new storage backend, moving data to a more cost-effective solution, or performing maintenance. This section provides a detailed guide on storage migration, covering strategies, tools, and best practices.

Overview of Storage Migration Storage migration can be complex due to the need to maintain data consistency and minimize downtime. Kubernetes facilitates this process through its extensible architecture and tools designed to manage data movement seamlessly.

Common Use Cases for Storage Migration:

- **Upgrading Storage Backend:** Moving to a new storage system with better performance or features.

- **Cost Optimization:** Transferring data to a more cost-effective storage solution.

- **Maintenance and Compliance:** Migrating data for maintenance, compliance, or disaster recovery planning.

Migration Strategies Different strategies can be employed for storage migration, depending on the specific requirements and constraints of your environment.

Cold Migration: Cold migration involves shutting down applications, copying data to the new storage, and then restarting the applications. This method is simple but incurs downtime.

Warm Migration: Warm migration minimizes downtime by keeping the application running in a limited capacity. Data is synchronized between the old and new storage systems, and the application is briefly paused to finalize the migration.

Hot Migration: Hot migration aims to eliminate downtime by continuously replicating data between the old and new storage systems while the application remains fully operational. This approach requires sophisticated tooling and careful planning.

Tools for Storage Migration Several tools and techniques are available to facilitate storage migration in Kubernetes:

Velero: Velero is an open-source tool designed for backup and migration of Kubernetes resources and persistent volumes. It supports snapshots and data transfer across different storage backends.

```
# Install Velero CLI
curl -LO https://github.com/vmware-tanzu/velero/releases/
download/v1.7.1/velero-v1.7.1-linux-amd64.tar.gz

tar -xzf velero-v1.7.1-linux-amd64.tar.gz
sudo mv velero /usr/local/bin/

# Install Velero in the cluster
velero install --provider aws --bucket <bucket-name>
--secret-file ./credentials-velero
```

Rsync: Rsync is a utility for efficiently transferring and synchronizing files across computer systems. It can be used for warm or hot migrations by continuously synchronizing data between storage systems.

```
# Example rsync command for synchronizing data
rsync -avz /mnt/old-storage/ /mnt/new-storage/
```

Storage Provider Tools: Many storage providers offer their own migration tools designed to facilitate data transfer between storage systems. For example, AWS DataSync, Google Cloud Storage Transfer Service, and Azure Data Box.

Steps for Performing Storage Migration   The following steps outline a typical storage migration process in Kubernetes:

1. Plan the Migration: Define the migration strategy (cold, warm, or hot), assess the data size, and determine the downtime tolerance. Identify the source and target storage systems and ensure compatibility.

2. Backup Data: Before starting the migration, take a backup of the data to prevent any potential data loss. Use tools like Velero to create snapshots of the PersistentVolumes.

```
# Create a backup using Velero
velero backup create <backup-name>
--include-namespaces <namespace>
```

3. Set Up Target Storage: Configure the target storage system and ensure it is ready to receive data. Create the necessary StorageClasses and PersistentVolumeClaims for the target storage.

```
# Example PersistentVolumeClaim for target storage
apiVersion: v1
kind: PersistentVolumeClaim
metadata:
  name: new-pvc
spec:
  accessModes:
  - ReadWriteOnce
  resources:
    requests:
      storage: 10Gi
  storageClassName: new-storage-class
```

4.   Data Synchronization: Use tools like rsync or storage provider-specific tools to synchronize data between the old and new storage systems. Ensure data consistency during this process.

5. Finalize the Migration: Depending on the chosen strategy, finalize the migration by shutting down the application (cold), briefly pausing it (warm), or performing a final sync (hot).   Update the PersistentVolumeClaims to point to the new storage volumes.

```
# Update PVC to point to the new PersistentVolume
kubectl patch pvc <pvc-name> -p
'{"spec":{"volumeName":"new-pv-name"}}'
```

6.   Verify the Migration: Validate the migration by checking data integrity and application functionality. Ensure that all data has been correctly transferred and that the application is performing as expected.

Best Practices for Storage Migration   Following best practices ensures a smooth and successful storage migration:

Minimize Downtime: Choose a migration strategy that aligns with your downtime tolerance and application requirements. Warm and hot migrations are preferable for minimizing disruption.

Test Migration Process: Conduct a test migration in a staging environment to identify and resolve potential issues before performing the actual migration.

Monitor and Log Migration Activities: Use monitoring and logging tools to track the progress of the migration and identify any errors or issues. This helps in troubleshooting and ensuring a successful migration.

Communicate with Stakeholders: Keep all stakeholders informed about the migration plan, timeline, and potential impact on services. Clear communication helps in managing expectations and coordinating efforts.

Conclusion Storage migration in Kubernetes is a critical process that enables administrators to upgrade, optimize, and maintain their storage systems without disrupting application availability. By understanding the various strategies, tools, and best practices, administrators can execute efficient and reliable storage migrations, ensuring data integrity and minimizing downtime. Proper planning, testing, and monitoring are essential to achieving a successful migration.

7.2   Storage Patterns

In Kubernetes, understanding the various storage patterns is crucial for designing and managing applications that efficiently use storage resources. This section will explore different access modes for PersistentVolumes, including ReadWriteOnce, ReadOnlyMany, and ReadWriteMany. Additionally, we will delve into the differences between ephemeral and persistent storage and outline best practices for managing storage in stateful applications. By the end of this section, you will have a comprehensive understanding of when and how to use each access mode and storage type to meet your application's requirements effectively.

7.2.1   ReadWriteOnce, ReadOnlyMany, and ReadWriteMany

In Kubernetes, storage patterns define how storage volumes can be accessed by containers running in the cluster. These patterns are determined by the access modes specified in PersistentVolumeClaims (PVCs) and PersistentVolumes (PVs). The primary access modes are ReadWriteOnce (RWO), ReadOnlyMany (ROX), and ReadWriteMany (RWX). Each mode has specific use cases and implications for how data is accessed and modified.

ReadWriteOnce (RWO) ReadWriteOnce is the most commonly used access mode. It allows a volume to be mounted as read-write by a single node at a time. This mode is suitable for scenarios where data consistency is critical and only one instance of an application or pod needs to write to the volume.

Key Characteristics of RWO:

- **Exclusive Access:** The volume can only be mounted as read-write by one node at a time.

- **Consistency:** Ensures data consistency by preventing concurrent writes from multiple nodes.

- **Typical Use Cases:** Databases, single-instance applications, and stateful services where write operations need to be tightly controlled.

Example PVC with RWO:

```yaml
apiVersion: v1
kind: PersistentVolumeClaim
metadata:
  name: example-rwo-pvc
spec:
  accessModes:
  - ReadWriteOnce
  resources:
    requests:
      storage: 10Gi
  storageClassName: standard
```

ReadOnlyMany (ROX) ReadOnlyMany allows a volume to be mounted as read-only by multiple nodes simultaneously. This mode is useful for scenarios where data needs to be shared across multiple pods without allowing any modifications.

Key Characteristics of ROX:

- **Shared Read Access:** Multiple nodes can mount the volume simultaneously, but only for read operations.

- **Data Integrity:** Ensures data integrity by preventing any write operations.

- **Typical Use Cases:** Shared configuration files, reference data, and any scenario where data needs to be consumed by multiple instances without modification.

Example PVC with ROX:

```
apiVersion: v1
kind: PersistentVolumeClaim
metadata:
  name: example-rox-pvc
spec:
  accessModes:
  - ReadOnlyMany
  resources:
    requests:
      storage: 10Gi
  storageClassName: standard
```

ReadWriteMany (RWX) ReadWriteMany allows a volume to be mounted as read-write by multiple nodes simultaneously. This mode is ideal for scenarios where multiple instances of an application need to write to the same storage volume concurrently.

Key Characteristics of RWX:

- **Concurrent Read-Write Access:** Multiple nodes can mount the volume simultaneously and perform both read and write operations.

- **Scalability:** Supports scaling out applications that need to share state or data across multiple instances.

- **Typical Use Cases:** Distributed file systems, shared logs, and collaborative applications where data needs to be accessed and modified by multiple pods concurrently.

Example PVC with RWX:

```
apiVersion: v1
kind: PersistentVolumeClaim
metadata:
  name: example-rwx-pvc
spec:
  accessModes:
```

```
- ReadWriteMany
resources:
  requests:
    storage: 10Gi
storageClassName: standard
```

Considerations for Choosing Access Modes When choosing an access mode for a PVC, consider the specific requirements of your application, including data consistency, concurrency, and performance. Here are some guidelines to help with the decision:

Guidelines:

- **Data Consistency:** If data consistency is crucial and only one instance needs to write to the volume, use RWO.

- **Shared Data Access:** If multiple instances need to read from the same data set without modification, use ROX.

- **Concurrent Writes:** If multiple instances need to write to the same volume, use RWX, but ensure your storage backend supports this mode effectively.

Storage Backend Support Not all storage backends support all access modes. Ensure that your chosen storage backend can handle the required access mode for your use case. Some backends may require additional configuration to support RWX or ROX access modes.

Example Backends and Supported Modes:

- **AWS EBS:** Primarily supports RWO.

- **Google Persistent Disks:** Supports RWO and ROX.

- **NFS:** Supports RWO, ROX, and RWX.

- **CephFS:** Supports RWO, ROX, and RWX.

Conclusion Understanding and selecting the appropriate access mode for your PersistentVolumes is crucial for ensuring the correct operation and performance of your applications. ReadWriteOnce, ReadOnlyMany, and ReadWriteMany each have specific use cases and considerations. By carefully evaluating your application's needs and the capabilities of your storage backend, you can make informed decisions that optimize data access and storage management in your Kubernetes environment.

7.2.2 Ephemeral vs Persistent Storage

In Kubernetes, storage can be broadly classified into two types: ephemeral and persistent. Understanding the differences between these types is essential for designing applications that effectively manage data based on their requirements for durability, availability, and scope of data retention.

Ephemeral Storage Ephemeral storage is temporary and is tied to the lifecycle of the pod that uses it. When a pod is deleted, the data in ephemeral storage is also deleted. This type of storage is suitable for use cases where data does not need to be retained beyond the lifecycle of a pod, such as caching, temporary data processing, and scratch space.

Key Characteristics of Ephemeral Storage:

- **Temporary Data:** Data is only available as long as the pod exists.

- **Fast Access:** Often resides on the node's local disk or memory, providing fast access.

- **Use Cases:** Caching, temporary data processing, scratch space, and session data.

Types of Ephemeral Storage:

- **EmptyDir:** A directory that initially starts empty and is deleted when the pod is removed.

- **ConfigMap:** Used to inject configuration data into pods.

- **Secret:** Used to pass sensitive information, such as passwords, into pods.

- **DownwardAPI:** Makes metadata about the pod available to the pod itself.

Example EmptyDir Volume:

```yaml
apiVersion: v1
kind: Pod
metadata:
  name: example-pod
spec:
  containers:
  - name: example-container
    image: busybox
    command: ["sh", "-c", "while true; do echo $(date) >>
/var/log/example.log; sleep 5; done"]
    volumeMounts:
    - mountPath: /var/log
      name: example-volume
  volumes:
  - name: example-volume
    emptyDir: {}
```

Persistent Storage Persistent storage retains data beyond the lifecycle of individual pods. It is designed for use cases where data durability and long-term storage are required. Persistent storage is managed using PersistentVolumes (PVs) and PersistentVolumeClaims (PVCs), allowing data to be decoupled from the lifecycle of pods and nodes.

Key Characteristics of Persistent Storage:

- **Durable Data:** Data persists beyond the lifecycle of pods and nodes.

- **Stateful Applications:** Ideal for databases, file storage, and other stateful applications.

- **Decoupled Lifecycle:** Data can be retained and reused across different pod instances and deployments.

Types of Persistent Storage:

- **PersistentVolume (PV):** A piece of storage in the cluster that has been provisioned by an administrator or dynamically provisioned using StorageClasses.

- **PersistentVolumeClaim (PVC):** A request for storage by a user that binds to a PV.

Example PersistentVolume and PersistentVolumeClaim:

```
apiVersion: v1
kind: PersistentVolume
metadata:
  name: example-pv
spec:
  capacity:
    storage: 10Gi
  accessModes:
    - ReadWriteOnce
  persistentVolumeReclaimPolicy: Retain
  storageClassName: manual
  hostPath:
    path: "/mnt/data"

---

apiVersion: v1
kind: PersistentVolumeClaim
metadata:
  name: example-pvc
spec:
  accessModes:
    - ReadWriteOnce
  resources:
    requests:
      storage: 10Gi
  storageClassName: manual
```

Choosing Between Ephemeral and Persistent Storage The choice between ephemeral and persistent storage depends on the specific requirements of your application:

Use Cases for Ephemeral Storage:

- **Temporary Data Processing:** Tasks that generate temporary data, such as intermediate files or caches.

- **Stateless Applications:** Applications where data persistence is not critical.

- **Configuration and Secrets:** Using ConfigMaps and Secrets to inject configuration and sensitive data into pods.

Use Cases for Persistent Storage:

- **Databases:** Stateful applications like databases that require data durability.

- **File Storage:** Applications that need to store and retrieve files.

- **Data Analytics:** Applications that process and store large datasets.

Conclusion Understanding the differences between ephemeral and persistent storage in Kubernetes is essential for designing applications that effectively manage data based on their requirements. Ephemeral storage is suited for temporary data and stateless applications, while persistent storage is necessary for stateful applications that require data durability. By selecting the appropriate storage type, you can optimize the performance, reliability, and scalability of your Kubernetes applications.

7.2.3   Best Practices for Storage in Stateful Applications

Managing storage for stateful applications in Kubernetes requires careful planning and adherence to best practices to ensure data durability, availability, and performance. This section outlines key best practices for effectively managing storage in stateful applications.

1. Use Persistent Volumes and Claims

Leverage PVs and PVCs: Always use PersistentVolumes (PVs) and PersistentVolumeClaims (PVCs) to manage storage for stateful applications. This approach decouples storage from the lifecycle of individual pods, ensuring data persistence even if pods are terminated or rescheduled.

```
apiVersion: v1
kind: PersistentVolumeClaim
metadata:
  name: stateful-app-pvc
spec:
  accessModes:
  - ReadWriteOnce
  resources:
    requests:
      storage: 20Gi
  storageClassName: standard
```

2. Choose the Appropriate Storage Class

Select Based on Performance and Features: Different storage classes offer varying performance characteristics and features. Choose a StorageClass that matches your application's performance requirements, such as IOPS and throughput, and supports necessary features like encryption and snapshots.

```
apiVersion: storage.k8s.io/v1
kind: StorageClass
metadata:
  name: high-performance
provisioner: kubernetes.io/aws-ebs
parameters:
  type: io1
  iopsPerGB: "10"
  fsType: ext4
reclaimPolicy: Retain
volumeBindingMode: WaitForFirstConsumer
```

3. Implement Backup and Disaster Recovery

Regular Backups: Implement a robust backup strategy to protect against data loss. Use tools like Velero to schedule regular backups of your PVs and PVCs, and ensure backups are stored in a secure, geographically diverse location.

```
# Schedule a Velero backup
velero create schedule daily-backup --schedule "0 2 * * *"
--include-namespaces <namespace>
```

Disaster Recovery Plan: Develop and regularly test a disaster recovery plan to quickly restore data and resume operations in the event of a failure. Ensure that backups are easily accessible and restorable.

4. Monitor and Optimize Performance

Performance Monitoring: Use monitoring tools such as Prometheus and Grafana to track the performance of your storage volumes. Monitor key metrics like IOPS, latency, and throughput to identify and address performance bottlenecks.

```
# Example Prometheus configuration for storage metrics
scrape_configs:
  - job_name: 'kubernetes-pvs'
    kubernetes_sd_configs:
      - role: pod
    relabel_configs:
      - source_labels: [__meta_kubernetes_pod_label_app]
        action: keep
        regex: my-storage-app
```

Optimize Resource Allocation: Adjust resource requests and limits for your PVCs to ensure they are allocated appropriately based on your application's needs. Avoid over-provisioning to reduce costs and under-provisioning to prevent performance degradation.

5. Ensure Data Security

Encryption: Use encryption for data at rest and in transit to protect sensitive information. Many storage providers offer built-in encryption options, or you can use tools like dm-crypt for encryption at the filesystem level.

```
# Example PVC with encryption parameters
apiVersion: v1
kind: PersistentVolumeClaim
metadata:
  name: encrypted-pvc
spec:
  accessModes:
  - ReadWriteOnce
  resources:
    requests:
      storage: 20Gi
  storageClassName: encrypted
```

Access Controls: Implement strict access controls to limit who can read or write to your storage volumes. Use Kubernetes Role-Based Access Control (RBAC) to manage permissions and ensure that only authorized users and services can access sensitive data.

```
# Example RBAC policy for PVC access
apiVersion: rbac.authorization.k8s.io/v1
kind: Role
metadata:
  namespace: default
  name: pvc-access-role
rules:
- apiGroups: [""]
  resources: ["persistentvolumeclaims"]
  verbs: ["get", "list", "watch"]
```

6. Use StatefulSets for Stateful Applications

StatefulSets: Use StatefulSets for deploying stateful applications. StatefulSets manage the deployment and scaling of pods, ensuring that each pod gets a unique, stable identifier and persistent storage.

```yaml
apiVersion: apps/v1
kind: StatefulSet
metadata:
  name: stateful-app
spec:
  serviceName: "stateful-app"
  replicas: 3
  selector:
    matchLabels:
      app: stateful-app
  template:
    metadata:
      labels:
        app: stateful-app
    spec:
      containers:
      - name: stateful-container
        image: my-stateful-app-image
        volumeMounts:
        - name: data
          mountPath: /data
  volumeClaimTemplates:
  - metadata:
      name: data
    spec:
      accessModes: ["ReadWriteOnce"]
      resources:
        requests:
          storage: 20Gi
```

Conclusion By following these best practices, you can ensure efficient, secure, and reliable storage management for stateful applications in Kubernetes. Leveraging PersistentVolumes and PersistentVolumeClaims, choosing the right StorageClass, implementing robust backup and disaster recovery strategies, monitoring performance, and ensuring data security are critical steps in managing storage effectively. Utilizing StatefulSets further enhances the management of stateful applications, providing stable identities and persistent storage across pod restarts and rescheduling.

Chapter 8

Cluster Operations

8.1 Autoscaling Strategies

8.1.1 Vertical Pod Autoscaling

Vertical Pod Autoscaling (VPA) in Kubernetes is a mechanism designed to automatically adjust the resource limits and requests (CPU and memory) for containers in a pod based on their actual usage. This ensures that applications have the necessary resources to operate efficiently without over-provisioning, which can lead to resource wastage and increased costs.

Overview of Vertical Pod Autoscaling VPA continuously monitors the resource utilization of containers and provides recommendations for the optimal resource requests and limits. It can either suggest the appropriate resource values or apply them automatically, helping maintain the performance and efficiency of applications.

Key Benefits of VPA:

- **Resource Optimization:** Ensures that applications are neither under-provisioned nor over-provisioned, optimizing resource usage.

- **Performance Improvement:** By providing the right amount of resources, VPA helps improve the performance and reliability of applications.

- **Cost Efficiency:** Reduces costs associated with over-provisioning by dynamically adjusting resource allocations.

- **Reduced Manual Intervention:** Automates the process of adjusting resource requests and limits, reducing the need for manual tuning.

How Vertical Pod Autoscaling Works VPA consists of three main components:

- **Recommender:** Continuously monitors resource usage and provides recommendations for optimal resource requests and limits.

- **Updater:** Automatically updates the resource requests and limits for pods based on the recommendations, if configured to do so.

- **Admission Controller:** Modifies the resource requests and limits of newly created or updated pods based on the recommendations.

Workflow of VPA:

1. The Recommender monitors the actual resource usage of containers and calculates the recommended resource requests and limits.

2. The Updater applies the recommendations to the running pods, if configured to do so.

3. The Admission Controller intercepts pod creation and update requests, adjusting resource specifications according to the recommendations.

Configuring Vertical Pod Autoscaler To use VPA, you need to install the VPA components and create a VerticalPodAutoscaler resource. Below are the steps to configure VPA in your Kubernetes cluster:

Installing VPA: The following commands install VPA components using kubectl:

```
# Clone the VPA repository
git clone https://github.com/kubernetes/autoscaler.git

# Navigate to the VPA directory
```

```
cd autoscaler/vertical-pod-autoscaler/

# Deploy the VPA components
kubectl apply -f vertical-pod-autoscaler/deploy/
```

Creating a VerticalPodAutoscaler Resource: Define a VerticalPodAutoscaler resource that specifies the target deployment and the update mode.

```
apiVersion: autoscaling.k8s.io/v1
kind: VerticalPodAutoscaler
metadata:
  name: example-vpa
spec:
  targetRef:
    apiVersion: "apps/v1"
    kind:       Deployment
    name:       example-deployment
  updatePolicy:
    updateMode: "Auto"
```

Update Modes: VPA supports three update modes:

- **Off:** VPA provides recommendations but does not automatically apply them.

- **Auto:** VPA automatically updates the resource requests and limits for pods.

- **Initial:** VPA only sets the initial resource requests and limits at pod creation time.

Monitoring and Tuning VPA Effective use of VPA involves monitoring its recommendations and adjustments to ensure they align with the application's performance needs. Regular tuning may be required to adjust the update modes or thresholds based on observed performance.

Monitoring VPA: Use tools like Prometheus and Grafana to monitor VPA metrics and track the impact of resource adjustments on application performance.

```
# Example Prometheus configuration for VPA metrics
scrape_configs:
  - job_name: 'vpa'
    static_configs:
      - targets: ['<vpa-metrics-endpoint>:8080']
```

Best Practices for Using VPA:

- **Start with Recommendations:** Initially configure VPA in recommendation mode to understand its suggestions before enabling automatic updates.

- **Gradual Rollout:** Apply VPA to a subset of pods or deployments to observe its impact before scaling it cluster-wide.

- **Combine with HPA:** Use Vertical Pod Autoscaler in conjunction with Horizontal Pod Autoscaler (HPA) for optimal scaling of both resource requests and the number of pods.

- **Regular Review:** Periodically review VPA recommendations and adjust settings as necessary to ensure optimal performance.

Conclusion Vertical Pod Autoscaling (VPA) is a powerful tool for dynamically adjusting the resource allocations of Kubernetes pods based on actual usage. By optimizing resource requests and limits, VPA enhances application performance, reduces costs, and simplifies resource management. Implementing VPA effectively requires careful configuration, monitoring, and tuning to align with the specific needs of your applications.

8.1.2 Horizontal Pod Autoscaling

Horizontal Pod Autoscaling (HPA) in Kubernetes automatically adjusts the number of pod replicas in a deployment, replica set, or stateful set based on observed CPU utilization, memory usage, or other custom metrics. This ensures that the right amount of resources is available to handle the application's load, enhancing performance and reliability while optimizing resource usage.

Overview of Horizontal Pod Autoscaling HPA dynamically scales the number of pods in response to the load on the application. It uses metrics provided by the Kubernetes Metrics Server or custom metrics from Prometheus or other monitoring tools to make scaling decisions.

Key Benefits of HPA:

- **Automatic Scaling:** Adjusts the number of pods automatically based on real-time metrics, ensuring applications can handle varying loads.

- **Improved Performance:** Maintains application performance by scaling up during high load and scaling down during low load.

- **Cost Efficiency:** Optimizes resource usage by scaling down unnecessary pods during periods of low demand.

- **Flexibility:** Supports scaling based on various metrics, including CPU, memory, and custom metrics.

How Horizontal Pod Autoscaling Works HPA operates by continuously monitoring the specified metrics and adjusting the number of pod replicas to maintain the desired performance level. The primary components involved in HPA include the HPA controller and the metrics provider.

Workflow of HPA:

1. The HPA controller retrieves metrics from the metrics provider (e.g., Metrics Server, Prometheus).

2. The controller compares the current metrics against the target values defined in the HPA configuration.

3. Based on the comparison, the controller scales the number of pod replicas up or down to match the desired performance criteria.

Configuring Horizontal Pod Autoscaler To use HPA, you need to ensure the Kubernetes Metrics Server is installed and then create a HorizontalPodAutoscaler resource that specifies the target deployment and scaling criteria.

Installing Metrics Server: The Metrics Server provides resource usage metrics to the HPA controller. Install it using the following commands:

```
# Deploy Metrics Server
kubectl apply -f https://github.com/kubernetes-sigs/
metrics-server/releases/latest/download/components.yaml
```

Creating a HorizontalPodAutoscaler Resource: Define a HorizontalPodAutoscaler resource that specifies the target deployment and the metrics for scaling.

```
apiVersion: autoscaling/v2
kind: HorizontalPodAutoscaler
metadata:
  name: example-hpa
spec:
  scaleTargetRef:
    apiVersion: apps/v1
    kind: Deployment
    name: example-deployment
  minReplicas: 2
  maxReplicas: 10
  metrics:
  - type: Resource
    resource:
      name: cpu
      target:
        type: Utilization
        averageUtilization: 50
```

Custom Metrics for HPA Besides CPU and memory metrics, HPA can also scale based on custom metrics provided by Prometheus or other monitoring tools. Custom metrics allow more granular and application-specific scaling decisions.

Example Custom Metric: To use a custom metric, you need to expose the metric via a monitoring tool like Prometheus and configure HPA to use it.

```
apiVersion: autoscaling/v2
kind: HorizontalPodAutoscaler
metadata:
  name: example-hpa-custom
spec:
  scaleTargetRef:
    apiVersion: apps/v1
    kind: Deployment
    name: example-deployment
  minReplicas: 2
  maxReplicas: 10
  metrics:
  - type: Pods
    pods:
      metric:
        name: transactions_per_second
      target:
        type: AverageValue
        averageValue: 100
```

Best Practices for Using HPA Effective use of HPA requires careful planning and monitoring to ensure that scaling actions align with application performance requirements and resource constraints.

Best Practices:

- **Start with CPU/Memory Metrics:** Begin with CPU and memory metrics before introducing custom metrics to simplify initial configuration and monitoring.

- **Set Reasonable Limits:** Define realistic minimum and maximum replica counts to avoid overloading the cluster or under-provisioning the application.

- **Monitor Scaling Events:** Use logging and monitoring tools to track scaling events and adjust the HPA configuration based on observed behavior.

- **Combine with VPA:** Use HPA in conjunction with Vertical Pod Autoscaler (VPA) for optimal scaling of both resource requests and the number of pods.

- **Regularly Review Metrics:** Periodically review the metrics and thresholds used for scaling to ensure they remain aligned with the application's performance needs.

Monitoring and Tuning HPA   Monitoring the performance of HPA and tuning its parameters is crucial for maintaining optimal application performance. Use tools like Prometheus and Grafana to visualize metrics and scaling events.

Example Prometheus Configuration:

```
# Example Prometheus configuration for HPA metrics
scrape_configs:
  - job_name: 'kubernetes-hpa'
    kubernetes_sd_configs:
      - role: pod
    relabel_configs:
      - source_labels: [__meta_kubernetes_pod_label_app]
        action: keep
        regex: example-app
```

Conclusion   Horizontal Pod Autoscaling (HPA) is an essential tool for dynamically adjusting the number of pod replicas based on application load. By scaling up during high demand and scaling down during low demand, HPA ensures optimal application performance and resource utilization. Proper configuration, monitoring, and tuning of HPA are critical to achieving the desired outcomes, making it a fundamental component of efficient Kubernetes cluster operations.

8.1.3   Cluster Autoscaler: Node Level Autoscaling

The Cluster Autoscaler automatically adjusts the number of nodes in your Kubernetes cluster based on the demands of your workloads. It monitors the resource usage of your cluster and adds or removes nodes to meet the current needs, optimizing resource allocation and cost efficiency.

Key Features

- **Automatic Scaling:** The Cluster Autoscaler can increase the cluster size by adding nodes when there are pending pods that cannot be scheduled due to resource constraints. It can also remove underutilized nodes when they are no longer needed.

- **Integration with Cloud Providers:** The Cluster Autoscaler integrates seamlessly with major cloud providers like AWS, GCP, and Azure, managing node pools and scaling operations using the native capabilities of these platforms.

- **Configurable Scaling Policies:** Users can define minimum and maximum cluster sizes, set specific conditions for scaling up or down, and manage node group configurations to ensure efficient resource utilization.

- **Support for Multiple Node Pools:** The autoscaler can manage multiple node pools with different instance types and configurations, optimizing the cluster for various types of workloads.

How Cluster Autoscaler Works The Cluster Autoscaler works by continuously monitoring the cluster's resource usage and making scaling decisions based on predefined policies. It scales up by adding nodes when the resources are insufficient and scales down by removing nodes that are underutilized.

Installation and Configuration To install and configure the Cluster Autoscaler, you typically use Helm charts or Kubernetes manifests. Here is an example of deploying the Cluster Autoscaler on an AWS EKS cluster using Helm:

Using Helm:

```
# Add the autoscaler Helm repository
helm repo add autoscaler https://kubernetes.github.io/
autoscaler

# Update the repository
helm repo update

# Install the Cluster Autoscaler
helm install cluster-autoscaler autoscaler/cluster-autoscaler \
  --namespace kube-system \
  --set autoDiscovery.clusterName=<your-cluster-name> \
  --set awsRegion=<your-region> \
  --set rbac.serviceAccount.create=true \
  --set rbac.serviceAccount.name=cluster-autoscaler
```

Configuration Example   Below is a configuration example for the Cluster Autoscaler using a Kubernetes manifest:

```
apiVersion: autoscaling.k8s.io/v1
kind: ClusterAutoscaler
metadata:
  name: cluster-autoscaler
  namespace: kube-system
spec:
  scaleTargetRef:
    apiVersion: v1
    kind: Node
    name: node-group-1
  minNodes: 1
  maxNodes: 10
  metrics:
    - type: Resource
      resource:
        name: cpu
        target:
          type: Utilization
          averageUtilization: 50
```

Monitoring and Debugging   Monitoring the Cluster Autoscaler involves checking the status of the autoscaler deployment and the logs to ensure it is functioning correctly. You can use kubectl commands to view the current status and logs:

```
# Check the status of the Cluster Autoscaler
kubectl get deployment cluster-autoscaler -n kube-system

# View the logs of the Cluster Autoscaler
kubectl logs deployment/cluster-autoscaler -n kube-system
```

Best Practices

Define Clear Scaling Policies: Set appropriate minimum and maximum limits for your cluster size to prevent over-provisioning and under-provisioning of resources.

Monitor Resource Utilization: Regularly monitor the resource utilization of your nodes and adjust the autoscaler settings as needed to optimize performance and cost.

Use Multiple Node Pools: Consider using multiple node pools with different configurations to handle varying workload requirements more efficiently.

Test Scaling Scenarios: Test your scaling scenarios under different load conditions to ensure that the Cluster Autoscaler responds correctly and meets your performance requirements.

Conclusion   The Cluster Autoscaler is a crucial tool for maintaining an efficient, scalable, and cost-effective Kubernetes environment. By automatically adjusting the number of nodes based on workload demands, it ensures optimal resource utilization and performance. Proper installation, configuration, and monitoring are essential to leverage the full benefits of the Cluster Autoscaler.

8.1.4   KEDA: Kubernetes Event-Driven Autoscaling

Kubernetes Event-Driven Autoscaling (KEDA) is a powerful tool that helps manage workloads in Kubernetes by automatically scaling them based on the number of events that need to be processed. Unlike traditional autoscalers that primarily focus on metrics like CPU and memory usage, KEDA allows you to scale your applications based on various event sources such as messaging queues, HTTP requests, or custom metrics.

Key Features

- **Event-Driven Scaling:** KEDA scales Kubernetes deployments based on events, allowing for more responsive and efficient resource utilization.

- **Wide Range of Scalers:** Supports various event sources including Azure Queue, Kafka, AWS SQS, Prometheus, and more.

- **Seamless Integration:** Works with Kubernetes Horizontal Pod Autoscaler (HPA) and can extend its capabilities to include event-driven metrics.

- **Custom Metrics Support:** Allows scaling based on custom metrics from sources like Prometheus, Datadog, or custom-built metrics adapters.

- **Multi-Cloud Support:** Compatible with multiple cloud providers, making it flexible for different deployment environments.

Installation and Configuration   To use KEDA, you need to install it on your Kubernetes cluster and configure the appropriate scalers for your applications. The installation process typically involves deploying KEDA using Helm or Kubernetes manifests.

Installing KEDA: You can install KEDA using Helm for simplicity and ease of management:

```
# Add the KEDA Helm repository
helm repo add kedacore https://kedacore.github.io/charts
```

```
# Update the repository
helm repo update

# Install KEDA
helm install keda kedacore/keda --namespace keda
--create-namespace
```

Configuring KEDA Scalers   KEDA uses ScaledObjects to define how a deployment should scale based on an event source. Here's an example configuration for scaling a deployment based on messages in an Azure Queue:

```
apiVersion: keda.sh/v1alpha1
kind: ScaledObject
metadata:
  name: azure-queue-scaledobject
  namespace: default
spec:
  scaleTargetRef:
    name: azure-queue-worker
  pollingInterval: 30  # Optional. Default: 30 seconds
  cooldownPeriod: 300  # Optional. Default: 300 seconds
  minReplicaCount: 0  # Optional. Default: 0
  maxReplicaCount: 10  # Optional. Default: 100
  triggers:
  - type: azure-queue
    metadata:
      queueName: myqueue
      connectionFromEnv: AzureWebJobsStorage
      queueLength: "5"  # Optional. Default: 5 messages
```

Example: Scaling with Prometheus Metrics   KEDA can also scale based on Prometheus metrics, allowing for highly customizable scaling strategies. Here's an example:

```
apiVersion: keda.sh/v1alpha1
kind: ScaledObject
metadata:
```

```
  name: prometheus-scaledobject
  namespace: default
spec:
  scaleTargetRef:
    name: prometheus-deployment
  pollingInterval: 30
  cooldownPeriod: 300
  minReplicaCount: 1
  maxReplicaCount: 10
  triggers:
  - type: prometheus
    metadata:
      serverAddress: http://prometheus-server.default.svc.
cluster.local
      metricName: http_requests_total
      threshold: "100"
```

Monitoring and Debugging   Effective monitoring and debugging are crucial for managing KEDA deployments. You can monitor the status of KEDA and its scaled objects using kubectl commands:

```
# Check the status of KEDA
kubectl get deployments -n keda


# View logs for KEDA operator
kubectl logs deployment/keda-operator -n keda
```

Best Practices

Define Clear Scaling Policies: Clearly define the scaling policies and ensure they align with your application's performance requirements and resource constraints.

Monitor Metrics and Events: Regularly monitor the metrics and events that drive scaling decisions to ensure they are accurate and reflect the current load.

Test Scaling Scenarios: Test different scaling scenarios to ensure KEDA scales your applications as expected under various load conditions.

Optimize Polling and Cooldown Intervals: Adjust the polling interval and cooldown period to balance responsiveness and stability, avoiding frequent scaling actions.

Conclusion KEDA enhances Kubernetes' autoscaling capabilities by introducing event-driven scaling. By leveraging KEDA, you can create more responsive and efficient applications that scale based on real-time events. Proper installation, configuration, and monitoring are key to maximizing the benefits of KEDA in your Kubernetes environment.

8.1.5 Best Practices and Considerations for Autoscaling

Autoscaling is a powerful feature in Kubernetes that ensures your applications have the necessary resources to handle varying loads. To fully leverage autoscaling, it's important to follow best practices and consider various factors that can impact its effectiveness and efficiency.

Define Clear Scaling Policies

- **Set Realistic Limits:** Define minimum and maximum replica counts for Horizontal Pod Autoscaler (HPA) and Cluster Autoscaler to prevent over-provisioning or under-provisioning of resources.

- **Understand Your Workloads:** Know the resource requirements of your applications and set scaling thresholds that reflect their typical and peak usage patterns.

- **Balance Responsiveness and Stability:** Configure cooldown periods and polling intervals to balance the need for rapid scaling with the stability of your applications.

Monitor and Analyze Metrics

- **Regular Monitoring:** Use monitoring tools like Prometheus, Grafana, and the Kubernetes Metrics Server to continuously monitor the performance and resource usage of your applications.

- **Analyze Scaling Events:** Review scaling events and logs to understand how your autoscalers are performing and to identify any patterns or anomalies.

- **Adjust Policies Based on Insights:** Use the insights gained from monitoring and analysis to refine your scaling policies and improve their effectiveness.

Optimize Resource Requests and Limits

- **Right-Size Resource Requests:** Set resource requests and limits based on the actual usage patterns of your applications to ensure efficient resource utilization.

- **Use Vertical Pod Autoscaler (VPA):** Implement VPA alongside HPA to automatically adjust resource requests and limits based on historical usage data.

Use Multiple Autoscaling Strategies

- **Combine HPA and VPA:** Use Horizontal Pod Autoscaler for scaling the number of replicas and Vertical Pod Autoscaler for adjusting resource requests and limits.

- **Leverage Cluster Autoscaler:** Use Cluster Autoscaler to manage the number of nodes in your cluster, ensuring there are enough resources to support your scaled workloads.

- **Incorporate Event-Driven Autoscaling:** Utilize KEDA to scale applications based on custom metrics and events, providing more granular and responsive scaling.

Test Scaling Scenarios

- **Simulate Load Conditions:** Test your autoscaling policies under various load conditions to ensure they behave as expected.

- **Perform Chaos Engineering:** Introduce controlled failures and disruptions to test the resilience and robustness of your autoscaling configurations.

Consider Cost Implications

- **Optimize for Cost Efficiency:** Balance the need for performance and reliability with cost considerations, avoiding unnecessary over-provisioning of resources.

- **Monitor Cloud Costs:** Use cloud cost monitoring tools to track the impact of autoscaling on your cloud expenses and adjust your policies to optimize costs.

Implement Security Best Practices

- **Secure Autoscaler Access:** Ensure that your autoscalers have the necessary permissions to perform scaling operations but follow the principle of least privilege.

- **Monitor Security Posture:** Regularly review the security configurations of your autoscaling components and ensure they comply with your organization's security policies.

Regularly Review and Update Policies

- **Continuous Improvement:** Regularly review your autoscaling policies and configurations to ensure they remain effective and aligned with your application and business needs.

- **Stay Updated:** Keep up-to-date with the latest developments in Kubernetes autoscaling features and best practices to continuously improve your autoscaling strategies.

Conclusion Effective autoscaling in Kubernetes requires careful planning, monitoring, and continuous improvement. By following these best practices and considering the various factors that influence autoscaling, you can ensure that your applications remain responsive, efficient, and cost-effective under varying load conditions. Proper implementation of autoscaling strategies enhances the resilience and performance of your Kubernetes clusters, providing a robust foundation for your applications.

8.2 Federation and Multi-Cluster Management

8.2.1 Introduction to Federation

Kubernetes Cluster Federation, also known as KubeFed, is a powerful tool that allows you to manage multiple Kubernetes clusters as a single entity. Federation provides a unified control plane, enabling consistent policy enforcement, resource management, and high availability across clusters located in different geographical regions or cloud providers.

What is Cluster Federation? Cluster Federation is designed to simplify the management of multiple clusters by enabling you to deploy and manage applications across clusters in a consistent manner. It abstracts the complexities involved in operating multiple clusters, offering a single point of control for deployment, policy enforcement, and monitoring.

Key Features of Cluster Federation:

- **Centralized Control:** A single control plane to manage multiple clusters.

- **Cross-Cluster Service Discovery:** Services can be discovered across clusters, improving service availability and failover capabilities.

- **Consistent Policy Enforcement:** Uniform policies can be enforced across all clusters, ensuring compliance and security.

- **Resource Distribution:** Efficiently distribute resources and workloads across clusters to optimize performance and cost.

- **High Availability and Disaster Recovery:** Enhance application availability and enable disaster recovery by replicating services across multiple clusters.

How Cluster Federation Works Cluster Federation works by creating a federated control plane that sits above individual Kubernetes clusters. This control plane manages the federated clusters using a set of APIs and controllers designed to synchronize resources and enforce policies across all member clusters.

Components of Cluster Federation:

- **Federation API Server:** Provides a RESTful interface for managing federated resources.

- **Federation Controller Manager:** Synchronizes resources and configurations across clusters.

- **Federated Resources:** Resources such as deployments, services, and secrets that are managed across clusters.

Setting Up Cluster Federation Setting up Cluster Federation involves deploying the federation control plane and registering individual clusters with it. This process typically includes the following steps:

Deploy the Federation Control Plane:

```
# Deploy Federation API server and Controller Manager
kubectl apply -f https://github.com/kubernetes-sigs/kubefed/
releases/download/v0.7.0/kubefed.yaml
```

Register Clusters with the Federation:

```
# Join clusters to the federation
kubefedctl join cluster1 --host-cluster-context=cluster1
--cluster-context=cluster1

kubefedctl join cluster2 --host-cluster-context=cluster1
--cluster-context=cluster2
```

Use Cases for Cluster Federation Cluster Federation is particularly useful in scenarios where high availability, geographic distribution, and multi-cloud strategies are critical. Some common use cases include:

- **Global Service Distribution:** Deploy services across clusters in different regions to reduce latency and improve user experience.

- **Disaster Recovery:** Ensure business continuity by replicating services across clusters to handle regional failures.

- **Compliance and Data Residency:** Manage data residency requirements by deploying clusters in specific geographic locations.

- **Resource Optimization:** Balance workloads across clusters to optimize resource utilization and reduce costs.

Conclusion Kubernetes Cluster Federation simplifies the management of multiple clusters, providing a unified control plane for consistent policy enforcement, resource distribution, and high availability. By leveraging Cluster Federation, organizations can achieve greater resilience, scalability, and flexibility in their Kubernetes deployments.

8.2.2   Managing Multiple Clusters

Managing multiple Kubernetes clusters effectively requires a combination of strategies, tools, and best practices to ensure consistency, reliability, and efficiency. Whether you're operating clusters in different regions, across multiple cloud providers, or in hybrid environments, these practices help streamline operations and enhance resilience.

Using kubeconfig Files The 'kubeconfig' file is essential for accessing and managing multiple clusters. It allows you to configure access credentials for different clusters and switch between them using contexts. Each context in a 'kubeconfig' file specifies a cluster, a user, and a namespace.

Creating a kubeconfig File:

```
apiVersion: v1
kind: Config
preferences: {}
clusters:
- name: development
  cluster:
    server: https://development-cluster.example.com
    certificate-authority: /path/to/ca.crt
```

```
- name: production
  cluster:
    server: https://production-cluster.example.com
    certificate-authority: /path/to/ca.crt
contexts:
- name: dev
  context:
    cluster: development
    user: dev-user
    namespace: dev-namespace
- name: prod
  context:
    cluster: production
    user: prod-user
    namespace: prod-namespace
current-context: dev
users:
- name: dev-user
  user:
    client-certificate: /path/to/dev-user.crt
    client-key: /path/to/dev-user.key
- name: prod-user
  user:
    client-certificate: /path/to/prod-user.crt
    client-key: /path/to/prod-user.key
```

Switching Contexts: Use the 'kubectl config use-context' command to switch between clusters:

```
# Switch to the production context
kubectl config use-context prod
```

Tools for Multi-Cluster Management Beyond kubeconfig, several tools can help manage multiple clusters efficiently:

- **Rancher:** Provides a centralized management platform for Kubernetes clusters, supporting multiple cloud providers and on-premises environments.

- **Anthos:** Google's platform for managing applications across hybrid and multi-cloud environments.

- **KubeSphere:** An open-source container platform that includes multi-cluster management, DevOps pipelines, and more.

Federation and Multi-Cluster Tools Cluster Federation (KubeFed) and other multi-cluster tools offer advanced capabilities for managing resources and policies across clusters.

Use Cases for Managing Multiple Clusters Effective multi-cluster management is crucial for various scenarios, such as disaster recovery, geo-distribution, and multi-cloud strategies:

- **Disaster Recovery:** Replicate critical workloads across clusters to ensure availability during regional failures.

- **Geo-distribution:** Deploy applications closer to users by leveraging clusters in different geographic regions, reducing latency.

- **Multi-cloud Strategy:** Avoid vendor lock-in and optimize costs by distributing workloads across multiple cloud providers.

Best Practices for Managing Multiple Clusters Implementing best practices is crucial for effective multi-cluster management:

- **Unified Monitoring and Logging:** Use centralized monitoring and logging solutions like Prometheus and Grafana to monitor all clusters from a single pane of glass.

- **Consistent Security Policies:** Ensure consistent security policies and configurations across clusters to maintain compliance and security standards.

- **Automated Resource Management:** Utilize tools like KubeFed and GitOps practices to automate the management and synchronization of resources across clusters.

- **Regular Backups:** Regularly back up critical data and configurations to enable quick recovery in case of failures.

Conclusion Managing multiple Kubernetes clusters requires careful planning and the right tools to ensure consistency, reliability, and efficiency. By leveraging kubeconfig files, Cluster Federation, and multi-cluster management tools, you can effectively manage complex multi-cluster environments and achieve high availability, disaster recovery, and optimized resource utilization.

8.2.3 Synchronizing Resources Across Clusters

Synchronizing resources across multiple Kubernetes clusters ensures consistency and reliability in a multi-cluster setup. This process involves replicating resources, configurations, and policies to maintain uniformity and enable seamless operations across clusters. Here are some strategies and tools for effective resource synchronization:

Using GitOps for Synchronization GitOps is an effective approach for synchronizing resources across clusters. It involves storing the desired state of your clusters in a Git repository and using tools like ArgoCD or FluxCD to automatically synchronize the actual state of the clusters with the desired state defined in Git.

Setting Up GitOps with FluxCD: FluxCD is a popular GitOps tool that automates the deployment of resources across multiple Kubernetes clusters. It continuously monitors your Git repositories and ensures that your cluster state matches the state defined in Git.

- **Define Desired State:** Store your Kubernetes manifests, Helm charts, and Kustomize configurations in a Git repository.

- **Deploy FluxCD:** Use the FluxCD CLI to install Flux controllers in your clusters.

- **Automate Synchronization:** Configure FluxCD to continuously sync the clusters with the repository, ensuring that any changes in Git are automatically applied.

Example FluxCD Configuration:

```yaml
apiVersion: source.toolkit.fluxcd.io/v1
kind: GitRepository
metadata:
  name: my-app
  namespace: flux-system
spec:
  interval: 5m
  url: https://github.com/my-org/my-app
  ref:
    branch: main
---
apiVersion: kustomize.toolkit.fluxcd.io/v1
kind: Kustomization
metadata:
  name: my-app
  namespace: flux-system
spec:
  interval: 10m
  path: "./deploy/prod"
  prune: true
  sourceRef:
    kind: GitRepository
    name: my-app
```

Using Custom Controllers and CRDs Custom controllers and Custom Resource Definitions (CRDs) can be used to manage and synchronize custom resources across clusters. This approach provides flexibility for handling specialized resources and complex synchronization logic.

Federation Resource Propagation For users already employing Kubernetes Federation (KubeFed), it allows defining Federated Resource types that specify which resources should be synchronized across clusters. These can include ConfigMaps, Secrets, Deployments, and more.

Example Federated Deployment:

```
apiVersion: types.kubefed.io/v1beta1
kind: FederatedDeployment
metadata:
  name: nginx
  namespace: default
spec:
  template:
    metadata:
      labels:
        app: nginx
    spec:
      replicas: 3
      template:
        metadata:
          labels:
            app: nginx
        spec:
          containers:
          - name: nginx
            image: nginx:1.15.4
            ports:
            - containerPort: 80
  placement:
    clusters:
    - name: cluster1
    - name: cluster2
```

Centralized Management Tools Tools like Rancher and KubeSphere offer centralized management platforms for multi-cluster environments. These platforms provide a single pane of glass for managing, monitoring, and synchronizing resources across clusters.

Rancher:

- Provides a unified dashboard for managing multiple clusters.

- Simplifies the deployment and synchronization of applications across clusters.

- Integrates with GitOps tools for seamless resource synchronization.

KubeSphere:

- Offers multi-cluster management and DevOps capabilities.

- Supports resource synchronization and centralized policy management.

- Provides comprehensive monitoring and logging across clusters.

Monitoring and Validation   Ensuring the consistency and integrity of synchronized resources is crucial. Implement monitoring and validation mechanisms to detect and resolve discrepancies.

Best Practices for Monitoring:

- **Centralized Logging:** Use centralized logging solutions to aggregate logs from all clusters and monitor synchronization events.

- **Metrics Collection:** Collect and visualize metrics related to resource synchronization using Prometheus and Grafana.

- **Automated Validation:** Implement automated checks to validate that resources are synchronized correctly across clusters.

Conclusion   Synchronizing resources across multiple Kubernetes clusters is essential for maintaining consistency, reliability, and efficiency in a multi-cluster environment. By leveraging tools like FluxCD, custom controllers, and centralized management platforms, administrators can ensure seamless operations and effective resource management across their clusters.

8.2.4   Disaster Recovery and Redundancy with Federation

Disaster recovery and redundancy are critical aspects of maintaining highly available and resilient Kubernetes environments. Kubernetes Federation (KubeFed) provides powerful mechanisms to enhance disaster recovery capabilities and ensure redundancy across multiple clusters. This section explores strategies for implementing disaster recovery and redundancy using Kubernetes Federation.

High Availability through Cluster Federation KubeFed allows you to distribute applications and services across multiple clusters, which can be located in different geographical regions or cloud providers. This geographic distribution ensures that your applications remain available even if one cluster experiences a failure. Federation enables the replication of resources and services, providing failover capabilities and reducing downtime.

Key Benefits:

- **Geographic Redundancy:** By spreading clusters across different regions, you can protect against localized failures.

- **Improved Resilience:** Federated clusters can share the load, and if one cluster goes down, others can take over seamlessly.

- **Reduced Downtime:** Automatic failover mechanisms ensure minimal disruption to services.

Disaster Recovery Strategies Implementing effective disaster recovery strategies with Kubernetes Federation involves several key practices:

Resource Propagation: KubeFed allows you to propagate resources such as Deployments, Services, ConfigMaps, and Secrets across federated clusters. This ensures that all clusters have the necessary resources to take over in case of a failure.

Automated Failover: Configure automated failover mechanisms to switch traffic to healthy clusters when a failure is detected. This can be achieved through Federated Ingress and DNS configurations that route traffic to the nearest available cluster.

Backup and Restore: Regularly backup your cluster configurations, including federated resources. Use tools like Velero for backing up and restoring Kubernetes resources across clusters. Ensure that backups are stored in multiple locations to prevent data loss.

```
# Install Velero for backup and restore
kubectl apply -f https://github.com/vmware-tanzu/velero/
```

```
releases/latest/download/velero-v1.7.1-linux-amd64.tar.gz

# Schedule regular backups
velero backup create cluster-backup --include-cluster-resources
--wait
```

Implementing Redundancy To achieve redundancy, configure your federation to ensure that critical applications and services are replicated across multiple clusters. Use the following practices:

Federated Deployments: Create Federated Deployments to ensure that your applications are consistently deployed across all clusters. Specify placement policies to control where and how resources are distributed.

```
apiVersion: types.kubefed.io/v1beta1
kind: FederatedDeployment
metadata:
  name: my-app
  namespace: default
spec:
  template:
    metadata:
      labels:
        app: my-app
    spec:
      replicas: 3
      template:
        metadata:
          labels:
            app: my-app
        spec:
          containers:
          - name: my-app-container
            image: my-app-image
  placement:
    clusters:
    - name: cluster1
    - name: cluster2
```

Federated Ingress: Use Federated Ingress to manage external traffic and provide load balancing across clusters. This setup ensures that user requests are directed to the nearest or most responsive cluster, improving performance and availability.

Monitoring and Management Continuous monitoring and proactive management are essential for maintaining a robust federated environment. Implement monitoring solutions that provide visibility into the health and performance of all clusters. Tools like Prometheus and Grafana can be integrated with KubeFed for comprehensive monitoring.

Example Monitoring Setup:

```
# Deploy Prometheus to monitor federated clusters
kubectl apply -f https://github.com/prometheus-operator/
prometheus-operator/releases/download/v0.47.0/bundle.yaml
```

Best Practices Adopting best practices for disaster recovery and redundancy with Kubernetes Federation ensures that your applications remain resilient and available:

- **Regular Testing:** Periodically test failover mechanisms and backup restores to ensure they work as expected.

- **Consistent Configuration:** Use tools like FluxCD or ArgoCD to maintain consistent configurations across clusters.

- **Documentation:** Maintain detailed documentation of your federation setup, including failover procedures and backup policies.

Conclusion Kubernetes Federation provides powerful tools for enhancing disaster recovery and redundancy across multiple clusters. By implementing effective strategies and best practices, you can ensure that your applications remain highly available and resilient in the face of failures and disruptions.

Chapter 9

Security Best Practices

9.1 Introduction to Kubernetes Security

Kubernetes security is a multi-faceted area critical for ensuring the integrity, confidentiality, and availability of containerized applications. As Kubernetes has become the leading platform for container orchestration, securing it has become paramount. This section provides a brief overview of security in Kubernetes and highlights the importance of security in containerized environments.

Overview of Security in Kubernetes Kubernetes is designed with a layered security approach, integrating various security mechanisms and best practices to protect workloads. These mechanisms include Role-Based Access Control (RBAC), network policies, secrets management, and admission control. The Kubernetes control plane components, such as the API server, etcd, and the scheduler, also play crucial roles in maintaining the security and stability of the cluster.

A critical aspect of Kubernetes security is its reliance on third-party integrations for comprehensive security solutions. Kubernetes itself provides the framework and APIs for security but delegates specific functionalities, such as user authentication and runtime security, to external tools and systems.

Importance of Security in Containerized Environments The adoption of containerized environments has revolutionized software development and deployment by providing scalability, flexibility, and efficiency. However, it also introduces new security challenges. Containers share the same kernel, making the attack surface larger if not properly isolated and secured.

Ensuring the security of a Kubernetes cluster is crucial for several reasons:

- **Protection of Sensitive Data:** Containers often handle sensitive information, and any breach could lead to significant data exposure.

- **Maintaining Service Availability:** Security incidents can disrupt services, leading to downtime and loss of trust.

- **Compliance Requirements:** Many industries have strict compliance requirements that necessitate robust security measures.

- **Preventing Lateral Movement:** In a compromised environment, an attacker might move laterally to exploit other containers and services. Proper security measures can mitigate this risk.

Kubernetes security encompasses multiple domains, including network security, workload security, and infrastructure security. Effective security practices involve not only securing the Kubernetes components but also ensuring that applications running on the cluster are secure throughout their lifecycle—from development to deployment and runtime.

By understanding and implementing robust security measures, organizations can safeguard their Kubernetes environments against various threats, ensuring the smooth and secure operation of their containerized applications.

9.2   Pod Security Admission

9.2.1   Introduction to PSA

Pod Security Admission (PSA) is the successor to PodSecurityPolicy (PSP) in Kubernetes. This transition was made to simplify and enhance security controls within Kubernetes clusters. PSP was deprecated in Kubernetes v1.21 and removed in v1.25 due to its complexity and limited adoption. PSA, introduced in Kubernetes v1.23 and stable since v1.25, offers a more streamlined approach by leveraging namespace labels to enforce security standards.

PSA works by checking incoming pod specifications against predefined security standards—Privileged, Baseline, and Restricted. These standards ensure that pods adhere to security best practices based on their operational needs. By using namespace labels, PSA can enforce different security profiles across various parts of the cluster, providing flexibility and ease of management.

9.2.2 Configuring PSA

Configuring PSA involves labeling namespaces to apply the desired security standards. This configuration is straightforward and can be done using 'kubectl' commands.

Steps to Configure PSA:

1. **Label the Namespace:**

```
# Apply the Baseline policy to the 'default' namespace
kubectl label namespace default \
  pod-security.kubernetes.io/enforce=baseline \
  pod-security.kubernetes.io/enforce-version=v1.30
```

2. **Verify the Configuration:**

```
# Check the labels on the namespace
kubectl get namespace default --show-labels
```

3. **Deploy Pods:** Deploy pods as usual. PSA will evaluate pod specifications against the policies defined by the namespace labels and enforce them accordingly.

9.2.3   PSA Modes

PSA operates in three modes: Enforce, Audit, and Warn. Each mode serves a different purpose and can be used individually or in combination to achieve comprehensive security enforcement.

Enforce Mode: Enforce mode blocks any pod creation or update that does not comply with the specified security policies. It ensures strict adherence to security standards.

Audit Mode: Audit mode does not block non-compliant pods but logs violations. This mode is useful for monitoring and assessing the impact of policies without enforcing them immediately.

Warn Mode: Warn mode notifies users of policy violations via warnings but does not block pod creation or updates. It helps users become aware of security requirements without immediate enforcement.

Example Configuration:

```
# Apply Enforce, Audit, and Warn modes to the
'default' namespace
kubectl label namespace default \
  pod-security.kubernetes.io/enforce=baseline \
  pod-security.kubernetes.io/audit=baseline \
  pod-security.kubernetes.io/warn=baseline \
  pod-security.kubernetes.io/enforce-version=v1.30 \
  pod-security.kubernetes.io/audit-version=v1.30 \
  pod-security.kubernetes.io/warn-version=v1.30
```

9.2.4   Examples and Best Practices

Applying PSA with different security levels helps in maintaining a secure and compliant Kubernetes environment. Below are practical examples and best practices for setting up PSA.

Privileged Policy: The Privileged policy is the least restrictive and allows all pod configurations. It is suitable for trusted system-level workloads.

Example Configuration:

```
# Apply the Privileged policy to the 'kube-system' namespace
kubectl label namespace kube-system \
  pod-security.kubernetes.io/enforce=privileged \
  pod-security.kubernetes.io/enforce-version=v1.30
```

Baseline Policy: The Baseline policy prevents known privilege escalations while allowing common pod configurations. It is suitable for most application workloads.

Example Configuration:

```
# Apply the Baseline policy to the 'default' namespace
kubectl label namespace default \
  pod-security.kubernetes.io/enforce=baseline \
  pod-security.kubernetes.io/enforce-version=v1.30
```

Restricted Policy: The Restricted policy is the most secure, following strict pod hardening best practices. It is ideal for high-security environments.

Example Configuration:

```
# Apply the Restricted policy to the 'secure-apps' namespace
kubectl label namespace secure-apps \
  pod-security.kubernetes.io/enforce=restricted \
  pod-security.kubernetes.io/enforce-version=v1.30
```

Best Practices:

- **Gradual Enforcement:** Start with Audit or Warn modes to identify potential issues before enforcing policies.

- **Namespace Segmentation:** Apply different security policies to different namespaces based on their security requirements.

- **Regular Reviews:** Periodically review and update security policies to align with evolving security best practices and application needs.

- **Automated Enforcement:** Integrate PSA configurations into CI/CD pipelines to ensure consistent security enforcement across environments.

By understanding and correctly implementing Pod Security Admission, Kubernetes administrators can significantly enhance the security posture of their clusters, ensuring that only compliant pods are allowed to run.

9.3   Network Segmentation and Zero Trust

Network segmentation and Zero Trust are critical components of modern Kubernetes security strategies. As Kubernetes environments become more complex and interconnected, traditional perimeter-based security models are no longer sufficient. This section will delve into the principles and practices of network segmentation and Zero Trust, focusing on their implementation in Kubernetes clusters.

9.3.1   Introduction to Network Segmentation and Zero Trust

Network Segmentation Network segmentation involves dividing a network into smaller, isolated segments to control and restrict traffic flow between them. This practice minimizes the attack surface by limiting the spread of potential threats within the network. In Kubernetes, network segmentation is achieved using network policies that define and enforce rules for communication between pods and services.

Zero Trust Security   Zero Trust is a security model based on the principle of "never trust, always verify." Unlike traditional models that assume entities within the network are trustworthy, Zero Trust assumes that threats can exist both inside and outside the network. It requires continuous verification of the identity and integrity of devices, users, and applications before granting access to resources.

9.3.2 Implementing Network Segmentation in Kubernetes

Network segmentation in Kubernetes is primarily managed through network policies. These policies control traffic flow at the pod level, ensuring that only authorized communication is allowed. Here are the key steps to implement effective network segmentation:

Define Network Policies Use Kubernetes NetworkPolicy resources to create rules that govern traffic between pods. For example, a network policy might restrict a frontend service from communicating directly with the database, allowing access only through an API service.

```
apiVersion: networking.k8s.io/v1
kind: NetworkPolicy
metadata:
  name: allow-app-to-db
  namespace: default
spec:
  podSelector:
    matchLabels:
      app: database
  ingress:
  - from:
    - podSelector:
        matchLabels:
          app: api
```

Enforce Default Deny Policies Begin with a default deny policy that blocks all traffic, then explicitly allow necessary communication. This approach ensures that no unintended traffic flows between pods.

```
apiVersion: networking.k8s.io/v1
kind: NetworkPolicy
metadata:
  name: default-deny-all
  namespace: default
spec:
```

```
podSelector: {}
policyTypes:
- Ingress
- Egress
```

9.3.3   Zero Trust Principles in Kubernetes

Least Privilege Access   Ensure that users, devices, and applications have the minimum necessary access rights. Implement Role-Based Access Control (RBAC) to enforce fine-grained permissions.

Continuous Monitoring and Verification Continuously monitor network traffic and user behavior to detect anomalies. Use tools like Prometheus and Grafana for real-time visibility and alerting.

Service-to-Service Authentication   Implement mutual TLS (mTLS) to authenticate and encrypt service-to-service communication. This ensures that only verified services can communicate within the cluster.

9.3.4   Combining Network Segmentation with Zero Trust

Combining network segmentation with Zero Trust principles enhances security by ensuring that even if one segment is compromised, the threat cannot easily spread. This approach requires a comprehensive strategy that includes:

Micro-Segmentation Apply micro-segmentation to create granular security zones within the Kubernetes cluster. Each segment should be isolated and protected by specific network policies.

Strong Identity Management Use Kubernetes service accounts, namespaces, and RBAC to manage identities and access controls. Integrate with external identity providers for robust authentication.

Encryption and TLS Encrypt all communication within and between Kubernetes clusters. Use TLS for data in transit and manage certificates securely using tools like Cert-Manager.

9.3.5 Best Practices for Network Segmentation and Zero Trust

- **Regular Audits:** Periodically review and update network policies and access controls to ensure they align with evolving security requirements.

- **Automated Policy Enforcement:** Integrate security policies into CI/CD pipelines to enforce them consistently across development, staging, and production environments.

- **Use of Service Mesh:** Implement a service mesh like Istio or Linkerd to enhance observability, security, and traffic management capabilities.

- **Comprehensive Monitoring:** Deploy monitoring solutions to continuously track network traffic, identify potential threats, and respond promptly.

- **Training and Awareness:** Educate developers and operators on the principles of Zero Trust and the importance of secure coding and configuration practices.

By implementing these practices, organizations can significantly enhance the security of their Kubernetes environments, ensuring robust protection against internal and external threats.

9.4 Hardening Nodes and the Control Plane

Securing a Kubernetes cluster requires diligent attention to both node and control plane security. This section provides detailed best practices for hardening nodes, securing the control plane, and configuring Role-Based Access Control (RBAC) to enhance your cluster's security posture.

9.4.1 Node Hardening

Node hardening involves securing the individual machines (virtual or physical) that make up your Kubernetes cluster. Here are key practices to follow:

Operating System Hardening

- **Use Minimal Base Images:** Utilize minimal operating system images, such as Ubuntu Minimal or Alpine Linux, to reduce the attack surface.

- **Regular Updates:** Keep the operating system and all installed packages up-to-date with the latest security patches.

- **Disable Unnecessary Services:** Turn off services that are not required for Kubernetes operations.

- **Configure Firewalls:** Use tools like `iptables` or `firewalld` to restrict access to only necessary ports.

- **File Integrity Monitoring:** Implement tools like AIDE or Tripwire to monitor and detect unauthorized changes to files.

Security Tools

- **SELinux:** Enable Security-Enhanced Linux (SELinux) to enforce mandatory access controls.

- **AppArmor:** Use AppArmor to restrict the capabilities of individual containers.

- **Auditd:** Deploy `auditd` to log system calls and monitor suspicious activity.

SELinux Security-Enhanced Linux (SELinux) is a Linux kernel security module that provides a mechanism for supporting access control security policies. It implements mandatory access control (MAC), which restricts the abilities of a program or user, preventing security breaches by containing the damage that can be caused by malicious code or compromised programs.

Configuring SELinux for Kubernetes Nodes:

- **Install SELinux:** Ensure that SELinux is installed and enabled on your Linux nodes.

```
# Install SELinux
sudo apt-get install selinux-utils selinux-basics

# Enable SELinux
sudo selinux-activate

sudo reboot
```

- **Set SELinux to Enforcing Mode:** The enforcing mode enforces SELinux policies, logging actions and denying access that is not explicitly allowed.

```
# Set SELinux to enforcing mode
sudo setenforce 1
```

- **Create SELinux Policies:** Custom policies can be written to define the security context for your Kubernetes workloads.

```
module my_k8s_module 1.0;

require {
    type container_t;
    class sock_file write;
}

# Allow containers to write to a specific socket file
allow container_t self:sock_file write;
```

AppArmor AppArmor (Application Armor) is a Linux security module that provides an effective way of implementing security policies to restrict program capabilities. It uses profiles loaded into the kernel to confine the behavior of applications.

Configuring AppArmor for Kubernetes Nodes:

- **Install AppArmor:** Ensure that AppArmor is installed and enabled on your nodes.

```
# Install AppArmor
sudo apt-get install apparmor apparmor-utils

# Enable AppArmor
sudo systemctl enable apparmor

sudo systemctl start apparmor
```

- **Create and Apply AppArmor Profiles:** AppArmor profiles can be created to define restrictions for your Kubernetes workloads.

```
# Example AppArmor profile for a container
profile my_k8s_profile flags=(attach_disconnected) {
    # Deny all file writes by default
    deny /** w,
    # Allow writes only to specific directories
    /var/log/myapp/ w,
    /data/myapp/ rwk,
}
```

- **Apply AppArmor Profiles:** Apply the AppArmor profiles to your containers.

```
apiVersion: v1
kind: Pod
metadata:
  name: apparmor-demo
  annotations:
    container.apparmor.security.beta.
kubernetes.io/nginx: localhost/my_k8s_profile
spec:
  containers:
  - name: nginx
```

```
image: nginx
securityContext:
  appArmorProfile: localhost/my_k8s_profile
```

Auditd Auditd is a userspace component to the Linux Auditing System, which provides a way to track security-relevant information on a system. It logs system calls and can be configured to monitor and audit events, providing a detailed trail of actions for security analysis.

Configuring Auditd for Kubernetes Nodes:

- **Install Auditd:** Ensure that Auditd is installed on your nodes.

```
# Install Auditd
sudo apt-get install auditd
```

- **Configure Audit Rules:** Define audit rules to specify which events should be logged.

```
# Example audit rule to log all access to /etc/passwd
-a always,exit -F dir=/etc/passwd -F perm=wa
-k passwd_changes
```

- **Review Audit Logs:** Use audit logs to review and analyze security events.

```
# Display recent audit logs
sudo ausearch -k passwd_changes
```

Non-Root User Configuration

Run as Non-Root: Configure containers to run as non-root users to limit the impact of potential compromises.

```
apiVersion: v1
kind: Pod
metadata:
  name: non-root-pod
```

```
spec:
  containers:
  - name: app
    image: nginx
    securityContext:
      runAsUser: 1000
      runAsGroup: 3000
      fsGroup: 2000
```

9.4.2 Control Plane Security

The control plane is the brain of the Kubernetes cluster, managing the state of the cluster and orchestrating operations. Securing the control plane components is crucial:

API Server Security

- **Enable TLS:** Ensure all communication with the API server is encrypted using Transport Layer Security (TLS).

- **Authentication:** Implement robust authentication mechanisms such as x509 certificates, OIDC, or LDAP.

- **Authorization:** Use Role-Based Access Control (RBAC) to limit what authenticated users and service accounts can do.

```
apiVersion: rbac.authorization.k8s.io/v1
kind: Role
metadata:
  namespace: default
  name: pod-reader
rules:
- apiGroups: [""]
  resources: ["pods"]
  verbs: ["get", "watch", "list"]
```

etcd Security

- **Encrypt Data:** Enable encryption for data at rest in etcd.

- **Restrict Access:** Limit access to etcd to only necessary components and use firewall rules to restrict network access.

Controller Manager and Scheduler Security

- **Network Segmentation:** Ensure that the controller manager and scheduler are only accessible by the API server and other necessary components.

- **Secure Configurations:** Use secure configurations and avoid exposing these components to the public internet.

9.4.3 RBAC (Role-Based Access Control)

RBAC is a critical security feature in Kubernetes that helps manage permissions and access control:

Configuring RBAC Define Roles and RoleBindings: Create roles that define a set of permissions and bind them to users or service accounts using RoleBindings or ClusterRoleBindings.

```
apiVersion: rbac.authorization.k8s.io/v1
kind: RoleBinding
metadata:
  name: read-pods
  namespace: default
subjects:
- kind: User
  name: jane
  apiGroup: rbac.authorization.k8s.io
roleRef:
  kind: Role
  name: pod-reader
  apiGroup: rbac.authorization.k8s.io
```

Best Practices for RBAC

- **Principle of Least Privilege:** Grant the minimum required permissions to users and service accounts.

- **Namespace Isolation:** Use namespaces to isolate resources and apply RBAC policies at the namespace level.

- **Regular Audits:** Regularly audit RBAC policies to ensure they meet current security requirements and adjust them as necessary.

Monitoring and Logging

- **Audit Logs:** Enable and review audit logs to monitor for unauthorized access or suspicious activities.

- **Monitoring Tools:** Use monitoring tools like Prometheus and Grafana to visualize and alert on security events.

Conclusion By following these best practices for node hardening, control plane security, and RBAC configuration, you can significantly enhance the security of your Kubernetes cluster. Regular audits, updates, and adherence to security principles are essential for maintaining a robust security posture.

9.5 Image Security: Scanning and Signing

Ensuring the security of container images is a critical aspect of maintaining a secure Kubernetes environment. This section covers tools and techniques for scanning container images for vulnerabilities, signing images to verify their integrity, and best practices for building and maintaining secure images.

9.5.1 Image Scanning

Image scanning is the process of analyzing container images to detect known vulnerabilities. Various tools are available to perform this task, each with its unique features and capabilities.

Trivy Trivy is an open-source vulnerability scanner for container images, file systems, and Git repositories. It is known for its simplicity and efficiency, making it a popular choice for image scanning.

Using Trivy to Scan Images:

```
# Install Trivy
sudo apt-get install trivy

# Scan a Docker image
trivy image your-image:latest
```

Clair Clair is an open-source project for the static analysis of vulnerabilities in application containers (currently including appc and docker). Clair performs static analysis on containers, enabling users to detect vulnerabilities within their images.

Using Clair to Scan Images:

```
# Run Clair as a service
docker run -d -p 5432:5432 --name db arminc/clair-db:latest
docker run -d -p 6060:6060 --link db:postgres --name clair
arminc/clair-local-scan:v2.0.6

# Use a Clair client to scan an image
clair-scanner your-image:latest
```

9.5.2 Image Signing

Image signing is a process used to verify the integrity and authenticity of a container image. This process ensures that the image has not been tampered with and comes from a trusted source.

Notary Notary is a tool for signing and verifying content. It allows users to sign their container images and ensure that they have not been altered.

Using Notary to Sign Images:

```
# Initialize Notary repository
notary init your-repo

# Sign an image
```

```
notary add your-repo your-image:latest

# Publish the signed image
notary publish your-repo
```

The Update Framework (TUF) TUF is a framework for securing software update systems. It helps developers protect their systems from various attacks by providing a robust method for signing and verifying updates.

Using TUF for Image Signing:

```
# Initialize TUF repository
tuf init your-repo

# Add a target file (image)
tuf add-target your-repo your-image:latest

# Sign the repository
tuf sign your-repo

# Publish the signed targets
tuf publish your-repo
```

9.5.3   Best Practices for Building Secure Images

Building secure container images involves following best practices to minimize vulnerabilities and ensure the integrity of the images.

Minimize Base Image Size Use minimal base images to reduce the attack surface. Alpine Linux and other minimal distributions are preferred for this purpose.

```
# Example Dockerfile using Alpine Linux
FROM alpine:3.12
RUN apk add --no-cache python3
COPY . /app
WORKDIR /app
CMD ["python3", "app.py"]
```

Regularly Update Images Ensure that the base images and all software packages are regularly updated to include the latest security patches. Automate the process of rebuilding images to integrate these updates.

Use Multi-Stage Builds Multi-stage builds help in creating lean images by separating the build environment from the runtime environment. This technique reduces the final image size and improves security.

```
# Example Dockerfile with multi-stage build
FROM golang:1.15 AS builder
WORKDIR /src
COPY . .
RUN go build -o myapp

FROM alpine:3.12
COPY --from=builder /src/myapp /app/myapp
CMD ["/app/myapp"]
```

Implement Security Testing in CI/CD Pipelines Integrate image scanning and signing into CI/CD pipelines to automate security checks. This ensures that only verified and secure images are deployed to the Kubernetes cluster.

```
# Example CI/CD pipeline step for image scanning
steps:
  - name: Scan image
    image: trivy:latest
    script:
      - trivy image your-image:latest
```

Conclusion By implementing these best practices for image scanning, signing, and building, you can significantly enhance the security of your container images. Regularly updating images, minimizing their size, and integrating security checks into CI/CD pipelines are essential steps to maintain a secure and robust Kubernetes environment.

9.6   Audit Logging and Monitoring Access

Audit logging and monitoring access are critical components of a comprehensive security strategy in Kubernetes. These practices ensure that all actions within the cluster are recorded, providing a detailed trail for security analysis, compliance, and forensic investigation. This section covers the importance of audit logging, tools and techniques for implementing it, and best practices for monitoring access to the Kubernetes cluster.

9.6.1   Audit Logging

Audit logging involves capturing and storing logs of all significant events within a Kubernetes cluster. These logs provide visibility into the activities occurring within the cluster, helping administrators detect unauthorized access, unusual behavior, and potential security incidents.

Setting Up Kubernetes Audit Logging   Kubernetes provides a built-in audit logging mechanism that can be configured to capture various events. The audit logs can be customized based on predefined policies to capture specific types of events.

Configuring Audit Policies:

```
# Example audit policy configuration
apiVersion: audit.k8s.io/v1
kind: Policy
rules:
- level: Metadata
  resources:
  - group: ""
    resources: ["pods", "secrets"]
- level: RequestResponse
  users: ["admin"]
  verbs: ["create", "update", "delete"]
```

Enabling Audit Logging: To enable audit logging, configure the API server to use the audit policy file.

```
# Update the API server manifest
--audit-policy-file=/etc/kubernetes/audit-policy.yaml
--audit-log-path=/var/log/kubernetes/audit.log
```

Centralizing and Storing Audit Logs   Centralizing audit logs helps in managing and analyzing them effectively. Tools like Elasticsearch, Fluentd, and Kibana (EFK stack) can be used to aggregate, store, and visualize audit logs.

Analyzing Audit Logs   Analyzing audit logs involves reviewing the logs to identify any unusual or suspicious activities. Kibana provides a user-friendly interface to query and visualize audit logs, making it easier to analyze the data.

Example Kibana Query:

```
# Query to find all delete actions by admin user
{
  "query": {
    "bool": {
      "must": [
        { "match": { "user": "admin" }},
        { "match": { "verb": "delete" }}
      ]
    }
  }
}
```

9.6.2   Monitoring Access

Monitoring access to the Kubernetes cluster ensures that only authorized users and processes are performing actions within the cluster. This practice helps in maintaining security and detecting potential breaches.

Role-Based Access Control (RBAC)   RBAC is a key mechanism for controlling access in Kubernetes. By defining roles and role bindings, administrators can specify what actions users and service accounts can perform within the cluster.

Configuring RBAC:

```
# Define a role that allows read access to pods
apiVersion: rbac.authorization.k8s.io/v1
kind: Role
metadata:
  namespace: default
  name: pod-reader
rules:
- apiGroups: [""]
  resources: ["pods"]
  verbs: ["get", "watch", "list"]

# Bind the role to a user
apiVersion: rbac.authorization.k8s.io/v1
kind: RoleBinding
metadata:
  name: read-pods
  namespace: default
subjects:
- kind: User
  name: jane
  apiGroup: rbac.authorization.k8s.io
roleRef:
  kind: Role
  name: pod-reader
  apiGroup: rbac.authorization.k8s.io
```

Using External Monitoring Tools   Using external monitoring tools for collecting and visualizing metrics and logs ensures that the monitoring infrastructure is decoupled from the monitored environment, providing better scalability and reliability.

Prometheus and Grafana: Prometheus is a powerful monitoring system and time series database. Grafana is used for visualizing the data collected by Prometheus. Using external setups for these tools enhances the robustness of the monitoring solution.

Best Practices for Audit Logging and Monitoring Access

- **Enable Detailed Audit Logs:** Capture detailed logs to ensure comprehensive visibility into cluster activities.

- **Regularly Review Logs:** Periodically review audit logs to detect any unauthorized access or unusual behavior.

- **Implement RBAC:** Use RBAC to enforce least privilege access, ensuring users and services have only the permissions they need.

- **Use External Monitoring Tools:** Leverage external tools like Prometheus, Grafana, and Loki to monitor access and activities within the cluster.

- **Automate Alerts:** Set up automated alerts for suspicious activities to enable prompt "'latex responses to potential security incidents.

Conclusion Implementing audit logging and monitoring access are crucial steps in securing a Kubernetes cluster. By capturing detailed logs, enforcing RBAC, and using external monitoring tools, administrators can ensure that their clusters are secure and any suspicious activities are promptly detected and addressed. Leveraging external EFK, Prometheus, Grafana, and Loki setups enhances the reliability and scalability of the monitoring infrastructure, providing robust security for Kubernetes environments.

9.7 Encryption: At Rest and In Transit

Encryption is a critical component of Kubernetes security, protecting sensitive data both when it's stored (at rest) and when it's being transmitted (in transit). This section explores the implementation of encryption in Kubernetes environments, covering both scenarios and providing best practices for maintaining robust security.

9.7.1 Encryption at Rest

Encryption at rest refers to the encryption of data when it is stored. In Kubernetes, this primarily applies to data stored in etcd, the distributed key-value store used to hold all cluster data.

Enabling Encryption at Rest in Kubernetes　To enable encryption at rest for Kubernetes secrets:

1. Create an encryption configuration file:

```
apiVersion: apiserver.config.k8s.io/v1
kind: EncryptionConfiguration
resources:
  - resources:
      - secrets
    providers:
      - aescbc:
          keys:
            - name: key1
              secret: <base64-encoded-key>
      - identity: {}
```

2. Configure the API server to use the encryption configuration:

```
--encryption-provider-config=/path/to/
encryption-config.yaml
```

3. Restart the API server to apply the changes.

Best Practices for Encryption at Rest

- Regularly rotate encryption keys to maintain security.

- Use strong encryption algorithms (e.g., AES-256).

- Securely manage and store encryption keys, preferably using a key management service (KMS).

- Encrypt all sensitive data, not just secrets.

9.7.2　Encryption in Transit

Encryption in transit ensures that data is protected as it moves between different components of the Kubernetes cluster or to external systems.

Implementing TLS for Kubernetes Components

1. Generate TLS certificates for Kubernetes components:

```
openssl genrsa -out ca.key 2048
openssl req -new -x509 -days 365 -key ca.key -out ca.crt
```

2. Configure the API server to use TLS:

```
--tls-cert-file=/path/to/server.crt
--tls-private-key-file=/path/to/server.key
```

3. Enable TLS for etcd:

```
--cert-file=/path/to/etcd.crt
--key-file=/path/to/etcd.key
--trusted-ca-file=/path/to/ca.crt
```

Securing Pod-to-Pod Communication   Implement a service mesh like Istio or Linkerd to enable automatic mTLS between pods:

```
apiVersion: security.istio.io/v1beta1
kind: PeerAuthentication
metadata:
  name: default
  namespace: istio-system
spec:
  mtls:
    mode: STRICT
```

Best Practices for Encryption in Transit

- Use TLS 1.2 or later for all network communication.

- Implement mutual TLS (mTLS) for service-to-service communication.

- Regularly update and patch TLS libraries to address vulnerabilities.

- Use strong cipher suites and disable weak protocols.

- Implement proper certificate management, including automated rotation and renewal.

9.7.3　Key Management

Effective key management is crucial for maintaining the security of encrypted data.

Using Cloud Provider Key Management Services　Integrate with cloud provider KMS for secure key storage and management:

```
apiVersion: apiserver.config.k8s.io/v1
kind: EncryptionConfiguration
resources:
  - resources:
      - secrets
    providers:
      - kms:
          name: myKMSPlugin
          endpoint: unix:///path/to/socket
          cachesize: 100
          timeout: 3s
      - identity: {}
```

Best Practices for Key Management

- Use a dedicated key management service (KMS) for storing and managing encryption keys.

- Implement key rotation policies to regularly update encryption keys.

- Use separate keys for different purposes (e.g., data encryption, signing).

- Implement access controls and auditing for key management operations.

9.7.4　Monitoring and Auditing Encryption

Regular monitoring and auditing of encryption practices are essential to maintain security.

Implementing Encryption Monitoring

- Use Prometheus to collect metrics on encryption operations:

```
apiVersion: monitoring.coreos.com/v1
kind: ServiceMonitor
metadata:
  name: encryption-monitor
spec:
  selector:
    matchLabels:
      app: kube-apiserver
  endpoints:
  - port: https
    scheme: https
    tlsConfig:
      caFile: /path/to/ca.crt
    bearerTokenFile: /path/to/bearer-token
```

- Set up alerts for encryption-related issues:

```
groups:
- name: EncryptionAlerts
  rules:
  - alert: EncryptionKeyExpiringSoon
    expr: kube_secret_encryption_key_expiration_time
< 7 * 24 * 3600
    for: 1h
    labels:
      severity: warning
    annotations:
      summary: "Encryption key expiring soon"
      description: "The encryption key will expire in
less than 7 days"
```

Auditing Encryption Practices

- Regularly review encryption configurations and key usage.

- Conduct penetration testing to identify potential vulnerabilities in encryption implementation.

- Use tools like kube-bench to check for encryption-related misconfigurations:

```
kubectl run kube-bench --rm -i --tty --image=
aquasec/kube-bench:latest -- --check="1.2.31,1.2.32"
```

9.7.5   Conclusion

Implementing robust encryption practices for data at rest and in transit is crucial for maintaining the security of a Kubernetes cluster. By following the best practices outlined in this section, including proper key management, regular monitoring, and auditing, organizations can significantly enhance their overall security posture. Remember that encryption is just one part of a comprehensive security strategy and should be implemented alongside other security measures such as access controls, network policies, and regular security updates.

Chapter 10

Advanced Development Practices

10.1 GitOps with Kubernetes

GitOps is a modern approach to continuous deployment for cloud-native applications. It uses Git as a single source of truth for declarative infrastructure and applications. This section explores how GitOps principles can be applied to Kubernetes environments, enhancing reliability, consistency, and automation in deployment processes.

10.1.1 Introduction to GitOps

GitOps is an operational model that applies DevOps best practices for application deployment and infrastructure management. It centers around using Git repositories as the canonical source of truth for declarative descriptions of infrastructure and applications.

Key Principles of GitOps

- **Declarative Configuration**: The entire system is described declaratively, typically using YAML files for Kubernetes resources.

- **Version Control**: All changes to the system are version controlled in Git, providing a complete audit trail and enabling easy rollbacks.

- **Automated Synchronization**: Automated processes ensure that the deployed system matches the desired state described in the Git repository.

- **Continuous Reconciliation**: The system continuously monitors for drift between Git-defined desired state and actual cluster state, reconciling any differences.

10.1.2 Implementing GitOps in Kubernetes

To implement GitOps in a Kubernetes environment, you need three main components:

1. A Git repository containing Kubernetes manifests

2. A Kubernetes cluster

3. A GitOps operator (e.g., Flux or ArgoCD)

Setting Up a GitOps Workflow

1. **Create a Git Repository**: This repository will contain all your Kubernetes manifests, Helm charts, and other configuration files.

2. **Install a GitOps Operator**: We'll use Flux as an example.

```
flux bootstrap github \
  --owner=$GITHUB_USER \
  --repository=flux-gitops \
  --branch=main \
  --path=./clusters/my-cluster \
  --personal
```

3. **Define Your Application**: Create Kubernetes manifests in your Git repository.

```
apiVersion: apps/v1
kind: Deployment
metadata:
```

```
      name: myapp
spec:
  replicas: 3
  selector:
    matchLabels:
      app: myapp
  template:
    metadata:
      labels:
        app: myapp
    spec:
      containers:
      - name: myapp
        image: myapp:v1.0.0
        ports:
        - containerPort: 8080
```

4. **Commit and Push**: Any changes pushed to the repository will be automatically applied to the cluster by the GitOps operator.

10.1.3 Benefits of GitOps in Kubernetes

Implementing GitOps in Kubernetes environments offers several advantages:

- **Improved Collaboration**: Developers and operations teams can collaborate more effectively using familiar Git workflows.

- **Enhanced Security**: Git's cryptographic integrity and the principle of least privilege improve overall security.

- **Faster Recovery**: In case of cluster failure, the entire system can be quickly reconstructed from the Git repository.

- **Consistency**: Ensures consistency between development, staging, and production environments.

- **Audibility**: Git's version history provides a comprehensive audit trail of all changes.

10.1.4   GitOps Tools for Kubernetes

Several tools are available to implement GitOps in Kubernetes:

Flux

Flux is a set of continuous and progressive delivery solutions for Kubernetes that are open and extensible.

```
apiVersion: kustomize.toolkit.fluxcd.io/v1beta2
kind: Kustomization
metadata:
  name: myapp
  namespace: flux-system
spec:
  interval: 5m
  path: "./kustomize"
  prune: true
  sourceRef:
    kind: GitRepository
    name: myapp
  validation: client
```

ArgoCD

ArgoCD is a declarative, GitOps continuous delivery tool for Kubernetes.

```
apiVersion: argoproj.io/v1alpha1
kind: Application
metadata:
  name: myapp
  namespace: argocd
spec:
  project: default
  source:
    repoURL: https://github.com/myorg/myapp.git
    targetRevision: HEAD
    path: kustomize
  destination:
```

```
  server: https://kubernetes.default.svc
  namespace: myapp
syncPolicy:
  automated:
    prune: true
    selfHeal: true
```

10.1.5   Best Practices for GitOps in Kubernetes

To effectively implement GitOps in Kubernetes, consider the following best practices:

- **Use Declarative Configurations**: Always use declarative configurations for your Kubernetes resources.

- **Implement Environment Parity**: Use the same GitOps workflow across all environments (dev, staging, production).

- **Secure Secrets Management**: Use tools like Sealed Secrets or external secret management systems to handle sensitive information.

- **Implement Proper Access Controls**: Use Git repository access controls and Kubernetes RBAC to manage permissions.

- **Monitor and Alert**: Set up monitoring and alerting for your GitOps processes to quickly detect and respond to issues.

- **Regular Audits**: Regularly audit your Git history and cluster state to ensure consistency and security.

10.1.6   Challenges and Considerations

While GitOps offers many benefits, it's important to be aware of potential challenges:

- **Learning Curve**: Teams may need time to adapt to the GitOps workflow.

- **Merge Conflicts**: As multiple team members contribute, merge conflicts may arise and need to be managed carefully.

- **Performance**: For large clusters or frequent updates, performance of the GitOps operator may become a consideration.

- **Secrets Management**: Proper handling of secrets requires additional tools and processes.

10.1.7   Conclusion

GitOps represents a powerful paradigm for managing Kubernetes clusters and applications. By leveraging Git as the single source of truth and implementing automated synchronization, organizations can achieve more reliable, consistent, and auditable deployments. While there are challenges to consider, the benefits of GitOps in terms of improved collaboration, faster recovery times, and enhanced security make it an attractive option for many Kubernetes-based projects. As the ecosystem of GitOps tools continues to evolve, we can expect even more sophisticated and streamlined approaches to implementing these principles in Kubernetes environments.

10.2   CI/CD in Kubernetes

Continuous Integration and Continuous Deployment (CI/CD) are essential practices in modern software development, enabling teams to deliver code changes more frequently and reliably. When combined with Kubernetes, CI/CD pipelines can leverage the platform's orchestration capabilities to automate the entire process from code commit to production deployment.

10.2.1   Understanding CI/CD in the Context of Kubernetes

In a Kubernetes environment, CI/CD pipelines typically involve the following stages:

1. **Code Integration**: Developers merge code changes into a central repository.

2. **Build**: The application is compiled and packaged into a container image.

3. **Test**: Automated tests are run against the built image.

4. **Push**: The image is pushed to a container registry.

5. **Deploy**: The image is deployed to Kubernetes clusters, often starting with development environments and progressing to production.

10.2.2 Setting Up CI/CD for Kubernetes

To implement CI/CD for Kubernetes, you'll need:

- A version control system (e.g., Git)

- A CI/CD platform (e.g., Jenkins, GitLab CI, GitHub Actions)

- A container registry (e.g., Docker Hub, Google Container Registry)

- Access to Kubernetes clusters

Example CI/CD Pipeline with GitHub Actions

Here's an example of a GitHub Actions workflow for a Kubernetes-based application:

```
name: CI/CD Pipeline

on:
  push:
    branches: [ main ]

jobs:
  build-and-deploy:
    runs-on: ubuntu-latest
    steps:
    - uses: actions/checkout@v2

    - name: Build and push Docker image
      uses: docker/build-push-action@v2
      with:
        push: true
```

```
      tags: user/app:${{ github.sha }}

  - name: Set up kubectl
    uses: azure/setup-kubectl@v1

  - name: Deploy to Kubernetes
    run: |
      kubectl set image deployment/myapp \
        myapp=user/app:${{ github.sha }}
    env:
      KUBE_CONFIG: ${{ secrets.KUBE_CONFIG }}
```

10.2.3   Key Components of CI/CD in Kubernetes

Container Builds

Building container images is a crucial step in the CI process. Tools like
Docker or Buildah can be used to create these images.

```
FROM node:14
WORKDIR /app
COPY package*.json ./
RUN npm install
COPY . .
EXPOSE 3000
CMD ["npm", "start"]
```

Testing in Kubernetes

Automated testing in a Kubernetes environment often involves:

- Unit tests within the CI pipeline

- Integration tests using ephemeral Kubernetes namespaces

- End-to-end tests on staging environments

Deployment Strategies

Kubernetes supports various deployment strategies:

- **Rolling Updates**: The default strategy, gradually replacing old pods with new ones.

- **Blue/Green Deployments**: Running two identical environments and switching traffic between them.

- **Canary Releases**: Gradually rolling out changes to a small subset of users.

Example of a rolling update deployment:

```yaml
apiVersion: apps/v1
kind: Deployment
metadata:
  name: myapp
spec:
  replicas: 3
  strategy:
    type: RollingUpdate
    rollingUpdate:
      maxSurge: 1
      maxUnavailable: 1
  # ... rest of the deployment spec
```

10.2.4 Best Practices for CI/CD in Kubernetes

- **Use Declarative Configurations**: Store Kubernetes manifests in version control.

- **Implement Immutable Deployments**: Use unique tags for each image build.

- **Utilize Helm Charts**: Package applications for easier management and deployment.

- **Implement Secrets Management**: Use tools like Sealed Secrets or Vault for secure secrets handling.

- **Set Resource Limits**: Define resource requests and limits for containers.

- **Implement Liveness and Readiness Probes**: Ensure proper health checking of applications.

- **Use Namespaces**: Separate resources logically using Kubernetes namespaces.

10.2.5   Monitoring and Observability

Integrating monitoring and observability into your CI/CD pipeline is crucial:

- Use tools like Prometheus and Grafana for metrics collection and visualization.

- Implement distributed tracing with Jaeger or Zipkin.

- Set up centralized logging with solutions like ELK stack or Loki.

Example Prometheus ServiceMonitor:

```
apiVersion: monitoring.coreos.com/v1
kind: ServiceMonitor
metadata:
  name: myapp-monitor
  labels:
    team: frontend
spec:
  selector:
    matchLabels:
      app: myapp
  endpoints:
  - port: web
```

10.2.6   Security Considerations

Security should be integrated throughout the CI/CD pipeline:

- Implement image scanning to detect vulnerabilities.

- Use pod security admission to enforce security profiles.

- Implement network policies to control traffic between pods.

- Regularly update and patch all components of the pipeline.

Example Network Policy:

```
apiVersion: networking.k8s.io/v1
kind: NetworkPolicy
metadata:
  name: myapp-network-policy
spec:
  podSelector:
    matchLabels:
      app: myapp
  policyTypes:
  - Ingress
  - Egress
  ingress:
  - from:
    - podSelector:
        matchLabels:
          role: frontend
  egress:
  - to:
    - podSelector:
        matchLabels:
          role: backend
```

10.2.7 Challenges and Considerations

Implementing CI/CD in Kubernetes comes with its own set of challenges:

- **Complexity**: Kubernetes adds an extra layer of complexity to CI/CD pipelines.

- **State Management**: Handling stateful applications requires careful consideration.

- **Resource Management**: Ensuring efficient use of cluster resources across environments.

- **Rollback Strategies**: Implementing effective rollback mechanisms for failed deployments.

- **Multi-cluster Deployments**: Managing deployments across multiple clusters or hybrid environments.

10.2.8   Tools and Platforms

Several tools and platforms can facilitate CI/CD in Kubernetes:

- **Jenkins X**: A CI/CD solution designed specifically for Kubernetes.

- **Spinnaker**: A multi-cloud continuous delivery platform.

- **Tekton**: A Kubernetes-native CI/CD framework.

- **Argo CD**: A declarative, GitOps continuous delivery tool for Kubernetes.

10.2.9   Conclusion

Implementing CI/CD in Kubernetes environments allows organizations to leverage the full potential of container orchestration for rapid, reliable software delivery. By automating the build, test, and deployment processes, teams can focus on developing features and fixing bugs, rather than managing complex deployment workflows. While there are challenges to overcome, the benefits of increased deployment frequency, faster time to market, and improved software quality make CI/CD an essential practice for Kubernetes-based projects. As the ecosystem continues to evolve, we can expect even more sophisticated tools and techniques to emerge, further streamlining the CI/CD process in Kubernetes environments.

10.3   Kubernetes in DevSecOps

DevSecOps is an approach that integrates security practices within the DevOps process. When applied to Kubernetes environments, it ensures that security is built into every stage of the application lifecycle, from development to deployment and operations. This section explores how Kubernetes can be leveraged in a DevSecOps context to enhance security, streamline operations, and maintain compliance.

10.3.1   Principles of DevSecOps in Kubernetes

The core principles of DevSecOps in Kubernetes include:

- **Shift Left Security**: Integrating security early in the development process.

- **Continuous Security**: Implementing security checks and practices throughout the CI/CD pipeline.

- **Automation**: Automating security processes to ensure consistency and reduce human error.

- **Immutability**: Treating infrastructure as immutable to enhance security and consistency.

- **Least Privilege**: Ensuring that all components operate with the minimum necessary permissions.

10.3.2   Implementing DevSecOps Practices in Kubernetes

Secure Development Practices

- Use secure coding practices and conduct regular code reviews.

- Implement pre-commit hooks to catch security issues early.

- Utilize static code analysis tools integrated into the development environment.

Example pre-commit hook for scanning Kubernetes manifests:

```
#!/bin/sh

for file in $(git diff --cached --name-only | grep -E
'\.(yaml|yml)$')
do
  kubesec scan $file
  if [ $? -ne 0 ]; then
    echo "Security issues found in $file"
    exit 1
  fi
done
```

Secure Container Images

- Use minimal base images to reduce the attack surface.

- Implement container image scanning in the CI pipeline.

- Ensure proper versioning and tagging of images.

Example Dockerfile for a secure base image:

```
FROM alpine:3.14
RUN apk add --no-cache ca-certificates && \
    adduser -D -H -u 10000 appuser
USER appuser
WORKDIR /app
COPY --chown=appuser:appuser . .
CMD ["./myapp"]
```

Kubernetes Security Features

Leverage Kubernetes built-in security features:

- **Pod Security Admission (PSA)**: Enforce security standards for pods.

- **RBAC**: Implement Role-Based Access Control for fine-grained permissions.

- **Network Policies**: Control traffic flow between pods and namespaces.

- **Secrets Management**: Securely handle sensitive information.

Example of applying Pod Security Standards:

```
# Label a namespace to enforce the "baseline" Pod Security
kubectl label --overwrite ns myapp \
  pod-security.kubernetes.io/enforce=baseline
```

Continuous Security Scanning

Implement continuous security scanning throughout the CI/CD pipeline:

- Static Application Security Testing (SAST)

- Dynamic Application Security Testing (DAST)

- Container image scanning

- Kubernetes manifest analysis

Example integration of container scanning in a CI pipeline (GitLab CI):

```
container_scanning:
  image: docker:stable
  services:
    - docker:dind
  script:
    - docker build -t myapp:$CI_COMMIT_SHA .
    - docker run --rm -v /var/run/docker.sock:/var/run/
docker.sock
      aquasec/trivy:latest image myapp:$CI_COMMIT_SHA
  only:
    - main
```

Runtime Security

Implement runtime security measures:

- Use runtime security tools like Falco for real-time threat detection.

- Implement pod security admission controllers.

- Enable audit logging for cluster activities.

Example Falco rule for detecting suspicious activities:

```
- rule: Detect Outbound Connections to Suspicious IPs
  desc: Detect outbound connections to known malicious IPs
  condition: outbound and dest.ip in (suspicious_ips)
  output: Outbound connection to suspicious IP
    (command=%proc.cmdline connection=%fd.name)
  priority: WARNING
  source: syscall
  tags: [network, mitre_exfiltration]
```

10.3.3   Compliance and Governance

Ensure compliance with relevant standards and regulations:

- Implement policy-as-code using tools like OPA Gatekeeper.

- Regular compliance scanning and reporting.

- Automated audit trails and logging.

Example OPA Gatekeeper policy to enforce resource limits:

```
apiVersion: constraints.gatekeeper.sh/v1beta1
kind: K8sRequiredResources
metadata:
  name: container-must-have-limits
spec:
  match:
    kinds:
      - apiGroups: [""]
```

```
      kinds: ["Pod"]
  parameters:
    limits:
      - cpu
      - memory
```

10.3.4   Monitoring and Incident Response

Implement robust monitoring and incident response mechanisms:

- Use tools like Prometheus and Grafana for monitoring and alerting.

- Implement a Security Information and Event Management (SIEM) system.

- Develop and regularly test incident response plans.

Example Prometheus alert rule:

```
groups:
- name: example
  rules:
  - alert: HighErrorRate
    expr: sum(rate(http_requests_total{status=~"5.."}[5m]))
          / sum(rate(http_requests_total[5m])) > 0.1
    for: 10m
    labels:
      severity: page
    annotations:
      summary: High HTTP error rate detected
```

10.3.5   Challenges and Considerations

Implementing DevSecOps in Kubernetes environments comes with challenges:

- **Complexity**: The distributed nature of Kubernetes adds complexity to security practices.

- **Skill Gap**: DevSecOps requires a broad skill set across development, operations, and security.

- **Tool Integration**: Integrating various security tools can be challenging.

- **Performance Impact**: Security measures can potentially impact performance and need to be optimized.

- **Keeping Up with Evolving Threats**: Continuous learning and adaptation are necessary to address new security challenges.

10.3.6   Best Practices

To effectively implement DevSecOps in Kubernetes:

- Foster a security-first culture across teams.

- Implement security measures at every stage of the application lifecycle.

- Automate security processes as much as possible.

- Regularly update and patch all components of the Kubernetes ecosystem.

- Conduct regular security audits and penetration testing.

- Provide ongoing security training for all team members.

- Implement a robust secrets management solution.

- Use infrastructure-as-code practices for consistent and secure deployments.

10.3.7   Conclusion

Integrating Kubernetes into a DevSecOps framework allows organizations to build security into their containerized applications from the ground up. By leveraging Kubernetes' native security features, implementing continuous security scanning, and fostering a culture of security awareness, teams can create more resilient and secure applications. While challenges exist, the benefits of a well-implemented DevSecOps strategy in Kubernetes environments include faster deployment cycles, reduced security risks, and improved compliance posture. As Kubernetes and the broader cloud-native ecosystem continue to evolve, DevSecOps practices will remain crucial in ensuring the security and reliability of containerized applications.

10.4   Canary, Blue-Green Deployments, and A/B Testing

Advanced deployment strategies in Kubernetes allow for more controlled and less risky rollouts of new application versions. This section explores three popular strategies: Canary Deployments, Blue-Green Deployments, and A/B Testing. These techniques enable teams to validate changes in production environments with minimal risk and maximize the benefits of Kubernetes' orchestration capabilities.

10.4.1   Canary Deployments

Canary deployments involve rolling out a new version of an application to a small subset of users or servers before deploying it to the entire infrastructure. This approach allows teams to test new features in a production environment with real user traffic while minimizing the risk of widespread issues.

Implementing Canary Deployments in Kubernetes

To implement a canary deployment in Kubernetes:

1. Deploy the new version alongside the existing version.

2. Route a small percentage of traffic to the new version.

3. Monitor the performance and behavior of the new version.

4. Gradually increase traffic to the new version if no issues are detected.

5. Complete the rollout by routing all traffic to the new version.

Example Canary Deployment Using Ingress

Here's an example of how to implement a canary deployment using Kubernetes Ingress:

```yaml
apiVersion: networking.k8s.io/v1
kind: Ingress
metadata:
  name: my-app-ingress
  annotations:
    nginx.ingress.kubernetes.io/canary: "true"
    nginx.ingress.kubernetes.io/canary-weight: "20"
spec:
  rules:
  - host: myapp.example.com
    http:
      paths:
      - path: /
        pathType: Prefix
        backend:
          service:
            name: myapp-canary-service
            port:
              number: 80
```

This configuration routes 20

10.4.2   Blue-Green Deployments

Blue-Green deployment is a technique that reduces downtime and risk by running two identical production environments called Blue and Green. At any time, only one of the environments is live, serving all production traffic.

Implementing Blue-Green Deployments in Kubernetes

To implement a Blue-Green deployment:

1. Deploy the new version (Green) alongside the current version (Blue).

2. Conduct testing on the Green environment.

3. Switch the router to direct all traffic to the Green environment.

4. Monitor for any issues.

5. If problems arise, switch back to the Blue environment.

Example Blue-Green Deployment Using Services

Here's an example of how to implement a Blue-Green deployment using
Kubernetes Services:

```
---
apiVersion: v1
kind: Service
metadata:
  name: myapp-blue
spec:
  selector:
    app: myapp
    version: v1
  ports:
  - protocol: TCP
    port: 80
    targetPort: 8080
---
apiVersion: v1
kind: Service
metadata:
  name: myapp-green
spec:
  selector:
    app: myapp
    version: v2
  ports:
  - protocol: TCP
    port: 80
    targetPort: 8080
---
apiVersion: v1
```

```
kind: Service
metadata:
  name: myapp-prod
spec:
  selector:
    app: myapp
    version: v1  # Switch this to v2 to activate Green
  ports:
  - protocol: TCP
    port: 80
    targetPort: 8080
```

To switch from Blue to Green, update the selector in the 'myapp-prod' service from 'version: v1' to 'version: v2'.

10.4.3   A/B Testing

A/B testing, also known as split testing, is a method of comparing two versions of an application to determine which one performs better. Unlike Canary or Blue-Green deployments, which are primarily focused on safe rollouts, A/B testing is used to make data-driven decisions about features or changes.

Implementing A/B Testing in Kubernetes

To implement A/B testing:

1. Deploy both versions of the application.

2. Configure traffic splitting between the two versions.

3. Collect metrics and user feedback for both versions.

4. Analyze the results to determine which version performs better.

5. Roll out the winning version to all users.

Example A/B Testing Using Istio

Istio, a service mesh for Kubernetes, provides powerful traffic management features that can be used for A/B testing. Here's an example configuration:

```
apiVersion: networking.istio.io/v1alpha3
kind: VirtualService
metadata:
  name: myapp-vsvc
spec:
  hosts:
  - myapp.example.com
  http:
  - route:
    - destination:
        host: myapp-v1
        subset: v1
      weight: 50
    - destination:
        host: myapp-v2
        subset: v2
      weight: 50
```

This configuration splits traffic 50/50 between version 1 and version 2 of the application.

10.4.4   Monitoring and Metrics

For all these deployment strategies, robust monitoring and metrics collection are crucial. Key areas to monitor include:

- Application performance (response times, error rates)

- User engagement metrics

- Infrastructure metrics (CPU, memory usage)

- Business metrics (conversion rates, revenue)

Tools like Prometheus and Grafana can be used to collect and visualize these metrics.

10.4.5   Best Practices

When implementing these deployment strategies:

- **Automate the Process:** Use CI/CD pipelines to automate deployments and rollbacks.

- **Implement Feature Flags:** Use feature flags to easily enable or disable features without redeploying.

- **Monitor Closely:** Set up comprehensive monitoring and alerting to quickly detect issues.

- **Plan for Rollbacks:** Always have a rollback strategy in place.

- **Test Thoroughly:** Conduct thorough testing before and during the deployment process.

- **Start Small:** Begin with a small percentage of traffic or users and gradually increase.

10.4.6   Challenges and Considerations

While these strategies offer many benefits, they also come with challenges:

- **Increased Complexity:** Managing multiple versions simultaneously can be complex.

- **Resource Usage:** Running multiple versions in parallel may require additional resources.

- **Database Migrations:** Care must be taken when dealing with database schema changes.

- **Session Management:** Ensuring consistent user experiences across versions can be challenging.

- **Metrics and Logging:** Proper tagging and separation of metrics and logs for different versions is crucial.

10.4.7 Conclusion

Canary Deployments, Blue-Green Deployments, and A/B Testing are powerful strategies that leverage Kubernetes' capabilities to provide safer, more controlled application rollouts. By allowing teams to validate changes in production environments with minimal risk, these techniques can significantly improve the reliability and quality of software deployments. While they require careful planning and implementation, the benefits in terms of reduced downtime, improved user experience, and data-driven decision making make them valuable tools in any Kubernetes practitioner's toolkit. As organizations continue to adopt cloud-native technologies and practices, these advanced deployment strategies will play an increasingly important role in managing complex, distributed systems.

Chapter 11

Performance and Optimization

Performance optimization is a critical aspect of managing Kubernetes clusters. As applications grow in complexity and scale, ensuring that the cluster operates efficiently becomes increasingly important. This chapter explores various strategies and best practices for optimizing Kubernetes performance.

11.1 Tuning for High Performance

Tuning a Kubernetes cluster for high performance involves optimizing various components, from the infrastructure layer to the application layer. This section will cover key areas of focus and provide practical guidance for enhancing cluster performance.

11.1.1 Infrastructure Optimization

The underlying infrastructure plays a crucial role in Kubernetes performance. Consider the following aspects:

Node Configuration

- **CPU and Memory:** Choose appropriate instance types with balanced CPU and memory resources.

- **Storage:** Use high-performance storage options like SSDs for etcd and container images.

- **Network:** Ensure low-latency, high-bandwidth network connections between nodes.

Example of node affinity to ensure pods run on high-performance nodes:

```yaml
apiVersion: v1
kind: Pod
metadata:
  name: high-performance-pod
spec:
  affinity:
    nodeAffinity:
      requiredDuringSchedulingIgnoredDuringExecution:
        nodeSelectorTerms:
        - matchExpressions:
          - key: node-type
            operator: In
            values:
            - high-performance
  containers:
  - name: app
    image: myapp:v1
```

Cluster Sizing

- Right-size the cluster based on workload requirements.

- Implement auto-scaling to handle varying loads efficiently.

11.1.2 Kubernetes Component Optimization

Optimizing Kubernetes components can significantly improve overall cluster performance.

API Server

- Increase `--max-requests-inflight` and `--max-mutating-requests-inflight` for high-traffic clusters.

- Enable API Priority and Fairness (APF) to prevent resource starvation.

Example API server configuration:

```
kube-apiserver
  --max-requests-inflight=1500
  --max-mutating-requests-inflight=500
  --enable-priority-and-fairness=true
```

etcd

- Use SSD storage for etcd data.

- Optimize etcd parameters like `--snapshot-count` and `--heartbeat-interval`.

Example etcd configuration:

```
etcd
  --snapshot-count=10000
  --heartbeat-interval=100ms
```

Scheduler

- Adjust `--kube-api-qps` and `--kube-api-burst` for faster scheduling in large clusters.

11.1.3 Workload Optimization

Optimizing individual workloads can lead to significant performance improvements.

Resource Requests and Limits

Set appropriate resource requests and limits for containers:

```
apiVersion: v1
kind: Pod
metadata:
  name: resource-optimized-pod
spec:
  containers:
  - name: app
    image: myapp:v1
    resources:
      requests:
        cpu: 100m
        memory: 128Mi
      limits:
        cpu: 500m
        memory: 512Mi
```

Horizontal Pod Autoscaler (HPA)

Implement HPA to automatically scale workloads based on metrics:

```
apiVersion: autoscaling/v2
kind: HorizontalPodAutoscaler
metadata:
  name: myapp-hpa
spec:
  scaleTargetRef:
    apiVersion: apps/v1
    kind: Deployment
    name: myapp
  minReplicas: 2
  maxReplicas: 10
  metrics:
  - type: Resource
    resource:
      name: cpu
      target:
        type: Utilization
        averageUtilization: 50
```

11.1.4   Networking Optimization

Optimizing network performance is crucial for distributed applications in Kubernetes.

CNI Plugin Selection

Choose a CNI plugin that best fits your performance requirements. For reference, see the comparisons in chapter 6.

Network Policies

Implement network policies to control traffic flow and reduce unnecessary network chatter:

```
apiVersion: networking.k8s.io/v1
kind: NetworkPolicy
metadata:
  name: allow-internal-traffic
spec:
  podSelector: {}
  policyTypes:
  - Ingress
  ingress:
  - from:
    - podSelector: {}
```

11.1.5   Monitoring and Profiling

Implement robust monitoring and profiling to identify performance bottlenecks.

Prometheus and Grafana

Set up Prometheus for metrics collection and Grafana for visualization:

```
apiVersion: monitoring.coreos.com/v1
kind: Prometheus
metadata:
```

```
name: prometheus
spec:
  serviceAccountName: prometheus
  serviceMonitorSelector:
    matchLabels:
      team: frontend
  resources:
    requests:
      memory: 400Mi
```

Kubernetes Metrics Server

Deploy the Kubernetes Metrics Server to collect resource metrics:

```
kubectl apply -f https://github.com/kubernetes-sigs/
metrics-server/releases/latest/download/components.yaml
```

11.1.6   Best Practices for Performance Tuning

- **Benchmark and Profile:** Regularly benchmark your applications and profile resource usage.

- **Incremental Changes:** Make small, incremental changes and measure their impact.

- **Use Production-like Environments:** Test performance optimizations in environments that closely resemble production.

- **Monitor Continuously:** Implement continuous monitoring to catch performance regressions early.

- **Optimize Images:** Use minimal base images and multi-stage builds to reduce image size and startup time.

- **Leverage Node Labels:** Use node labels and selectors to match workloads with appropriate node types.

- **Consider Pod Topology Spread Constraints:** Use topology spread constraints to distribute pods across nodes effectively.

11.1.7 Advanced Techniques

NUMA-aware Scheduling

For CPU-intensive workloads, consider NUMA-aware scheduling:

```
apiVersion: performance.kubelet.io/v1alpha1
kind: NUMATopologyHint
metadata:
  name: myapp
spec:
  preferredCPUBindPolicy: strictPerThread
```

CPU Manager Policies

Utilize CPU Manager policies for workloads that require dedicated CPU cores:

```
--cpu-manager-policy=static
```

Huge Pages

For memory-intensive applications, consider using huge pages:

```
apiVersion: v1
kind: Pod
metadata:
  name: huge-pages-pod
spec:
  containers:
  - name: example
    image: example/image
    volumeMounts:
    - mountPath: /hugepages
      name: hugepage
    resources:
      limits:
        hugepages-2Mi: 100Mi
  volumes:
  - name: hugepage
```

```
emptyDir:
  medium: HugePages
```

11.1.8   Conclusion

Tuning Kubernetes for high performance is an ongoing process that requires a deep understanding of both Kubernetes internals and application requirements. By focusing on infrastructure optimization, fine-tuning Kubernetes components, optimizing workloads, and implementing effective monitoring, you can significantly enhance the performance of your Kubernetes clusters. Remember that performance tuning often involves trade-offs, and what works best will depend on your specific use case and requirements. Regular testing, monitoring, and iteration are key to maintaining high-performance Kubernetes environments.

11.2   Optimizing Cost in Cloud Environments

While Kubernetes can significantly improve resource utilization and application deployment efficiency, managing costs in cloud environments requires careful planning and optimization. This section explores strategies and best practices for optimizing costs when running Kubernetes clusters in cloud environments.

11.2.1   Understanding Cloud Costs

Before diving into optimization strategies, it's crucial to understand the components that contribute to cloud costs in a Kubernetes environment:

- Compute resources (CPU, memory)

- Storage (persistent volumes, object storage)

- Network traffic (ingress, egress, load balancers)

- Managed Kubernetes services fees

- Additional cloud services (monitoring, logging, etc.)

11.2.2 Resource Optimization

Efficient resource utilization is key to cost optimization in Kubernetes.

Right-sizing Resources

Ensure that pods are allocated appropriate resources:

```
apiVersion: v1
kind: Pod
metadata:
  name: resource-optimized-pod
spec:
  containers:
  - name: app
    image: myapp:v1
    resources:
      requests:
        cpu: 100m
        memory: 128Mi
      limits:
        cpu: 500m
        memory: 512Mi
```

Use tools like Vertical Pod Autoscaler (VPA) to automatically adjust resource requests:

```
apiVersion: autoscaling.k8s.io/v1
kind: VerticalPodAutoscaler
metadata:
  name: my-app-vpa
spec:
  targetRef:
    apiVersion: "apps/v1"
    kind: Deployment
    name: my-app
  updatePolicy:
    updateMode: "Auto"
```

Cluster Autoscaler

Implement Cluster Autoscaler to dynamically adjust the number of nodes based on workload:

```
apiVersion: autoscaling.k8s.io/v1
kind: ClusterAutoscaler
metadata:
  name: default
spec:
  scaleDown:
    enabled: true
    delayAfterAdd: 10m
    delayAfterDelete: 10s
    delayAfterFailure: 3m
  scaleDownUnneededTime: 10m
  scaleDownUnreadyTime: 20m
```

11.2.3   Node Strategies

Optimize node selection and management to reduce costs.

Spot Instances

Utilize spot instances for non-critical workloads:

```
apiVersion: apps/v1
kind: Deployment
metadata:
  name: spot-deployment
spec:
  replicas: 3
  selector:
    matchLabels:
      app: myapp
  template:
    metadata:
      labels:
        app: myapp
```

```
spec:
  nodeSelector:
    lifecycle: spot
  containers:
  - name: myapp
    image: myapp:v1
```

Node Pools

Create separate node pools for different workload types:

- General-purpose nodes for mixed workloads

- CPU-optimized nodes for compute-intensive tasks

- Memory-optimized nodes for data-intensive applications

11.2.4 Storage Optimization

Optimize storage usage to reduce costs.

Storage Classes

Define appropriate storage classes for different use cases:

```
apiVersion: storage.k8s.io/v1
kind: StorageClass
metadata:
  name: standard
provisioner: kubernetes.io/aws-ebs
parameters:
  type: gp2
```

Volume Snapshot Classes

Implement volume snapshots for efficient backup and restore:

```
apiVersion: snapshot.storage.k8s.io/v1
kind: VolumeSnapshotClass
metadata:
```

```
  name: csi-hostpath-snapclass
driver: hostpath.csi.k8s.io
deletionPolicy: Delete
```

11.2.5 Networking Optimization

Optimize network usage to reduce data transfer costs.

Ingress Controllers

Use Ingress controllers to consolidate incoming traffic and reduce load balancer costs:

```
apiVersion: networking.k8s.io/v1
kind: Ingress
metadata:
  name: minimal-ingress
  annotations:
    kubernetes.io/ingress.class: nginx
spec:
  rules:
  - http:
      paths:
      - path: /testpath
        pathType: Prefix
        backend:
          service:
            name: test
            port:
              number: 80
```

Network Policies

Implement network policies to control and optimize traffic flow:

```
apiVersion: networking.k8s.io/v1
kind: NetworkPolicy
metadata:
  name: limit-egress
```

```
spec:
  podSelector: {}
  policyTypes:
  - Egress
  egress:
  - to:
    - namespaceSelector:
        matchLabels:
          purpose: production
```

11.2.6   Cost Visibility and Monitoring

Implement tools for cost visibility and monitoring.

Kubernetes Cost Monitoring Tools

Utilize tools like Kubecost or OpenCost for detailed cost breakdowns:

```
helm repo add kubecost https://kubecost.github.io/cost-analyzer
helm install kubecost kubecost/cost-analyzer
--namespace kubecost --create-namespace
```

Cloud Provider Cost Management Tools

Leverage cloud provider-specific cost management tools:

- AWS Cost Explorer

- Google Cloud Cost Management

- Azure Cost Management

11.2.7   Best Practices for Cost Optimization

- **Regular Audits:** Conduct regular cost audits to identify optimization opportunities.

- **Implement Tagging:** Use consistent tagging strategies for resources to track costs by team, project, or environment.

- **Use Reserved Instances:** For stable, long-running workloads, consider using reserved instances for significant cost savings.

- **Optimize CI/CD Pipelines:** Ensure CI/CD processes are efficient to reduce costs associated with build and test environments.

- **Implement Cost Allocation:** Use namespaces and labels to allocate costs to specific teams or projects.

- **Educate Teams:** Provide training on cost optimization best practices to all teams working with Kubernetes.

11.2.8 Advanced Cost Optimization Techniques

Multi-Cloud Strategy

Consider a multi-cloud strategy to optimize costs across different providers:

- Use tools like Crossplane for multi-cloud resource provisioning

- Implement a consistent abstraction layer for cloud resources

Serverless Kubernetes

Explore serverless Kubernetes options for certain workloads:

- AWS Fargate for EKS

- Azure Container Instances (ACI) with AKS virtual nodes

- Google Cloud Run for Anthos

FinOps Practices

Implement FinOps (Financial Operations) practices:

- Establish a FinOps team or role

- Implement showback or chargeback models

- Set up cost anomaly detection and alerting

11.2.9 Conclusion

Optimizing costs in cloud environments for Kubernetes requires a multifaceted approach, combining resource optimization, strategic use of cloud services, and implementation of cost management tools and practices. By following these strategies and best practices, organizations can significantly reduce their cloud spending while maintaining the flexibility and scalability benefits of Kubernetes. Remember that cost optimization is an ongoing process that requires regular attention and adjustment as your applications and infrastructure evolve. Balancing cost optimization with performance, reliability, and scalability is key to a successful Kubernetes deployment in the cloud.

11.3 Load Testing and Simulating Failures

Load testing and failure simulation are crucial practices in ensuring the reliability and performance of Kubernetes-based applications. These techniques help identify bottlenecks, verify system behavior under stress, and ensure that applications can gracefully handle various failure scenarios. This section explores strategies and tools for effective load testing and failure simulation in Kubernetes environments.

11.3.1 Load Testing in Kubernetes

Load testing involves simulating high traffic or workload conditions to assess system performance and identify bottlenecks.

Tools for Load Testing

Several tools are available for load testing Kubernetes applications:

- **Apache JMeter**: A popular open-source load testing tool.

- **Gatling**: Scala-based load testing tool with good Kubernetes integration.

- **Locust**: Python-based load testing tool that's easy to extend.

- **k6**: A modern load testing tool built for developer happiness.

Implementing Load Tests

Here's an example of how to run a load test using k6 in Kubernetes:

```
apiVersion: k6.io/v1alpha1
kind: K6
metadata:
  name: k6-sample
spec:
  script:
    configMap:
      name: my-test
      file: test.js
  runner:
    image: loadimpact/k6:latest
  arguments: --vus 10 --duration 30s
```

The corresponding test script (test.js) might look like this:

```
import http from 'k6/http';
import { check, sleep } from 'k6';

export default function() {
  let res = http.get(
'http://my-service.default.svc.cluster.local');
  check(res, { 'status was 200': (r) => r.status == 200 });
  sleep(1);
}
```

Best Practices for Load Testing

- Start with baseline tests to understand normal performance.

- Gradually increase load to identify breaking points.

- Test different components (e.g., API endpoints, databases) separately.

- Monitor resource usage (CPU, memory, network) during tests.

- Use realistic data and scenarios in your tests.

- Automate load tests as part of your CI/CD pipeline.

11.3.2 Simulating Failures

Failure simulation, also known as chaos engineering, involves intentionally introducing failures to test system resilience.

Types of Failures to Simulate

- Pod failures

- Node failures

- Network partitions

- Resource constraints (CPU, memory)

- Disk failures

- DNS failures

Tools for Failure Simulation

Several tools are available for simulating failures in Kubernetes:

- **Chaos Mesh**: A cloud-native chaos engineering platform.

- **Litmus Chaos**: An open-source chaos engineering platform for Kubernetes.

- **Gremlin**: A commercial chaos engineering platform with Kubernetes support.

Implementing Failure Simulations

Here's an example of how to use Chaos Mesh to simulate a pod failure:

```
apiVersion: chaos-mesh.org/v1alpha1
kind: PodChaos
metadata:
  name: pod-failure-example
spec:
  action: pod-failure
  mode: one
```

```
duration: '30s'
selector:
  namespaces:
    - default
  labelSelectors:
    'app': 'web-server'
```

Best Practices for Failure Simulation

- Start with small-scale experiments in non-production environments.

- Gradually increase the complexity and scope of failure scenarios.

- Monitor system behavior and user experience during experiments.

- Have a rollback plan for each experiment.

- Document findings and improvements after each simulation.

- Automate failure simulations as part of your testing pipeline.

11.3.3   Monitoring and Observability During Tests

Effective monitoring and observability are crucial during load tests and failure simulations.

Key Metrics to Monitor

- Response times

- Error rates

- Resource utilization (CPU, memory, disk I/O, network)

- Throughput

- Latency

Observability Tools

Use a combination of tools for comprehensive observability:

- **Prometheus**: For metrics collection and alerting.

- **Grafana**: For metrics visualization.

- **Jaeger or Zipkin**: For distributed tracing.

- **Elasticsearch, Fluentd, and Kibana (EFK) stack**: For log aggregation and analysis.

Example Prometheus configuration for scraping custom metrics:

```
apiVersion: monitoring.coreos.com/v1
kind: ServiceMonitor
metadata:
  name: example-app
  labels:
    team: frontend
spec:
  selector:
    matchLabels:
      app: example-app
  endpoints:
  - port: web
```

11.3.4   Analyzing and Acting on Results

After conducting load tests and failure simulations, it's crucial to analyze the results and take appropriate actions.

Analyzing Results

- Identify performance bottlenecks and their root causes.

- Assess the effectiveness of auto-scaling and self-healing mechanisms.

- Evaluate the impact of failures on user experience and business metrics.

- Compare results against defined Service Level Objectives (SLOs).

Taking Action

Based on the analysis, take actions such as:

- Optimizing resource allocation and scaling policies.

- Improving error handling and retry mechanisms.

- Enhancing monitoring and alerting systems.

- Updating disaster recovery and incident response plans.

- Refining application architecture for better resilience.

11.3.5 Advanced Techniques

Continuous Chaos Engineering

Implement continuous chaos engineering practices:

- Integrate failure simulations into CI/CD pipelines.

- Conduct regular "game days" to simulate complex failure scenarios.

- Use AI/ML to predict and simulate potential failure modes.

Multi-cluster and Multi-region Testing

Extend load testing and failure simulations across multiple clusters and regions:

- Test global load balancing and failover mechanisms.

- Simulate region-wide outages and assess business continuity.

- Evaluate cross-region data replication and consistency.

11.3.6 Conclusion

Load testing and failure simulation are essential practices for ensuring the reliability and performance of Kubernetes-based applications. By systematically testing your systems under various load conditions and failure scenarios, you can identify weaknesses, optimize performance, and build more resilient applications. Remember that these are ongoing processes – as your applications evolve, so should your testing strategies. Regularly conducting these tests and integrating them into your development lifecycle will help maintain the health and reliability of your Kubernetes environments.

Chapter 12

Disaster Recovery and Business Continuity

Disaster recovery and business continuity are critical aspects of managing Kubernetes clusters in production environments. These practices ensure that your applications and data can be recovered quickly in the event of a disaster, minimizing downtime and data loss. This chapter explores various strategies and tools for implementing robust disaster recovery and business continuity plans in Kubernetes environments.

12.1 Backup Strategies: Stash, Velero, and More

Effective backup strategies are the foundation of any disaster recovery plan. In Kubernetes, several tools and approaches can be used to create comprehensive backup solutions. This section will focus on popular backup tools such as Stash and Velero, as well as other strategies for ensuring data persistence and recoverability.

12.1.1 Importance of Kubernetes Backups

Kubernetes backups are crucial for several reasons:

- **Data Protection**: Safeguard against accidental deletions or corruption.

- **Disaster Recovery**: Quickly restore services in case of cluster failure.

- **Compliance**: Meet regulatory requirements for data retention and protection.

- **Migration**: Facilitate cluster migration or upgrades.

- **Testing and Development**: Create realistic test environments using production data.

12.1.2   Key Components to Back Up

When developing a backup strategy for Kubernetes, consider backing up the following components:

- Persistent Volumes (PVs)

- Kubernetes API Objects (Deployments, Services, ConfigMaps, Secrets, etc.)

- Etcd data

- Custom Resource Definitions (CRDs) and Custom Resources

- Cluster configuration

12.1.3   Backup Tools

Velero

Velero (formerly Heptio Ark) is a popular open-source tool for backing up and restoring Kubernetes clusters.

Key Features of Velero:

- Backs up cluster resources and persistent volumes

- Supports multiple storage providers (AWS S3, Google Cloud Storage, Azure Blob Storage, etc.)

- Provides hooks for custom actions during backup and restore

- Supports cluster migration

Installing Velero:

```
# Install Velero CLI
curl -LO https://github.com/vmware-tanzu/velero/releases/
download/v1.7.1/velero-v1.7.1-linux-amd64.tar.gz

tar -xzf velero-v1.7.1-linux-amd64.tar.gz
sudo mv velero /usr/local/bin/

# Install Velero in the cluster
velero install --provider aws --bucket my-backup-bucket \
--secret-file ./credentials-velero
```

Creating a Backup with Velero:

```
velero backup create my-backup --include-namespaces
my-namespace
```

Restoring from a Backup:

```
velero restore create --from-backup my-backup
```

Stash

Stash is another powerful backup solution for Kubernetes, developed by AppsCode.

Key Features of Stash:

- Supports backup of volumes and Kubernetes resources

- Provides database-aware backups for popular databases

- Offers encryption and compression of backups

- Supports incremental backups

Installing Stash:

```
helm repo add appscode https://charts.appscode.com/stable/
helm repo update
helm install stash appscode/stash \
  --version v2023.05.31 \
  --namespace kube-system
```

Creating a Backup with Stash:

```
apiVersion: stash.appscode.com/v1beta1
kind: BackupConfiguration
metadata:
  name: sample-backup
  namespace: demo
spec:
  schedule: "*/5 * * * *"
  repository:
    name: gcs-repo
  target:
    ref:
      apiVersion: apps/v1
      kind: Deployment
      name: sample-deployment
  runtimeSettings:
    container:
      resources:
        requests:
          cpu: "200m"
          memory: "128Mi"
        limits:
          cpu: "200m"
          memory: "128Mi"
  retentionPolicy:
    name: 'keep-last-5'
    keepLast: 5
    prune: true
```

12.1.4 Other Backup Strategies

Etcd Snapshots

Regularly backing up etcd is crucial as it stores the entire state of the cluster.

Creating an etcd Snapshot:

```
ETCDCTL_API=3 etcdctl --endpoints=https://127.0.0.1:2379 \
  --cacert=/etc/kubernetes/pki/etcd/ca.crt \
  --cert=/etc/kubernetes/pki/etcd/server.crt \
  --key=/etc/kubernetes/pki/etcd/server.key \
  snapshot save
/backup/etcd-snapshot-$(date +%Y-%m-%d_%H:%M:%S).db
```

Custom Scripts

For specific use cases, custom scripts can be developed to backup particular resources or data.

Example Backup Script:

```bash
#!/bin/bash
NAMESPACE="my-namespace"
BACKUP_DIR="/path/to/backups"

# Backup all resources in the namespace
kubectl get all -n $NAMESPACE -o yaml >
$BACKUP_DIR/all_resources.yaml

# Backup specific custom resources
kubectl get mycustomresource -n $NAMESPACE -o yaml >
$BACKUP_DIR/custom_resources.yaml

# Backup secrets (consider encryption for sensitive data)
kubectl get secrets -n $NAMESPACE -o yaml >
$BACKUP_DIR/secrets.yaml
```

12.1.5 Best Practices for Kubernetes Backups

- **Regular Scheduling**: Automate backups on a regular schedule.

- **Retention Policies**: Implement retention policies to manage backup storage efficiently.

- **Encryption**: Encrypt backups, especially when storing sensitive data.

- **Testing**: Regularly test the restore process to ensure backups are valid and usable.

- **Monitoring**: Set up monitoring and alerting for backup jobs.

- **Documentation**: Maintain clear documentation of backup and restore procedures.

- **Geo-Redundancy**: Store backups in geographically diverse locations.

- **Version Control**: Keep track of backup versions and cluster state.

12.1.6 Challenges and Considerations

- **Stateful Applications**: Backing up stateful applications may require application-specific strategies.

- **Consistency**: Ensure backups are consistent, especially for distributed systems.

- **Performance Impact**: Consider the impact of backups on cluster performance.

- **Large Clusters**: Develop strategies for efficiently backing up large-scale clusters.

- **Regulatory Compliance**: Ensure backup strategies meet relevant compliance requirements.

12.1.7 Conclusion

Implementing robust backup strategies is crucial for disaster recovery and business continuity in Kubernetes environments. Tools like Velero and Stash provide powerful, Kubernetes-native solutions for backing up both cluster resources and persistent data. By combining these tools with best practices such as regular testing, encryption, and geo-redundancy, organizations can ensure that their Kubernetes clusters are resilient to disasters and can be quickly restored if needed. Remember that backup strategies should be tailored to your specific needs and regularly reviewed and updated as your cluster and applications evolve.

12.2 Planning and Practicing Disaster Recovery Scenarios

Effective disaster recovery in Kubernetes environments goes beyond having backup strategies in place. It requires careful planning, regular practice, and continuous improvement. This section explores how to plan for various disaster scenarios and implement practices to ensure your team is prepared to handle unexpected events efficiently.

12.2.1 Identifying Potential Disaster Scenarios

The first step in disaster recovery planning is to identify potential disaster scenarios. In a Kubernetes environment, these might include:

- **Cluster-wide failures**: Complete loss of a cluster due to infrastructure issues or region-wide outages.

- **Data corruption**: Corruption of etcd data or persistent volumes.

- **Security breaches**: Unauthorized access or malicious activities within the cluster.

- **Application failures**: Critical bugs or misconfigurations causing application downtime.

- **Network partitions**: Network issues causing split-brain scenarios or isolation of cluster components.

- **Resource exhaustion**: Unexpected spikes in resource usage leading to service degradation.

12.2.2 Developing Disaster Recovery Plans

For each identified scenario, develop a detailed recovery plan. A typical disaster recovery plan should include:

- **Detection methods**: How to identify that a disaster has occurred.

- **Response team**: Who should be notified and involved in the recovery process.

- **Recovery steps**: Detailed, step-by-step procedures for recovery.

- **Communication plan**: How to communicate with stakeholders during the recovery process.

- **Recovery time objective (RTO)**: The target time within which systems should be restored.

- **Recovery point objective (RPO)**: The maximum acceptable amount of data loss.

Example: Cluster-wide Failure Recovery Plan

```
1. Detection:
   - Monitor cluster health using Prometheus alerts
   - Set up external monitoring for cluster availability

2. Response Team:
   - Primary: On-call DevOps engineer
   - Secondary: Cluster administrator
   - Escalation: Head of Infrastructure

3. Recovery Steps:
   a. Verify cluster state and extent of failure
   b. Attempt to recover existing cluster if possible
   c. If recovery is not possible, initiate cluster rebuild:
      - Create new cluster using Infrastructure as Code (IaC)
```

```
      - Restore etcd data from latest backup
      - Reapply Kubernetes object definitions from backup
   d. Verify cluster health and application functionality
   e. Update DNS and load balancers to point to new cluster

4. Communication:
   - Notify internal teams via Slack
   - Update status page for external communication
   - Send email updates to key stakeholders

5. RTO: 4 hours
6. RPO: 15 minutes (based on backup frequency)
```

12.2.3 Implementing Disaster Recovery Drills

Regular disaster recovery drills are essential to ensure that your team is prepared and your plans are effective.

Types of Drills

- **Tabletop exercises**: Team discussions walking through disaster scenarios.

- **Functional exercises**: Simulated disasters in a test environment.

- **Full-scale drills**: Exercises that involve actual recovery procedures in a production-like environment.

Conducting a Drill

- **Preparation**

  - Define the scenario and objectives

  - Prepare the environment (if applicable)

  - Brief participants on their roles

- **Execution**

  - Simulate the disaster scenario

- Follow the disaster recovery plan

- Document actions and decisions

- **Evaluation**

  - Assess the effectiveness of the recovery process

  - Identify areas for improvement

  - Update the disaster recovery plan based on findings

12.2.4 Tools and Techniques for Disaster Recovery Practice

Several tools can assist in implementing and practicing disaster recovery scenarios in Kubernetes:

Chaos Engineering Tools

Use chaos engineering tools to simulate failures and practice recovery:

```
# Example: Using Chaos Mesh to simulate a node failure
apiVersion: chaos-mesh.org/v1alpha1
kind: PodChaos
metadata:
  name: pod-failure
spec:
  action: pod-failure
  mode: one
  duration: '300s'
  selector:
    namespaces:
      - default
    labelSelectors:
      'app': 'web-server'
```

Infrastructure as Code (IaC)

Use IaC tools like Terraform to quickly recreate clusters:

```
# Example: Terraform configuration for GKE cluster
resource "google_container_cluster" "primary" {
  name     = "my-gke-cluster"
  location = "us-central1"

  initial_node_count = 3

  master_auth {
    client_certificate_config {
      issue_client_certificate = false
    }
  }
}
```

GitOps for Disaster Recovery

Implement GitOps practices to store and version all cluster configurations:

```
# Example: Using Flux to automatically sync cluster state
apiVersion: source.toolkit.fluxcd.io/v1beta1
kind: GitRepository
metadata:
  name: flux-system
  namespace: flux-system
spec:
  interval: 1m
  url: https://github.com/example/k8s-gitops
  ref:
    branch: main
---
apiVersion: kustomize.toolkit.fluxcd.io/v1beta1
kind: Kustomization
metadata:
  name: flux-system
  namespace: flux-system
spec:
  interval: 10m
  path: "./clusters/production"
```

```
prune: true
sourceRef:
  kind: GitRepository
  name: flux-system
validation: client
```

12.2.5 Best Practices for Disaster Recovery Planning and Practice

- **Regular Updates**: Review and update disaster recovery plans regularly.

- **Automated Testing**: Implement automated tests for recovery procedures.

- **Cross-training**: Ensure multiple team members are familiar with recovery procedures.

- **Documentation**: Maintain clear, up-to-date documentation of all recovery processes.

- **Post-mortem Analysis**: Conduct thorough post-mortem analyses after real incidents and major drills.

- **Continuous Improvement**: Use insights from drills and real incidents to continuously improve recovery plans.

12.2.6 Challenges and Considerations

- **Realistic Simulations**: Creating truly realistic disaster scenarios can be challenging.

- **Resource Constraints**: Allocating time and resources for regular drills can be difficult.

- **Keeping Plans Updated**: Ensuring disaster recovery plans stay current with evolving infrastructure.

- **Balancing Security and Accessibility**: Making recovery tools and information accessible while maintaining security.

12.2.7 Conclusion

Planning and practicing disaster recovery scenarios is crucial for ensuring the resilience of Kubernetes environments. By identifying potential disasters, developing comprehensive recovery plans, and regularly practicing through drills, organizations can significantly improve their ability to respond to unexpected events. Leveraging tools for chaos engineering, infrastructure as code, and GitOps can enhance the effectiveness of disaster recovery practices. Remember that disaster recovery planning is an ongoing process that requires continuous evaluation and improvement to keep pace with evolving technologies and business needs.

12.3 Business Continuity Planning in Kubernetes Environments

Business Continuity Planning (BCP) in Kubernetes environments focuses on ensuring that critical business functions can continue during and after a disaster. While disaster recovery often deals with technical aspects of restoring systems, business continuity encompasses broader organizational strategies to maintain operations. This section explores how to develop and implement effective business continuity plans in Kubernetes-based infrastructures.

12.3.1 Understanding Business Continuity in the Context of Kubernetes

Business continuity in Kubernetes environments involves:

- Identifying critical business processes and their supporting applications

- Ensuring high availability and resilience of Kubernetes clusters

- Implementing strategies to minimize downtime and data loss

- Establishing procedures for failover and failback

- Defining communication protocols during incidents

12.3.2　Key Components of a Business Continuity Plan

A comprehensive business continuity plan for Kubernetes environments should include:

Business Impact Analysis (BIA)

Conduct a BIA to identify:

- Critical business functions

- Recovery Time Objectives (RTO) for each function

- Recovery Point Objectives (RPO) for data

- Dependencies between applications and services

Risk Assessment

Identify potential risks to your Kubernetes infrastructure:

- Infrastructure failures (hardware, network, cloud provider outages)

- Application-level issues (bugs, misconfigurations)

- Security threats (DDoS attacks, unauthorized access)

- Human errors

Continuity Strategies

Develop strategies to ensure business continuity:

- Multi-cluster deployments

- Geo-distributed clusters

- Automated failover mechanisms

- Data replication and backup strategies

12.3.3 Implementing Business Continuity in Kubernetes

Multi-Cluster Architectures

Implement multi-cluster architectures to enhance resilience:

```
# Example: Using kubefed to manage multiple clusters
apiVersion: types.kubefed.io/v1beta1
kind: FederatedDeployment
metadata:
  name: test-deployment
  namespace: test-namespace
spec:
  template:
    metadata:
      labels:
        app: nginx
    spec:
      replicas: 3
      selector:
        matchLabels:
          app: nginx
      template:
        metadata:
          labels:
            app: nginx
        spec:
          containers:
          - image: nginx
            name: nginx
  placement:
    clusters:
    - name: cluster1
    - name: cluster2
```

Automated Failover

Implement automated failover using tools like Kubernetes Federation or custom controllers:

```
# Example: Simple failover controller pseudo-code
while True:
    primary_cluster_status = check_cluster_health(primary_cluster)
    if primary_cluster_status != "Healthy":
        switch_traffic_to_backup_cluster()
        notify_operations_team()
    sleep(check_interval)
```

Data Replication

Ensure data consistency across clusters using tools like Velero for Kubernetes resources and database-specific replication mechanisms:

```yaml
# Example: Velero backup schedule
apiVersion: velero.io/v1
kind: Schedule
metadata:
  name: daily-backup
  namespace: velero
spec:
  schedule: "0 1 * * *"
  template:
    snapshotVolumes:
      - name: persistent-volume-claim
        driver: csi
    includeClusterResources: null
    storageLocation: default
    ttl: 240h
```

12.3.4 Testing and Validation

Regularly test your business continuity plan:

- Conduct failover drills

- Simulate various disaster scenarios

- Validate RTO and RPO objectives

- Test communication procedures

12.3.5 Monitoring and Alerting

Implement robust monitoring and alerting to quickly detect and respond to issues:

```
# Example: Prometheus alert rule for high error rate
groups:
- name: example
  rules:
  - alert: HighErrorRate
    expr: sum(rate(http_requests_total{code=~"5.."}[5m]))
          / sum(rate(http_requests_total[5m])) > 0.1
    for: 10m
    labels:
      severity: page
    annotations:
      summary: High HTTP error rate detected
```

12.3.6 Communication and Documentation

Establish clear communication protocols:

- Define escalation procedures

- Create contact lists for key personnel

- Prepare templates for stakeholder communications

- Maintain up-to-date documentation of all systems and procedures

12.3.7 Continuous Improvement

Regularly review and update your business continuity plan:

- Conduct post-mortem analyses after incidents or drills

- Incorporate lessons learned into the plan

- Stay updated with evolving Kubernetes best practices and tools

- Regularly train team members on continuity procedures

12.3.8 Challenges in Kubernetes Business Continuity Planning

- **Complexity**: Kubernetes environments can be complex, making it challenging to account for all failure scenarios.

- **Rapid Change**: The fast-paced nature of Kubernetes development may require frequent updates to continuity plans.

- **Stateful Applications**: Managing continuity for stateful applications in Kubernetes requires special consideration.

- **Multi-Cloud Strategies**: Implementing continuity across multiple cloud providers can introduce additional complexities.

12.3.9 Best Practices

- **Automate Everything**: Use Infrastructure as Code (IaC) and GitOps practices to automate deployments and configuration management.

- **Implement Chaos Engineering**: Regularly introduce controlled chaos to test system resilience.

- **Use Kubernetes-Native Tools**: Leverage tools designed for Kubernetes, such as Operators, for managing complex applications.

- **Embrace Immutable Infrastructure**: Treat infrastructure as immutable to simplify recovery processes.

- **Implement Least Privilege**: Use RBAC and Pod Security Policies to minimize the impact of security breaches.

- **Regular Audits**: Conduct regular audits of your Kubernetes configurations and continuity plans.

12.3.10 Conclusion

Business Continuity Planning in Kubernetes environments requires a holistic approach that combines technical solutions with organizational strategies. By leveraging Kubernetes' native capabilities for resilience and scalability, implementing robust monitoring and automation, and regularly testing and updating continuity plans, organizations can ensure their critical business functions remain operational even in the face of disruptions. Remember that business continuity is an ongoing process that requires continuous attention and adaptation to changing business needs and technological landscapes.

Chapter 13

Ecosystem and Integration

The Kubernetes ecosystem is rich with tools and platforms that extend its functionality and simplify various aspects of cluster management and application deployment. This chapter explores key components of this ecosystem and how they integrate with Kubernetes to enhance its capabilities.

13.1 Helm: Package Management for Kubernetes

Helm is the de facto package manager for Kubernetes, simplifying the process of defining, installing, and upgrading even the most complex Kubernetes applications. This section focuses on Helm 3, which brought significant improvements over its predecessors.

13.1.1 Introduction to Helm

Helm uses a packaging format called charts. A chart is a collection of files that describe a related set of Kubernetes resources. Helm provides the following key features:

- Templating of Kubernetes manifest files

- Release management

- Chart repositories for sharing and reusing configurations

- Rollback capabilities

13.1.2   Key Concepts in Helm

- **Chart**: A package of pre-configured Kubernetes resources

- **Release**: An instance of a chart running in a Kubernetes cluster

- **Repository**: A place where charts can be collected and shared

- **Values**: Configuration values that are supplied to the chart during release

13.1.3   Installing Helm

To install Helm, you can use package managers or download the binary directly:

```
# Using Homebrew (macOS)
brew install helm

# Using Chocolatey (Windows)
choco install kubernetes-helm

# Using apt (Debian/Ubuntu)
curl https://baltocdn.com/helm/signing.asc | gpg --dearmor |
sudo tee /usr/share/keyrings/helm.gpg > /dev/null

sudo apt-get install apt-transport-https --yes

echo "deb [arch=$(dpkg --print-architecture) signed-by=
/usr/share/keyrings/helm.gpg] https://baltocdn.com/helm/
stable/debian/ all main" | sudo tee /etc/apt/sources.list.d/
helm-stable-debian.list

sudo apt-get update

sudo apt-get install helm
```

13.1.4   Creating a Helm Chart

To create a new Helm chart:

```
helm create mychart
```

This creates a directory structure for your chart:

```
mychart/
  Chart.yaml  # A YAML file containing information
              # about the chart
  values.yaml # The default configuration values for
              # this chart
  charts/     # A directory containing any charts upon
              # which this chart depends
  templates/  # A directory of templates that, when
              # combined with values, will generate
              # valid Kubernetes manifest files
```

13.1.5   Helm Chart Example

Here's an example of a simple Helm chart for a web application:

Chart.yaml

```
apiVersion: v2
name: mywebapp
description: A Helm chart for a simple web application
version: 0.1.0
appVersion: "1.16.0"
```

values.yaml

```
replicaCount: 2

image:
  repository: nginx
  tag: "1.21.0"
  pullPolicy: IfNotPresent
```

```
service:
  type: ClusterIP
  port: 80

ingress:
  enabled: false
```

templates/deployment.yaml

```
apiVersion: apps/v1
kind: Deployment
metadata:
  name: {{ include "mywebapp.fullname" . }}
  labels:
    {{- include "mywebapp.labels" . | nindent 4 }}
spec:
  replicas: {{ .Values.replicaCount }}
  selector:
    matchLabels:
      {{- include "mywebapp.selectorLabels" . | nindent 6 }}
  template:
    metadata:
      labels:
        {{- include "mywebapp.selectorLabels" . | nindent 8 }}
    spec:
      containers:
        - name: {{ .Chart.Name }}
          image: "{{ .Values.image.repository }}:{{ .Values.image.tag }}"
          imagePullPolicy: {{ .Values.image.pullPolicy }}
          ports:
            - name: http
              containerPort: 80
              protocol: TCP
```

templates/service.yaml

```
apiVersion: v1
kind: Service
metadata:
  name: {{ include "mywebapp.fullname" . }}
  labels:
    {{- include "mywebapp.labels" . | nindent 4 }}
spec:
  type: {{ .Values.service.type }}
  ports:
    - port: {{ .Values.service.port }}
      targetPort: http
      protocol: TCP
      name: http
  selector:
    {{- include "mywebapp.selectorLabels" . | nindent 4 }}
```

13.1.6   Installing a Chart

To install a chart:

```
helm install myrelease ./mychart
```

13.1.7   Upgrading a Release

To upgrade a release:

```
helm upgrade myrelease ./mychart
```

13.1.8   Rolling Back a Release

To roll back to a previous release:

```
helm rollback myrelease 1
```

13.1.9   Working with Repositories

Add a repository:

```
helm repo add bitnami https://charts.bitnami.com/bitnami
```

Search for charts:

```
helm search repo bitnami
```

13.1.10   Best Practices for Helm Charts

- Use semantic versioning for your charts

- Provide clear documentation in the README.md and NOTES.txt files

- Use helpers and named templates to reduce duplication

- Use conditionals and control structures for flexible charts

- Implement RBAC resources in your charts

- Use subcharts for complex applications

13.1.11   Security Considerations

- Always verify the source of Helm charts

- Use Helm's provenance and integrity features

- Implement proper RBAC for Tiller (in Helm 2) or use Helm 3 which doesn't require Tiller

- Regularly update charts to include security patches

13.1.12   Conclusion

Helm simplifies the management of Kubernetes applications by providing a powerful templating and package management system. By using Helm, teams can standardize their Kubernetes deployments, easily share configurations, and manage complex application lifecycles more effectively. As the Kubernetes ecosystem continues to evolve, Helm remains a crucial tool for managing applications in Kubernetes environments.

13.2 Kustomize: Configuration Management for Kubernetes

Kustomize is a standalone tool to customize Kubernetes configurations in a template-free way. It's also integrated directly into kubectl, making it a powerful native option for managing Kubernetes manifests. This section explores how Kustomize works and how it can be used to manage complex Kubernetes deployments.

13.2.1 Introduction to Kustomize

Kustomize allows you to customize raw, template-free YAML files for multiple purposes, leaving the original files untouched and usable as-is. It operates on the concept of bases and overlays, where a base contains a set of YAML configurations, and overlays specify customizations to be applied to the base.

Key features of Kustomize include:

- Template-free customization of Kubernetes YAML files

- Integration with kubectl

- Support for multiple environments using overlays

- Patching mechanisms for fine-grained customizations

13.2.2 Basic Concepts

- **Base**: A directory with a set of Kubernetes YAML files and a kustomization.yaml file.

- **Overlay**: A directory that refers to a base and specifies customizations to be applied.

- **Kustomization file**: A file named kustomization.yaml that describes how to generate or transform Kubernetes objects.

- **Patch**: A partial YAML file used to modify existing Kubernetes objects.

13.2.3   Basic Kustomize Structure

A typical Kustomize project structure might look like this:

```
.
|-- base
|   |-- deployment.yaml
|   |-- service.yaml
|   '-- kustomization.yaml
'-- overlays
    |-- development
    |   |-- kustomization.yaml
    |   '-- patch.yaml
    '-- production
        |-- kustomization.yaml
        '-- patch.yaml
```

13.2.4   Example Kustomize Configuration

Base Configuration

base/deployment.yaml:

```yaml
apiVersion: apps/v1
kind: Deployment
metadata:
  name: myapp
spec:
  replicas: 1
  selector:
    matchLabels:
      app: myapp
  template:
    metadata:
      labels:
        app: myapp
    spec:
      containers:
      - name: myapp
```

```
        image: myapp:1.0.0
        ports:
        - containerPort: 8080
```

base/service.yaml:

```
apiVersion: v1
kind: Service
metadata:
  name: myapp
spec:
  selector:
    app: myapp
  ports:
  - port: 80
    targetPort: 8080
```

base/kustomization.yaml:

```
apiVersion: kustomize.config.k8s.io/v1beta1
kind: Kustomization
resources:
- deployment.yaml
- service.yaml
```

Development Overlay

overlays/development/kustomization.yaml:

```
apiVersion: kustomize.config.k8s.io/v1beta1
kind: Kustomization
bases:
- ../../base
patchesStrategicMerge:
- patch.yaml
```

overlays/development/patch.yaml:

```
apiVersion: apps/v1
kind: Deployment
```

```
metadata:
  name: myapp
spec:
  replicas: 2
```

13.2.5 Using Kustomize

To apply a Kustomize configuration:

```
kubectl apply -k overlays/development
```

To view the generated manifests without applying:

```
kubectl kustomize overlays/development
```

13.2.6 Advanced Kustomize Features

ConfigMap and Secret Generators

Kustomize can generate ConfigMaps and Secrets from files or literals:

```
apiVersion: kustomize.config.k8s.io/v1beta1
kind: Kustomization
configMapGenerator:
- name: myapp-config
  files:
  - config.properties
secretGenerator:
- name: myapp-secret
  literals:
  - API_KEY=secret-value
```

Image Tag Transformer

You can update image tags across all resources:

```
apiVersion: kustomize.config.k8s.io/v1beta1
kind: Kustomization
images:
- name: myapp
  newTag: 2.0.0
```

Namespace Transformer

Set a namespace for all resources:

```
apiVersion: kustomize.config.k8s.io/v1beta1
kind: Kustomization
namespace: my-namespace
resources:
- deployment.yaml
- service.yaml
```

13.2.7   Best Practices for Using Kustomize

- Keep base configurations generic and environment-agnostic

- Use overlays for environment-specific configurations

- Leverage patches for fine-grained customizations

- Use ConfigMap and Secret generators for better secret management

- Implement a clear directory structure for bases and overlays

- Version control your Kustomize configurations

13.2.8   Kustomize vs. Helm

While both Kustomize and Helm are used for managing Kubernetes configurations, they have different approaches:

- Kustomize is template-free and focuses on patching existing YAML

- Helm uses a templating engine and focuses on packaging and distributing charts

- Kustomize is built into kubectl, while Helm is a separate tool

- Kustomize has a flatter learning curve but may be less powerful for complex scenarios

- Helm has a rich ecosystem of pre-built charts but introduces additional complexity

Many teams use both tools, leveraging Helm for third-party applications and Kustomize for fine-tuning their own applications.

13.2.9   Conclusion

Kustomize provides a powerful, template-free way to manage Kubernetes configurations. Its integration with kubectl and its intuitive overlay system make it an excellent choice for teams looking to manage multiple environments or customize third-party manifests. By understanding and leveraging Kustomize's features, teams can create more maintainable, flexible, and environment-specific Kubernetes configurations.

13.3   Operators and Operator Framework

Kubernetes Operators are a powerful way to extend Kubernetes functionality and automate complex application management tasks. This section explores the concept of Operators, their benefits, and how to create and manage them using the Operator Framework.

13.3.1   Introduction to Kubernetes Operators

Operators are software extensions to Kubernetes that make use of custom resources to manage applications and their components. They act as application-specific controllers, encapsulating the operational knowledge of managing a specific application.
Key benefits of Operators include:

- Automating application-specific operational tasks

- Extending Kubernetes API with custom resources

- Simplifying complex stateful application management

- Enabling consistent application deployments across different environments

13.3.2   How Operators Work

Operators follow the Kubernetes principle of reconciliation loops. They:

1. Observe the current state of the cluster

2. Compare it with the desired state defined in custom resources

3. Take actions to bring the current state in line with the desired state

13.3.3   Custom Resource Definitions (CRDs)

Operators typically introduce Custom Resource Definitions (CRDs) to extend the Kubernetes API. Here's an example of a simple CRD for a hypothetical database:

```
apiVersion: apiextensions.k8s.io/v1
kind: CustomResourceDefinition
metadata:
  name: mydatabases.myapp.example.com
spec:
  group: myapp.example.com
  versions:
    - name: v1
      served: true
      storage: true
      schema:
        openAPIV3Schema:
          type: object
          properties:
            spec:
              type: object
              properties:
                size:
                  type: integer
                version:
                  type: string
  scope: Namespaced
  names:
```

```
plural: mydatabases
singular: mydatabase
kind: MyDatabase
shortNames:
- mdb
```

13.3.4   The Operator Framework

The Operator Framework is a toolkit for managing Operators. It includes:

- Operator SDK: For building Operators

- Operator Lifecycle Manager (OLM): For installing, updating, and managing Operators

- Operator Metering: For usage reporting of Operators

13.3.5   Creating an Operator with Operator SDK

Here's a basic workflow for creating an Operator using the Operator SDK:

1. Install the Operator SDK:

   ```
   # Example for Linux
   export ARCH=$(case $(uname -m) in x86_64) echo -n amd64 ;;
   aarch64) echo -n arm64 ;; *) echo -n $(uname -m) ;; esac)

   export OS=$(uname | awk '{print tolower($0)}')

   export OPERATOR_SDK_DL_URL=https://github.com/
   operator-framework/operator-sdk/releases/download/v1.28.0

   curl -LO ${OPERATOR_SDK_DL_URL}/operator-sdk_${OS}_${ARCH}

   chmod +x operator-sdk_${OS}_${ARCH} && sudo mv
   operator-sdk_${OS}_${ARCH} /usr/local/bin/operator-sdk
   ```

2. Create a new Operator project:

```
operator-sdk init --domain example.com --repo github.com/
example/myoperator
```

3. Create an API (which creates a CRD and a Controller):

```
operator-sdk create api --group myapp --version v1
--kind MyApp --resource --controller
```

4. Implement the Controller logic in the generated controller file.

5. Build and push the Operator image:

```
make docker-build docker-push IMG=
<some-registry>/myoperator:v0.0.1
```

6. Deploy the Operator:

```
make deploy IMG=<some-registry>/myoperator:v0.0.1
```

13.3.6   Operator Lifecycle Management

The Operator Lifecycle Manager (OLM) helps manage the lifecycle of
Operators in a Kubernetes cluster. Here's an example of an OLM
ClusterServiceVersion (CSV) for our hypothetical Operator:

```
apiVersion: operators.coreos.com/v1alpha1
kind: ClusterServiceVersion
metadata:
  annotations:
    capabilities: Basic Install
  name: myoperator.v0.0.1
  namespace: placeholder
spec:
  displayName: My Operator
  description: This is an example Operator.
  version: 0.0.1
  install:
    strategy: deployment
```

```yaml
  spec:
    deployments:
    - name: myoperator-controller-manager
      spec:
        replicas: 1
        selector:
          matchLabels:
            control-plane: controller-manager
        template:
          metadata:
            labels:
              control-plane: controller-manager
          spec:
            containers:
            - image: <some-registry>/myoperator:v0.0.1
              name: manager
installModes:
- supported: true
  type: OwnNamespace
- supported: true
  type: SingleNamespace
- supported: false
  type: MultiNamespace
- supported: true
  type: AllNamespaces
```

13.3.7   Best Practices for Operator Development

- Follow the Kubernetes Controller pattern

- Use finalizers for cleanup operations

- Implement proper error handling and logging

- Use status subresources to report Operator and managed resource status

- Implement proper RBAC for the Operator

- Version your CRDs and provide upgrade paths

- Use the Operator Capability Levels as a guide for feature implementation

13.3.8 Challenges and Considerations

- Complexity in managing stateful applications

- Ensuring Operators are scalable and performant

- Maintaining compatibility across Kubernetes versions

- Security considerations when Operators have cluster-wide permissions

- Testing Operators thoroughly, including failure scenarios

13.3.9 Conclusion

Kubernetes Operators provide a powerful way to extend Kubernetes and automate complex application management tasks. By encapsulating operational knowledge into software, Operators enable more efficient and consistent management of applications on Kubernetes. The Operator Framework, with its SDK and Lifecycle Manager, provides a comprehensive set of tools for developing, deploying, and managing Operators. As the Kubernetes ecosystem continues to evolve, Operators will play an increasingly important role in managing complex, stateful applications in Kubernetes environments.

13.4 Integration with Cloud Native Landscape: CNCF Projects and More

Kubernetes is at the heart of the cloud native ecosystem, but it's just one part of a vast landscape of projects and tools. This section explores how Kubernetes integrates with other Cloud Native Computing Foundation (CNCF) projects and additional tools in the cloud native ecosystem, enhancing its capabilities and extending its functionality.

13.4.1   Overview of the Cloud Native Landscape

The Cloud Native Landscape, curated by the CNCF, provides a map of the myriad projects and commercial products in the cloud native ecosystem. It's organized into several categories:

- Provisioning

- Runtime

- Orchestration & Management

- Application Definition & Development

- Observability & Analysis

- Platforms

Kubernetes serves as a focal point, with many projects designed to integrate with or extend its functionality.

13.4.2   Key CNCF Projects Integrating with Kubernetes

Containerd

Containerd is a industry-standard container runtime that can be used as the container runtime for Kubernetes.

Example configuration in kubelet:

```
--container-runtime=remote
```

```
--container-runtime-endpoint=unix:///run/containerd/
containerd.sock
```

Prometheus

Prometheus is a monitoring and alerting toolkit that integrates well with Kubernetes for metrics collection.

Example Prometheus Operator CustomResource:

```
apiVersion: monitoring.coreos.com/v1
kind: Prometheus
metadata:
  name: prometheus
spec:
  serviceAccountName: prometheus
  serviceMonitorSelector:
    matchLabels:
      team: frontend
  ruleSelector:
    matchLabels:
      team: frontend
  resources:
    requests:
      memory: 400Mi
```

Envoy

Envoy is a high-performance proxy that can be used as an ingress controller or service mesh in Kubernetes.

Example Envoy configuration as an ingress controller:

```
apiVersion: networking.k8s.io/v1
kind: Ingress
metadata:
  name: example-ingress
  annotations:
    kubernetes.io/ingress.class: envoy
spec:
  rules:
  - host: example.com
```

```
http:
  paths:
  - path: /
    pathType: Prefix
    backend:
      service:
        name: example-service
        port:
          number: 80
```

Jaeger

Jaeger is a distributed tracing system that can be used to monitor and troubleshoot microservices-based applications in Kubernetes.

Example Jaeger Operator deployment:

```
apiVersion: jaegertracing.io/v1
kind: Jaeger
metadata:
  name: simple-prod
spec:
  strategy: production
  storage:
    type: elasticsearch
    options:
      es:
        server-urls: http://elasticsearch:9200
```

13.4.3   Integration with Other Cloud Native Tools

Istio

Istio is a service mesh that provides traffic management, security, and observability for Kubernetes-based applications.

Example Istio VirtualService:

```
apiVersion: networking.istio.io/v1alpha3
```

```
kind: VirtualService
metadata:
  name: reviews-route
spec:
  hosts:
  - reviews.prod.svc.cluster.local
  http:
  - route:
    - destination:
        host: reviews.prod.svc.cluster.local
        subset: v2
      weight: 25
    - destination:
        host: reviews.prod.svc.cluster.local
        subset: v1
      weight: 75
```

Argo CD

Argo CD is a declarative, GitOps continuous delivery tool for Kubernetes.

Example Argo CD Application:

```
apiVersion: argoproj.io/v1alpha1
kind: Application
metadata:
  name: guestbook
  namespace: argocd
spec:
  project: default
  source:
    repoURL: https://github.com/argoproj/argocd-example-apps.git
    targetRevision: HEAD
    path: guestbook
  destination:
    server: https://kubernetes.default.svc
    namespace: guestbook
```

Linkerd

Linkerd is a lightweight service mesh for Kubernetes.

Example Linkerd ServiceProfile:

```
apiVersion: linkerd.io/v1alpha2
kind: ServiceProfile
metadata:
  name: nginx-service.default.svc.cluster.local
  namespace: default
spec:
  routes:
  - name: GET /
    condition:
      method: GET
      pathRegex: /
    responseClasses:
    - condition:
        status:
          min: 500
          max: 599
      isFailure: true
```

13.4.4   Kubernetes Ecosystem for Different Aspects

Storage

- Rook: Cloud-native storage orchestrator for Kubernetes

- Longhorn: Distributed block storage system for Kubernetes

Networking

- Cilium: eBPF-based Networking, Observability, and Security

- Calico: Networking and network security solution

Security

- Falco: Cloud-native runtime security project

- Open Policy Agent (OPA): Policy-based control for cloud native environments

Serverless

- Knative: Kubernetes-based platform to build, deploy, and manage serverless workloads

- OpenFaaS: Serverless Functions Made Simple

13.4.5 Best Practices for Integration

- Use Helm or Operators for deploying and managing complex applications

- Implement a service mesh for microservices communication and security

- Use GitOps principles with tools like Argo CD or Flux for continuous delivery

- Implement comprehensive monitoring and observability using tools like Prometheus, Grafana, and Jaeger

- Leverage CRDs and Operators to extend Kubernetes functionality

- Use policy engines like OPA for fine-grained control over cluster resources

13.4.6 Challenges and Considerations

- Increased complexity with multiple tools and integrations

- Ensuring compatibility between different tools and Kubernetes versions

- Managing the learning curve for teams adopting multiple cloud native technologies

- Balancing the benefits of new tools against the operational overhead they introduce

- Ensuring security across the entire cloud native stack

13.4.7 Conclusion

The integration of Kubernetes with the broader cloud native landscape significantly enhances its capabilities, allowing organizations to build more robust, scalable, and manageable cloud native applications. By leveraging CNCF projects and other cloud native tools, teams can address complex challenges in areas such as networking, storage, security, and observability. However, it's crucial to carefully consider which tools to adopt based on specific needs and to manage the added complexity that comes with a more diverse technology stack. As the cloud native ecosystem continues to evolve, staying informed about new projects and best practices will be key to leveraging the full potential of Kubernetes and related technologies.

Chapter 14

Real-World Case Studies

Understanding how large enterprises have adopted and benefited from Kubernetes provides valuable insights for organizations considering or in the process of their own Kubernetes journey. This chapter explores real-world examples of Kubernetes implementations, challenges faced, and lessons learned.

14.1 Adoption Stories from Large Enterprises

This section presents case studies from various industries, highlighting the motivations, processes, and outcomes of Kubernetes adoption in large-scale environments.

14.1.1 Financial Services: Capital One

Capital One, one of the largest banks in the United States, embraced Kubernetes as part of its cloud-native transformation.

Motivation

- Improve application deployment speed and reliability

- Enhance infrastructure utilization

- Support a microservices architecture

Implementation

- Implemented a multi-cluster strategy across multiple cloud providers

- Created internal developer platforms for streamlined application deployment

Outcomes

- Reduced application deployment time from weeks to minutes

- Improved resource utilization by 40%

- Enhanced ability to meet regulatory compliance requirements

Lessons Learned

- Importance of cultural change and developer education

- Need for robust security measures in a highly regulated industry

- Value of gradual migration starting with non-critical applications

14.1.2   E-commerce: Shopify

Shopify, a leading e-commerce platform, adopted Kubernetes to support its rapidly growing global merchant base.

Motivation

- Scale infrastructure to support millions of online stores

- Improve reliability during high-traffic events (e.g., Black Friday)

- Enhance developer productivity

Implementation

- Migrated from a monolithic architecture to microservices

- Developed custom tools for Kubernetes management, including "Krane" for deployments

- Implemented a global, multi-region Kubernetes infrastructure

Outcomes

- Successfully handled record-breaking Black Friday traffic

- Reduced deployment times from hours to minutes

- Improved application reliability and fault isolation

Lessons Learned

- Importance of building internal tools to simplify Kubernetes operations

- Need for comprehensive monitoring and observability solutions

- Value of gradual migration and thorough testing

14.1.3   Media Streaming: Netflix

Netflix, the world's leading streaming entertainment service, adopted Kubernetes to enhance its content delivery infrastructure.

Motivation

- Improve global content delivery efficiency

- Enhance ability to scale during peak viewing times

- Standardize deployment processes across different regions

Implementation

- Developed Titus, a container management platform built on Kubernetes

- Implemented a hybrid cloud strategy, running Kubernetes on both AWS and their own CDN

- Created custom scheduling algorithms to optimize content delivery

Outcomes

- Achieved consistent performance across global regions

- Improved resource utilization, leading to cost savings

- Enhanced ability to quickly deploy and update content delivery applications

Lessons Learned

- Importance of adapting Kubernetes to specific use cases

- Need for robust automation in large-scale deployments

- Value of contributing back to the open-source community

14.1.4   Automotive: BMW Group

BMW Group adopted Kubernetes to support its digital transformation and connected car initiatives.

Motivation

- Accelerate development of in-vehicle and cloud-based services

- Improve scalability of backend systems for connected cars

- Standardize application deployment across hybrid cloud environments

Implementation

- Developed a Kubernetes-based hybrid cloud platform

- Implemented GitOps practices for continuous deployment

- Created a self-service portal for developers to deploy applications

Outcomes

- Reduced time-to-market for new digital services

- Improved resource utilization and cost efficiency

- Enhanced ability to scale services based on real-time demand

Lessons Learned

- Importance of standardizing processes across different teams

- Need for comprehensive security measures in IoT environments

- Value of fostering a DevOps culture alongside technological changes

14.1.5 Common Themes in Enterprise Kubernetes Adoption

Across these case studies, several common themes emerge:

- **Gradual Migration**: Most enterprises opted for a phased approach, starting with non-critical applications.

- **Custom Tooling**: Many organizations developed custom tools to simplify Kubernetes operations for their specific needs.

- **Cultural Shift**: Successful adoption often required significant changes in development and operations practices.

- **Hybrid and Multi-Cloud Strategies**: Many enterprises implemented Kubernetes across multiple environments, including on-premises and various cloud providers.

- **Focus on Security**: Especially in regulated industries, robust security measures were a critical part of Kubernetes adoption.

- **Emphasis on Automation**: Automation of deployment, scaling, and management processes was key to realizing the benefits of Kubernetes.

14.1.6 Conclusion

These case studies demonstrate that while adopting Kubernetes at an enterprise scale comes with significant challenges, it can also bring substantial benefits in terms of scalability, efficiency, and developer productivity. The experiences of these large enterprises provide valuable lessons for organizations at any stage of their Kubernetes journey, highlighting the importance of careful planning, gradual implementation, and a focus on both technological and cultural aspects of the transition.

14.2 Lessons from Production Failures

Production failures in Kubernetes environments can provide valuable insights for improving system reliability, security, and performance. This section explores common types of failures encountered in Kubernetes deployments and the lessons learned from these incidents.

14.2.1 Common Types of Kubernetes Production Failures

Resource Exhaustion

- Inadequate resource limits leading to node failures

- Misconfigurations causing resource leaks

- Unexpected spikes in traffic overwhelming clusters

Networking Issues

- DNS failures causing service discovery problems

- Misconfigured network policies leading to communication breakdowns

- Load balancer misconfigurations affecting traffic distribution

Configuration Errors

- Incorrect deployment specifications causing rollout failures

- Mismanaged secrets leading to application crashes

- Incompatible version upgrades causing cluster instability

Dependency Failures

- External service outages affecting application availability

- Database connection issues causing data inconsistencies

- Container registry failures preventing deployments

14.2.2 Case Study: Resource Exhaustion in a Microservices Architecture

While not attributing this to a specific company, let's examine a common scenario many organizations face.

Scenario

A company running a microservices architecture on Kubernetes experienced a major outage when one service began consuming excessive CPU and memory, causing cascading failures across the cluster.

Root Causes

- Lack of proper resource limits on pods

- Inadequate monitoring and alerting for resource usage

- Absence of circuit breakers in inter-service communication

Impact

- 4-hour service downtime

- Significant revenue loss

- Damage to company reputation

Lessons Learned

- Implement and regularly review resource limits for all deployments

- Set up comprehensive monitoring and alerting for both cluster and application-level metrics

- Implement circuit breakers and fallback mechanisms in microservices architecture

- Conduct regular load testing to identify potential bottlenecks

14.2.3   Key Lessons from Production Failures

Importance of Proper Resource Management

- Always set appropriate resource requests and limits for containers

- Regularly review and adjust resource allocations based on actual usage

- Implement cluster autoscaling to handle unexpected load increases

Example of setting resource limits:

```
apiVersion: v1
kind: Pod
metadata:
  name: frontend
spec:
  containers:
  - name: app
    image: images.my-company.example/app:v4
    resources:
      requests:
        memory: "64Mi"
        cpu: "250m"
      limits:
        memory: "128Mi"
        cpu: "500m"
```

Robust Monitoring and Alerting

- Implement comprehensive monitoring covering both cluster and application metrics

- Set up proactive alerting to catch issues before they escalate

- Use tools like Prometheus and Grafana for effective monitoring

Example Prometheus alert rule:

```
groups:
- name: example
  rules:
  - alert: HighCPUUsage
    expr: 100 - (avg by(instance) (rate(node_cpu_seconds_total
{mode="idle"}[2m])) * 100) > 80
    for: 5m
    labels:
      severity: warning
    annotations:
      summary: High CPU usage detected on {{$labels.instance}}
      description: CPU usage is above 80% on
{{$labels.instance}}
```

Importance of Testing and Gradual Rollouts

- Conduct thorough testing, including chaos engineering practices

- Implement canary deployments and blue-green deployment strategies

- Use feature flags to control the rollout of new features

Example of a canary deployment:

```
apiVersion: networking.k8s.io/v1
kind: Ingress
metadata:
  name: my-ingress
  annotations:
    kubernetes.io/ingress.class: nginx
```

```yaml
        nginx.ingress.kubernetes.io/canary: "true"
        nginx.ingress.kubernetes.io/canary-weight: "20"
spec:
  rules:
  - host: myapp.example.com
    http:
      paths:
      - path: /
        pathType: Prefix
        backend:
          service:
            name: myapp-canary
            port:
              number: 80
```

Network Policy and Security

- Implement and regularly audit network policies

- Use Pod Security Admission to enforce security standards

- Regularly update and patch all components, including the Kubernetes version

Example Network Policy:

```yaml
apiVersion: networking.k8s.io/v1
kind: NetworkPolicy
metadata:
  name: default-deny-ingress
spec:
  podSelector: {}
  policyTypes:
  - Ingress
```

Dependency Management

- Implement circuit breakers for external service calls

- Use liveness and readiness probes effectively

- Consider implementing service meshes for better traffic management

Example of liveness and readiness probes:

```yaml
apiVersion: v1
kind: Pod
metadata:
  name: myapp-pod
spec:
  containers:
  - name: myapp-container
    image: myapp:v1
    livenessProbe:
      httpGet:
        path: /healthz
        port: 8080
      initialDelaySeconds: 15
      periodSeconds: 10
    readinessProbe:
      httpGet:
        path: /ready
        port: 8080
      periodSeconds: 5
```

14.2.4 Conclusion

Production failures, while challenging, provide invaluable lessons for improving Kubernetes deployments. Key takeaways include the importance of proper resource management, robust monitoring and alerting, thorough testing and gradual rollouts, effective network policies and security measures, and careful dependency management. By learning from these experiences and implementing best practices, organizations can build more resilient, secure, and efficient Kubernetes environments. Remember, the goal is not to avoid all failures, which is impossible, but to build systems that can gracefully handle and quickly recover from inevitable issues.

Chapter 15

Certification

As we conclude this comprehensive guide to Kubernetes administration, it's important to consider how to apply this knowledge in a practical setting. One way to validate your Kubernetes expertise is through the Certified Kubernetes Administrator (CKA) exam. This section provides valuable tips and strategies to help you prepare for and succeed in the CKA exam.

15.1 Certified Kubernetes Administrator (CKA) Exam Tips

The CKA exam is a hands-on, performance-based test that assesses your ability to deploy and manage Kubernetes clusters. Here are some key tips to help you prepare and succeed:

15.1.1 Exam Format and Structure

- The exam is 2 hours long and consists of 15-20 performance-based tasks.

- You'll be working in real Kubernetes clusters via a browser-based terminal.

- The exam is proctored remotely.

- A score of 66% is required to pass.

15.1.2   Key Areas of Focus

Based on the exam curriculum, focus on these core areas:

- Cluster Architecture, Installation & Configuration

- Workloads & Scheduling

- Services & Networking

- Storage

- Troubleshooting

15.1.3   Preparation Strategies

Hands-on Practice

- Set up a personal Kubernetes cluster (e.g., using minikube or kind).

- Practice creating and managing various Kubernetes resources.

- Simulate real-world scenarios and troubleshoot issues.

Command Line Proficiency

- Master kubectl commands and their options.

- Practice using kubectl explain for quick reference.

- Become comfortable with bash commands for file manipulation.

Example of using kubectl explain:

```
kubectl explain pod.spec.containers
```

Time Management

- Practice working under time constraints.

- Learn to quickly navigate the Kubernetes documentation.

- Prioritize questions based on their weight and your confidence.

15.1.4   Exam Day Tips

Environment Setup

- Familiarize yourself with the exam environment.

- Set up aliases and autocomplete for kubectl.

Example bash aliases:

```
alias k=kubectl
alias kgp='kubectl get pods'
alias kgd='kubectl get deployments'
```

Efficient Problem Solving

- Read each question carefully and identify the key requirements.

- Use imperative commands for quick resource creation.

- Leverage kubectl's dry-run option to generate YAML templates.

Example of using dry-run:

```
kubectl create deployment nginx --image=nginx --dry-run=client
-o yaml > nginx-deployment.yaml
```

Troubleshooting Techniques

- Master log analysis using kubectl logs.

- Understand how to use kubectl describe for detailed resource information.

- Practice debugging common issues (e.g., misconfigured services, RBAC issues).

15.1.5   Key Commands and Concepts to Master

Essential kubectl Commands

- kubectl get, describe, create, apply, delete

- kubectl exec for running commands in containers

- kubectl logs for viewing pod logs

- kubectl port-forward for accessing services

Important Concepts

- Pod lifecycle and health probes

- Service types and network policies

- Persistent volumes and storage classes

- RBAC and security contexts

- Cluster maintenance tasks (e.g., upgrades, backup and restore)

15.1.6   Practice Exercises

To prepare effectively, try these practice exercises:

1. Create a deployment with 3 replicas, then scale it to 5.

2. Set up a service to expose a deployment, then troubleshoot connectivity issues.

3. Configure persistent storage for a stateful application.

4. Implement RBAC for a service account with specific permissions.

5. Perform a simulated cluster upgrade.

15.1.7 Additional Resources

- Official Kubernetes Documentation: `https://kubernetes.io/docs/`

- Kubernetes the Hard Way by Kelsey Hightower: `https://github.com/kelseyhightower/kubernetes-the-hard-way`

- CKA Curriculum: `https://github.com/cncf/curriculum`

- Practice exams and simulators (various online providers)

15.1.8 Final Thoughts

Remember, the CKA exam is designed to test your practical skills in managing Kubernetes clusters. Focus on hands-on experience, efficient problem-solving, and a deep understanding of Kubernetes concepts. With thorough preparation and practice, you'll be well-equipped to succeed in the exam and demonstrate your expertise as a Kubernetes administrator. Good luck with your CKA exam!